The Money Compass

The Money Compass

WHERE YOUR MONEY WENT AND HOW TO GET IT BACK

Mark A. Grimaldi
G. Stevenson Smith

Published by John Wiley & Sons, Inc., Hoboken, New Jersey.
Published simultaneously in Canada.

The Grimaldi Way is a creation of Mark A. Grimaldi, patent pending. EFS ID 17275606.
Application number 14068508. Title: Method of Identifying Relative Strength of Mutual Funds.

For general information on our other products and services or for technical support, please
contact our Customer Care Department within the United States at (800) 762-2974, outside
the United States at (317) 572-3993 or fax (317) 572-4002.

Wiley publishes in a variety of print and electronic formats and by print-on-demand. Some
material included with standard print versions of this book may not be included in e-books
or in print-on-demand. If this book refers to media such as a CD or DVD that is not included
in the version you purchased, you may download this material at http://booksupport.wiley.
com. For more information about Wiley products, visit www.wiley.com.

Library of Congress Cataloging-in-Publication Data

Grimaldi, Mark.
    The money compass : where your money went and how to get it back / Mark Grimaldi
and Stevenson G. Smith.
        pages   cm
    Includes index.
    ISBN 978-1-118-61445-7 (hardback) — ISBN 978-1-118-61465-5 (ePDF) —
    ISBN 978-1-118-61461-7 (ePub)
        1. Finance, Public—United States.   2. Investments—United States.
    I. Smith, Stevenson G.   II. Title.
    HG179.G7457   2014
    332.024—dc23   2013039125

Printed in the United States of America
10 9 8 7 6 5 4 3 2 1

*To my amazing wife and children and
all those who believed in a broken boy.
Especially you Mom and Dad.*

—Mark Grimaldi

*This book is dedicated to the America
that once was.*

—Steve Smith

Contents

Preface

This book was written for those who know someone who has lost a great deal of their net worth during the Great Recession. It is written for those who know someone who has been disenfranchised by their government, educational system, or banking institutions. These organizations are on a path to separate Americans into two financial groups: the haves and the have nots.

Each chapter in the book makes suggestions as to how to fight back against the trend of separation by increasing your financial net worth. Some of the suggestions are small steps that anyone can take and others require more financial resources in order to implement. These steps are for the individual. They are not recommendations for passing new laws, special interest groups, or political parties.

The book is oriented toward all financial groups. It makes suggestions as to how to get back at the credit card companies that charge exorbitant rates and fees. It shows you how to use the current tax code to your advantage and not as a wealth destroyer. It identifies the worst piece of advice given to the small investor *and* the person who preaches it. It tells the story of the single biggest economic event of this century and how it helped cause the Great Recession. It forecasts the next big economic shock *and* how to *profit* from it. It identifies what you have lost in future potential because of a dysfunctional educational system and how to deal with that loss. The authors describe specific stock choices that will allow you to overcome all the losses you have been handed and forecasts are provided about what is coming up next in the economy.

If you believe the financial events that have been affecting your life are just inevitable coincidences and your financial situation is unchangeable, then you need to read this book and find out that concept is false. This book will give you the tools to stop being a victim of the system and start profiting from the system!

Acknowledgments

A special thanks to Laura Phillips, CFS; Julie Scheaffer; Frank Fabio, CPA; and my entire staff.

CHAPTER 1

Introduction

THE INVISIBLE HAND OF CONFISCATION

In the absence of the gold standard, there is no way to protect savings from confiscation through inflation. There is no safe store of value.
  The financial policy of the welfare state requires that there be no way for the owners of wealth to protect themselves.
    —Alan Greenspan, "Gold and Economic Freedom,"
                          The Objectivist (1966)

"**Why have I lost my money? And who took it?**" That's the theme of this book. Millions of once rich and well-off Americans have watched their assets disappear in the Great Recession. These Americans are unemployed, and after years of work many have lost their homes, and their once rock-solid retirement plans are in ruins. Was it based on stupid financial decisions? Probably. Was it based on making financial decisions without a high level of financial literacy? Probably. Was it greed? Probably. Was it based on actions over which they had no control? Probably. Many Americans have become poorer, and the rest are worried.

The "Probablies" are not the only answer to these questions. This book looks at specific political and financial events that put Americans into complex situations where they are required to make decisions that they are unskilled to make. On the surface these financial choices appeared simple. Buy a house. Sign a mortgage. Invest in stocks.

Yet signing a mortgage is a complex decision, and the forces and policies behind the financing are hidden. Oh, and we want to note at the beginning of this book: Stocks don't always go up.

Topics to be covered in this book include:

- What to do about the housing depression.
- Bank credit cards and uneducated borrowers—an interesting combination
- Making choices in fund investments
- Greenspan depression and the coming Recession
- 36 days of infamy in the 2000 Presidential election
- The federal debt bomb
- Collapsing educational systems
- What's going on with unemployment?

But first—Chapter 1 discusses four aspects of today's economy that have led to the financial pickle the United States and you are facing today. It begins with the fourth branch of government.

The Fourth Branch: K Street Government

Remember high school civics class? It was one of those groaning classes where a boring teacher talked about Congress, Justices, the prez, and, oh yeah, the founding of our democracy. Ooops—it's a republic. But what about the opposing groups in that republic? Are they equal to one another? Does one faction oppose and have the ability to override the interests of others?

Going back to the development of the United States and the Federalist Papers, James Madison (1787) wrote about strong groups who promote their interests over the rights of others and the public good. Among those he mentioned were those with resources and those without:

> But the most common and durable source of factions has been the various and unequal distribution of property. Those who hold and those who are without property have ever formed distinct interests in society. Those who are creditors, and those who are debtors, fall under a like discrimination. A landed interest, a manufacturing interest, a mercantile interest, a moneyed interest, with many lesser interests, grow up of necessity

in civilized nations, and divide them into different classes, actu-
ated by different sentiments and views.

It is in vain to say that enlightened statesmen will be able to
adjust these clashing interests, and render them all subservient
to the public good. Enlightened statesmen will not always be at
the helm.

Today, those factions Madison wrote about are alive and well.
They are found largely on K Street in Washington, D.C. K Street
consists of lobbying groups, various special interest committees,
and their service providers. The sole purpose of these groups is
to influence public policy and legislation using huge amounts of
money they collect from corporations, foreign governments, and
others. They have special access in our federal government,
and in some cases, these groups have written legislation that has
been introduced in Congress. Banks, investment banks, foreign
governments, industry groups, cigarette manufacturers (hey, cigarettes did great for 100 years), even congressmen use these groups
to change policies in the United States. Special interests and some
in our Congress are paid to support those who pay them the cash.

Where's the Cash?

Randy "Duke" Cunningham, the California Republican congressman
resigned on Monday after admitting he took $2.4 million in bribes ("A
Culture of Bribery in Congress," *Christian Science Monitor*, December 2, 2005,
www.csmonitor.com/2005/1202/p08s01-comv.html).

Former congressman William J. Jefferson was convicted of cor-
ruption charges Wednesday in a case made famous by the $90,000 in
bribe money stuffed into his freezer (Jerry Markon and Brigid Schulte,
"Jefferson Convicted in Bribery Scheme," *Washington Post*, August 6, 2009,
www.washingtonpost.com/wp-dyn/content/article/2009/08/05/AR200908
0503195.html).

Jack Abramoff, an influential Washington, D.C., lobbyist, was sentenced
to a four-year prison term for fraud and corrupting public officials. Swept
up in the fraud was Steve Griles, a coal industry lobbyist and deputy secretary at the Department of Interior, for obstruction of justice; 18th District
Ohio Congressman Bob Ney, in a trade of political favors for gifts; David
Safavian, former chief of staff in the General Services Administration; and

(Continued)

(Continued)

nine others. In addition, Tom DeLay, although not currently convicted of wrongdoing, had to step down as House Majority Leader and left Congress.

Senator Ted Stevens was accused of taking $250,000 in gifts. The Department of Justice later dropped the case due to technicalities.

Tom DeLay, the former House Majority Leader, resigned his post and at the time of this writing his guilty verdict on money laundering is being appealed. He is accused of laundering $190,000 of corporate money to Texas politicians in 2002 (www.statesman.com).

Charlie Rangel is found guilty of 11 ethical violations by a congressional House ethics committee. The violations include influence peddling, hiding $600,000 in income, misuse of federal funds, inaccurate financial disclosure statements, and soliciting donations for the Rangel Center for Public Policy in a manner that led to questions of influence peddling (http://cbsnews .com and www.house.gov).

If easy mortgage loans support their clients' interest, special interests are pushing that policy into Congress for the "public interest." If these loans go bad, they are there pushing for a bailout, for the "public interest." Either side works.

Do you remember your civics teacher talking about checks and balances in the U.S. government? Well, that's mainly true about the three branches of government, but it is not true about the fourth branch. There are no checks on the power of lobbyists in our country.

Reason number 1 why you lost your money—there is an unauthorized fourth branch of the government. This branch is very organized, and it is stuffed full of money. The money is used to influence government policies, not just government legislation. The objective of that influence is to ensure that policies go into effect that protect certain groups or make them richer. If it's not about money, it's about getting favors.

More Income Tax and More Debt, Too

Let's take a look at that statement. Prior to the income tax, the U.S. government received a large share of its revenues from a tariff tax.

The 16th Amendment made it legal to tax individual income in 1913. Originally, in 1894, the Supreme Court had determined that a 2 percent tax on incomes over $4,000 was unconstitutional, but beginning in 1909 and extending over a four-year period, the states ratified the 16th Amendment to the Constitution. The 16th Amendment allowed the federal government to levy a 1 percent tax against people's income (i.e., those with high income), and there was no need to apportion the collected revenues among the states according to their populations. The idea was that those with large amounts of wealth should support the government. Initially, the tax applied only to 4 percent of the U.S. population. And so it began.

And Collections Gets Bigger

In its first year in operation, income taxes were responsible for raising less than 10 percent of federal revenues. By contrast, the income tax accounted for 45 percent of federal revenues in 1950 and nearly 73 percent in 1985 (Answers.com, www.answers.com/topic/federal-income-tax-of-1913; accessed October 30, 2010).

In 2008, corporate and individual income taxes represent approximately 50 percent of the federal government's revenues (www.taxpolicycenter .org/briefing-book/background/numbers/revenue.cfm; accessed October 30, 2010).

But what really began with an income tax?

The federal government's ability to generate significant revenues is what began in 1913, and with it the idea to spread the wealth of the nation. Remember, the percentage of U.S. citizens paying taxes is no longer 4 percent as when the 16th Amendment was originally passed. Today, more of us are involved in spreading the wealth due to wasteful government programs.

Government spending is unchecked. There appears to be no limit on the level of government spending, and, consequently, tax revenues can't cover the expenditures. So government borrows. Expenditures must be funded with debt. Forty cents of each dollar spent must be borrowed.

I Asked

I once asked a congressman at a public meeting where the money for the 2008 stimulus was going to come from and he laughed off the question and said, "We'll just borrow it." He was reelected in the November 2010 elections.

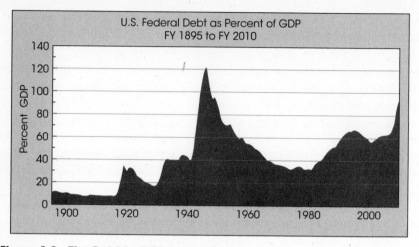

Figure 1.1   The Debt-to-GDP Ratio Chart
Source: usgovernmentspending.com, www.usgovernmentspending.com/federal_debt_chart
.html.

When revenues become insufficient for government excessiveness, the government simply borrows based on its ability to generate tax revenues. Everyone knows from their own personal finances that the higher their income, the more they can borrow. As long as the income stream continues, the federal government can borrow. But when our salaries can no longer support our continued borrowing, we have to stop borrowing. The federal government doesn't. If the tax revenues are not enough, the government can simply print money down at the Treasury building.

Figure 1.1 shows the relationship between federal debt and gross domestic product (GDP). This information is the best way to compare net worth and debt for a government. As individuals, we can sign for a first and second mortgage on our homes. Yes, the government does have assets to mortgage, but, politically, the federal government can't mortgage the Washington Monument—at least not yet. But who knows, maybe the Chinese are looking for a good investment. So for a government the debt-to-GDP ratio in Figure 1.1 is the closest comparison to an individual's net worth-to-debt ratio.

Notice the debt can be more than GDP, as it was in 1945 at the end of World War II. Also notice that the percentage relationship was around 15 percent until the passage of the 16th Amendment and the beginning of World War I. As the amount of income taxes collected from U.S. citizens increased to higher and higher dollar amounts, so did the government's debt level. Today, the percentage is approaching 100 percent. Basically, everything the government can hock has been hocked.

As Figure 1.1 is reviewed, several questions can be asked: Did the United States ever have a war before WWI? Oh, yes. "Remember the *Maine*" and the Spanish-American War? Did it raise the debt-to-GDP ratio above 15 percent? No. Even during the Civil War, it was not beyond 32 percent.

Looking at the debt-to-GDP ratio for the following selected time periods, we see how distorted it has become in 2010 (research .stlouisfed.org/fred2/series/GFDEGDQ188S).

During World War I:

Year	Debt-to-GDP
1914	7.98
1915	7.9
1916	7.28
1917	9.58
1918	19.25

During the Great Depression:

Year	Debt-to-GDP
1929	16.34
1930	17.75
1931	21.96
1932	33.2
1933	39.96
1934	40.99
1935	39.16
1936	40.31
1937	39.64

During World War II:

Year	Debt-to-GDP
1941	38.64
1942	44.73
1943	68.83
1944	91.45
1945	116

Past Eight Years:

Year	Debt-to-GDP
2005	62.77
2006	63.49
2007	63.99
2008	69.15
2009	83.29
2010	94.27
2011	95.2
2012	99.0

Looking at these time periods, it can be seen that our current debt-to-GDP ratio is out of whack with the political situation the United States is facing . . . we are not fighting WWII . . . we are just on a debt binge to fund special interests represented by the fourth branch of government. Additionally, the trend of the debt-to-GDP ratio should be seen as alarming.

Reason number 2: You are losing your wealth due to the collection of income taxes by the federal government. It is not because of the dollar totals collected. You are losing your wealth because of the effect those collections have on government's inability to adequately support this level of national debt. Without a stronger revenue base, the government's main choice to support this level of debt is to print money, and that leads to the next topic—the monetization of U.S. debt and increases in the cost of everything.

Monetization of the Debt: Say What?

This is a big monkey. This is the one that will be a killer. To get out from under a pile of debt, the government has to monetize it.

The Merriam-Webster dictionary (www.merriam-webster.com) describes the term *monetize* as the purchasing of public or private debt and thereby free for other uses moneys that would have been devoted to debt service. Well, that's not quite it.

Monetization of the debt occurs when the Federal Reserve buys back outstanding Treasury bonds. The holder of the Treasury bond receives a cash payment from the Fed. Where did the Fed get the money to buy back the bond? It prints money—one dollar after another. Thousands of these transactions occur, and the result is billions or trillions of U.S. dollars in the hands of everyone (especially banks). Although that doesn't sound bad, more money leads to more spending, but the effect can be a disaster.

First, with more money flowing around, everything becomes more expensive as inflation starts to kick in. On top of a surge in inflation, there is a drop in the value of the dollar compared to other currencies because there are just too many dollars floating around the world. The Fed wants this to occur so that the federal government can repay its debt with cheap dollars.

The consequence for U.S. citizens is an inability to buy certain products that are imported into the United States, like cars. Today, it is difficult to find a product that is completely manufactured in the United States. So get ready for a lower standard of living. Another consequence is an increase in interest rates, as the United States has to pay a higher rate on its debt as every creditor knows they are going to be paid back with cheaper dollars. Every borrower gets whacked with higher interest rates.

There are only three ways to pay off the enormous outstanding U.S. federal debt. One way is to default on the debt. Not a likely choice. A second alternative is to increase taxes to a high enough level to pay off the debt. Not possible given the debt burden.

I Asked

In my undergraduate economics course, I asked the professor if the United States could go bankrupt. With confidence, he replied that the United States can't go bankrupt because the government can tax you for everything that you have.

If I had been smarter, I would have asked: "Gee, don't you think someone would object?"

And the third and most viable choice is to inflate your way out of the debt.

The Fed is currently on the road to creating inflation so that debt obligations can be repaid with money that has less value. Possibly good for the government, but bad for us. Those of us who have worked and saved and put money aside for our retirement will find that the $1 million nest egg that your investment adviser told you was needed for a comfortable retirement won't do now. You are likely to need around $3 million after the effects of coming inflation and money printing work their way through the financial system.

Again, the government is not confiscating assets by taxing you at a higher rate—after all, they said they wouldn't raise taxes, and a promise is a promise. Rather, they are taking your money away by making any saved dollars in your possession worth less. Remember the old communists begging on the street corners of Moscow? They were still receiving the pensions they had been promised. Pass the vodka!

Well, maybe not. With the right level of inflation and drop in purchasing power, a bottle of vodka may be only for the rich. In five years, an imported bottle of vodka could cost $81 when the drop in the value of the dollar and the inflation rate shown in Table 1.1 are taken into account.

Reason number 3: So, who took my money? You are losing your wealth because the government is printing money and trying to inflate its way out of debt. Any monies that you saved or are scheduled to receive will be worth less and less. But no one increased your taxes. Hurray, we are lucky! Let's vote the incumbents in again.

Table 1.1   The Printing of Money, Inflation, and the Cost of a Bottle of Vodka

Today 2010		After 1 Year: 2011*		After 5 Years: 2015	
Cost of a bottle of vodka	$40		$52		$81
*Assume the following:					
	Year 1	Year 2	Year 3	Year 4	Year 5
Drop in value of the dollar	20%	5%	2%	1%	1%
Inflation rate	4%	8%	10%	10%	8%

The Last Biggie: Repeal of Glass-Steagall and Gamblers Gone Wild

The Glass-Steagall Act, passed in 1933, was a major banking revision act. It was enacted because of the fraud, margin trading, and investment excesses that occurred in banks before the 1929 market crash and depression. Prior to the 1929 market crash, all banks were involved in speculative investments. After the crash, it was apparent that local banks were involved in stock market investment activities in which they had little understanding of the risk or even the exact nature of their investments. The Act separated banks into two different types.

Commercial banks are those banks where individual depositors keep their checking and savings accounts and buy certificates of deposit. This is what I call a "Peoria bank" or a limited risk bank. Investment banks are the typical Wall Street banks that are organized to create mergers and acquisitions, issue bonds backed by mortgage loans, organize buyouts, trade derivatives, and underwrite stock issuances by large companies. These banks develop new and esoteric investment products for rich investors. This is what I call a "Las Vegas bank" or a high-roller bank.

The Glass-Steagall Act separated banks into commercial and investment banks. It walled off speculative activities from commercial banking. The objective was to limit risky capital investment activities to investment banks and depositor activities to commercial banks. Well, banks sought to find loopholes in the law and they paid the fourth branch of government—that is, the lobbyists—to change the law. The reason: More money can be made outside of commercial banking.

From 1933 to 1999, commercial and investment banks were separated from one another. During this period, the local town banks began to be merged into larger and larger banks. In 1934, there were 14,146 FDIC-insured commercial banks in the United States. In 1984, the high-water mark for these banks, there were 14,496 such banks. In 2009, the number was 6,839, which is more than a 50 percent drop in 25 years. Today, in many small towns and cities the only evidence of these former busy commercial banks are old vacant bank buildings which once bustled with customers. Figure 1.2 shows the decline in independent commercial banks.

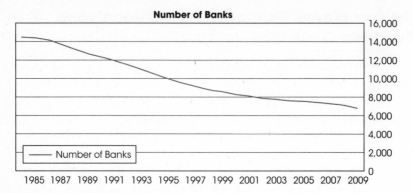

Figure 1.2   Number of Commercial Banks in the United States
Source: FDIC, www2.fdic.gov/hsob/hsobRpt.asp.

In 1999, the Glass-Steagall Act was repealed with the passage of Gramm-Leach-Bliley (GLB) Act. This new act repealed the separation of banking activities that had been in place for 66 years. The consequence of the repeal was that commercial banks could become investment banks. So could insurance companies. Everyone could bet on everything.

And that's why many of you lost money. Peoria banks became Las Vegas gamblers.

In 1987, a reason for separating risky operations from the commercial operations was noted.

> Securities activities can be risky, leading to enormous losses. Such losses could threaten the integrity of deposits. In turn, the Government insures deposits and could be required to pay large sums if depository institutions were to collapse as the result of securities losses.
>
> —Jackson, 2010, p. 3

Gee! You think? Is $750 billion a lot of money? How about another $600 billion?

Less than 10 years after the repeal of the Glass-Steagall Act, a financial crisis occurred in the United States that affected countries and financial institutions around the world.

The effect of the financial crisis of 2008 has left many financial institutions in ruins. GLB allowed commercial banks, investment banks, and insurance companies to become one. The unperceived investment risk for these institutions rose into the stratosphere. The number of failed banks in 2009 was 140, which was 2 percent of all commercial banks.

And the consolidations continued—until the institutions became too big to fail.

Recently, the congressionally enacted Dodd-Frank Act has back-pedaled on some of the cowboy financing and trading that occurred after the repeal of Glass-Steagall. Now there is a requirement for the disclosure of information about some derivatives, and there will be a council of "systematic risk oversight" created. The council's job is to analyze the risk in the financial system, especially banking, to determine if risk levels are reaching a point where extreme events could cause the whole system to collapse. Further, the law restricts investments in hedge funds by banks and the use of bank assets in risky trading ventures. The exact meaning of the legislation is being worked out by the government agencies tasked with the law's enforcement.

Now all that's left to do is for banks to find the loopholes in Dodd-Frank or delay its implementation while lobbying to lift certain unfavorable restrictions in the new legislation.

Reason number 4: Although a gambling casino looks like it is the place where the biggest bets are made, it's not. Bigger and more risky bets are placed at banks. When losses are incurred in a casino, it is the responsibility of the individual. Las Vegas has more suicides than any other similar-sized city. When banks lose their bets, it is the responsibility of the taxpayer. The taxpayer pays either one way or the other. And that's the fourth reason you are losing your wealth: paying for the bank's mistakes.

Summary

So what is the government doing in the background of your everyday life that is causing your money and net worth to disappear?

The government is:

- Strongly influenced by the fourth branch—the special interests.
- Issuing unsustainable amounts of debt.
- Monetizing the debt and creating the scenario for inflation by printing money.
- Allowing for high levels of financial failure risk to exist in the banking system.

As you get your morning coffee, the federal government is borrowing more money from China. By the time you get to work, the government has printed millions of dollars to put into the financial system. During your workday, the fourth branch is plying congressmen and senators with gifts and money to get access and influence so that their clients are better off than you.

In this book, areas of financial danger will be analyzed, and suggestions will be made to help prevent the invisible hand of confiscation from grabbing you.

References

Jackson, William D. *Glass-Steagall Act: Commercial vs. Investment Banking.* Washington, DC. UNT Digital Library. http://digital.library.unt.edu/ark:/67531/metacrs9065. Accessed November 12, 2010.

Madison, J. 1787. The Federalist No. 10, "The Utility of the Union as a Safeguard Against Domestic Faction and Insurrection." *Daily Advertiser,* November 22.

Greenspan and the Growing Bubble

The height of the bubble was reached in the winter of 1636–1637. Tulip traders were making (and losing) fortunes regularly. A good trader could earn up to 60,000 florins in a month—approximately $61,710 adjusted to current U.S. dollars. With profits like those to be had, nothing local governments could do stopped the frenzy of trading. Then one day in Haarlem a buyer failed to show up and pay for his bulb purchase. The ensuing panic spread across Holland, and within days tulip bulbs were worth only a hundredth of their former prices. The tulip bubble had burst.

—Cynthia Wood[1]

If you ask Americans what they consider the most important date for the U.S. economy in their generation, many will say September 11, 2001. I disagree. The most important date, in my opinion, was actually a series of dates, starting on November 7, 2000, when the presidential election was contested, and ending on December 12, 2000, when the U.S. Supreme Court ruled in favor of George Bush. Before I explain why, however, let me tell a story.

"Daddy, did you have a bad day?" I asked my father.

I could see that he did, but I wanted to ask anyway.

"Yes, Mark, I did," he replied grimly.

I was sorry to hear that, and asked if there was anything I could do to cheer him up. He suggested a drive to the corner drugstore, so we hopped in the car. The ride was short, and we didn't speak— but when we pulled into the store parking lot, my father looked at me with a piercing gaze.

"Mark, I had a very bad day today," he said. "Everything I touched turned to garbage."

No son wants to hear that from his father. I told him I was sorry.

"That's all right," he said, "I have a plan."

That relieved me. If there was one thing I could count on throughout my childhood, it was that my father *always* had a plan. But what could his plan have to do with a drugstore? I thought better of asking him, however, and decided to go with the flow. We got out of the car and walked into the store hand in hand, which my father always liked, and went directly to the aisle that had the items he wanted, which was his style. He found what he wanted—vitamins, I recall—and headed to the cashier. When we were next in line, my father grabbed my hand, bent down, and whispered in my ear.

"Mark, here's our chance to do something good for a stranger."

"What do you mean?" I whispered back.

"I read somewhere that if you have a bad day, you should do something good for a stranger, and all the bad will melt away," he replied.

My father looked to our left, and I followed his gaze, where I saw an elderly man with a walker slowly approaching. He had a bottle of pills in his hand, and a grimace on his face appeared when he saw the long line. I saw my father's face brighten.

"Please, go ahead of us," he said to the elderly man.

A few people behind us were annoyed, but my father didn't let that ruin his plan. The elderly man warmly acknowledged the kind gesture and eased his way to the counter. My father glowed; I could see that he was proud of himself. And then, all the "bad" in the day was gone. My father's plan had worked.

Yet he didn't stop there. In a move that confounded me, my father said he would like to pay for the elderly man's prescription. But it was right, and I was proud of my father. The elderly man replied that he was on a fixed income and would accept my father's help, and he gave us a look of gratitude.

My father took the elderly man's prescription and put it in on the counter with his vitamins. Then it happened. My father paused as he looked at the elderly man's prescription.

"Why aren't you buying generic?" he asked. It was a simple question.

I learned an important lesson from this experience: Even a good thing can be bad if pushed too far. The elderly gentleman hadn't asked for my father's help; the opportunity to help had just presented itself. Neither party wanted to examine the offer too closely, because it seemed simple enough. Both parties were happy with the arrangement and wanted to complete the transaction.

What could possibly go wrong? Well, it ended badly, and the old man paid for his own prescription.

The story about my dad is similar to what happened during the formation of the housing market bubble and subsequent housing market crash.

Simple Plans Often Become Complicated

Looking back, you'll recall that in the early part of the last decade, interest rates on mortgages dropped to their lowest levels since World War II. This change, combined with political incentives designed to increase homeownership, made it easier to borrow than ever before. An opportunity presented itself, and no one involved questioned the deal, because it seemed simple enough.

Even simple plans can have unexpected effects as I learned that day in the corner store with my father, and the financial plans for the housing market were not anywhere near simple.

This book is not about the housing bust, but the crash in the housing market is closely related to what occurred at the Federal Reserve Board at the beginning of the millennium. The result has been the loss of billions of dollars in wealth for the people of the United States. The story we are going to tell is all true and the names haven't been changed.

"On Friday, January 25, 2008, Alan Greenspan, said, 'You don't gradually fall into recession, you jump.' . . . I would never accuse the master of money supply of playing politics, but the only thing I want to know is if he said that with a straight face. Even he knows recessions do not just appear from nowhere."

—*Mark Grimaldi*, The Navigator, *February 2008*

Let's go back in time and see how the seeds for the Great Recession were sowed. Four years after President Clinton was elected, financial changes started to be made that set the scene for the 2008 Great Recession. It started in 1994 when the Clinton administration followed a determined policy to expand homeownership to more Americans. It was a simple plan, and two documents were at the foundation of that change.

One of those documents was the *Policy Statement on Discrimination in Lending* (Policy Statement). First, it needs to be stated that no one should be denied access to credit markets because of discrimination. In 1994, the Policy Statement was issued by an Interagency Task Force on Fair Lending set up by Clinton and chaired by then-HUD Secretary Henry Cisneros.[2] The stated objective of the policy, which applied to banks providing housing loans and other credit instruments, was to stop discriminatory lending practices to "protected classes" of citizens. The outcome of the Policy Statement was to loosen credit standards for loans. For example, in regard to mortgages, the door was thrown open:

> For example, ability to repay the loan is measured by suggested ratios of monthly housing expense to income (28%) and total obligations to income (36%). However, these guidelines allow considerable discretion on the part of the primary lender. In addition, the secondary market guidelines have in some cases been made more flexible, for example, with respect to factors such as stability of income (rather than stability of employment) and use of nontraditional ways of establishing good credit and ability to pay (e.g., use of past rent and utility payment records). Lenders should ensure that their loan processors and underwriters are aware of the provisions of the secondary market guidelines that provide various alternative and flexible means by which applicants may demonstrate their ability and willingness to repay their loans. Fannie Mae and Freddie Mac not infrequently purchase mortgages exceeding the suggested ratios, and their guidelines contain detailed discussions of the compensating factors that can justify higher ratios (and which must be documented by the primary lender).
>
> —*Policy Statement on Discrimination in Lending*, p. 15

A second change that loosened the rules of mortgage lending was the Community Reinvestment Act (CRA), originally enacted in 1977 and revised in 1995. The purpose of the CRA was to provide homeownership opportunities for underserved populations and small businesses by lowering standards for lending.[3] The CRA provided the means to ensure that banks provided financing for affordable community housing.[4] Every 24 months, banks subject to the CRA are numerically evaluated on how well they are meeting the regulatory approval under the law. In 1995, under pressure from the Clinton administration, the CRA was revised. The consequence was an expansion of home loans to low- and moderate-income borrowers and small businesses. Countrywide Financial was a major player in this market.[5] The revisions in the CRA allowed for the securitization of subprime mortgage loans, which began in 1997 with Bear Stearns.[6] Securitization of loans allowed for a mortgage to be divided and reorganized into an asset pool of other mortgages of which portions are sold to investors, thus, reducing the risk to the investor. . . uh-huh, okay, sure. In this manner, subprime mortgage loans could be sold off like stocks by the bank issuing the mortgages, and if that were the case, why worry too much about the quality of the mortgage?[7]

Other rule changes in the CRA allowed Fannie Mae and Freddie Mac to leverage themselves to the hilt in the mortgage market. They only needed 2.5 percent of the loan as collateral to guarantee a mortgage. Thus, loans to almost all borrowers could be made without worrying about repayments. Coupled with the fraudulent mortgage documents that other mortgage lenders developed, the blocks were being put in place for the coming meltdown. With lowered lending standards and pressure from the federal government to make loans, all that was needed was to wait for a drop in the interest rates, ala Alan Greenspan.

Moving On . . .

Let's move forward five years to 1999 to see how the simple plan was working. After the great stock market run of 1995 to 1999, the country was flush with capital. Watching the market had become the most popular American pastime. Local eateries had CNBC on the TV, and customers watched the Nasdaq Composite Index soar from 2000 in July 1998 to an all-time high of 5409 on March 10, 2000. Everyone seemed to have a story about a dot-com millionaire. Retirement plans were assuming growth rates of 10 percent to 12 percent per a year. Hoorah!

The new century was sure to bring more of the same, people thought. Investment advisers were telling people to take out a second mortgage on their homes and invest it in the stock market. The newest investors believed the stock market never went down. When the U.S. Federal Reserve Board (Fed) met on March 21, 2000, that certainly seemed to be the case: The Nasdaq Composite Index, though it had declined, was still at 4712. "That's just normal market volatility" was the thought. Travelers in high-end hotels at international airports told each other in casual lobby conversations not to sell their stocks.

My Fed, Your Fed

On December 23, 1913, Congress created the Federal Reserve System, which serves as the nation's central bank. The system consists of a seven-member board of governors headquartered in Washington, D.C., and 12 reserve banks located in major cities throughout the United States.

The seven members of the board of governors are appointed by the president and confirmed by the Senate to serve 14-year terms of office. The most important policymaking body of the Federal Reserve System is the Federal Open Market Committee (FOMC). The FOMC is composed of 12 members—the seven members of the board of governors and five of the 12 reserve bank presidents. The FOMC holds eight regularly scheduled meetings per year. At these meetings, the FOMC reviews economic and financial conditions and determines the appropriate actions to take, if any.

Yet, there was a big storm "a-coming." By the time the FOMC (Fed) met on May 16, 2000, the Nasdaq Composite Index had declined by 21 percent, to 3718. But here's where it gets interesting. Despite the precipitous market decline, the Fed didn't cut interest rates. In fact, it increased the federal funds rate by 0.50 percent.[8]

The downward spiral continued: By the time the Fed met on October 3, 2000, the Nasdaq Composite Index was down to 3456.

In other words, it had lost 1950 points, or 36 percent, from its March 10, 2000, high. The Fed, in response, did nothing, noting in its commentary that "the risks are weighted mainly towards situations that may generate heightened inflation pressures in the future." The federal funds rate stayed at 6.50 percent.

By the Fed's next meeting, on November 15, 2000, the Nasdaq Composite Index was down to 2920. That was 2489 points, or 46 percent, below its March 10, 2000, high. Again, the Fed did nothing, issuing virtually the same commentary about inflation.

The Fed's last meeting of the year took place on December 19, 2000. At the time, the Nasdaq Composite Index was down to 2512. That was 2897 points, or 53 percent, below its March 10, 2000, high. The index had lost more than half of its value. Again, the Fed did nothing. This time, however, it issued an unrealistic commentary.

> "The drag on demand and profits from rising energy costs, as well as eroding consumer confidence, reports of substantial shortfalls in sales and earnings, and stress in some segments of the financial markets suggest that economic growth may be slowing further," the Fed wrote. "While some inflation risks persist, they are diminished by the more moderate pace of economic activity and by the absence of any indication that longer-term inflation expectations have increased. The committee will continue to monitor closely the evolving economic situation."

At the time, this statement was puzzling. To start, the Fed referenced "stress in some segments of the financial markets," which was the understatement of the year. The Nasdaq Composite Index had lost half of its value in nine months. Microsoft alone had lost more than $270 billion in market capitalization. Yet it kept the federal funds rate at 6.50 percent. Figure 2.1 depicts the unchanging federal funds rate from May to December 2000 as the Nasdaq Composite Index kept losing value. During the period from January 3 to December 29, 2000, the Dow Jones Industrial Average lost 5 percent of its value, as shown in Table 2.1. The recession's effect on the Dow was delayed, and consequently the Fed may have been influenced by the smaller drop in the Dow as compared to the Nasdaq. The Dow was not spared during the Great Recession, and it lost around 22 percent of its capitalization from January 3 to December 29, 2008.

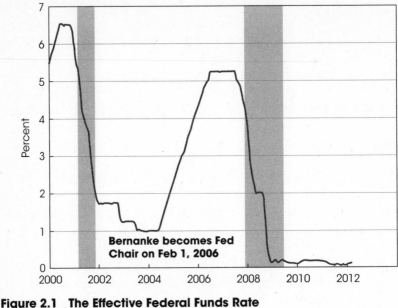

Figure 2.1   The Effective Federal Funds Rate
Source: Board of Governors of the Federal Reserve System.

Just weeks later, on the first business day of 2001, January 3, the Fed suddenly changed its tune. The economic situation wasn't "evolving," as the Fed had noted in its December 19 comments; in fact, it had fallen into distress, if the Fed's actions are any indication. On January 3, the Fed cut the federal funds rate by 0.50 percent. More rate cuts followed quickly. In fact, in the 13 months following its November 15, 2000, meeting—in which the Fed declared that "risks are weighted mainly towards situations that may generate heightened inflation pressure in the foreseeable future"—the policymakers decreased rates 11 times, by a total of 4.75 percent. They cut again on November 6, 2002, by 0.50 percent and June 25, 2003, by 0.25 percent. By the time the Fed was finished, the federal funds rate had fallen from 6.50 percent to 1.00 percent.

Why so much so fast? Because rates should have been cut in the fourth quarter of 2000, in which case the effect would have been felt in the economy starting in 2001. Because there were no 2000 rate cuts, however, the cuts had to come fast in order to be felt quickly.

Table 2.1 A Timeline of Interest Rates, Median Income, and a Falling Nasdaq Index

Date	Feb. 2, 2000	March 21, 2000	May 16, 2000	August 22, 2000	October 3, 2000	Nov. 15, 2000	Dec. 19, 2000
Core inflation	2.7%	3.2%	3.1%	3.7%	3.5%	3.4%	3.4%
Unemployment rate	4.0%	4.1%	3.8%	4.0%	3.9%	3.9%	3.9%
GDP	7.3%[a]	7.3%[a]	7.3%[a]	1.0%[a]	-0.50%[a]	-0.50%[a]	
Median household income	$40,696[b]	$40,696[b]	$40,696[b]	$40,696[b]	$40,696[b]	$40,696[b]	$40,696[b]
Median home price	$163,500	$162,400	$162,600	$169,000	$171,500	$176,300	$176,300
Federal funds rate	5.75%	6.00%	6.50%	6.50%	6.50%	6.50%	6.50%
Nasdaq Composite Index close	4073.96	4711.70	3717.57	3958.22	3455.57	2920.25	2511.70[c]
Dow Jones Industrial Average (rounded)	11003	10907	109935	11139	10700	10708	10584[d]

[a]Measured quarterly, as of most recent quarter-end: 12/31/99 for February 2, March 21, and May 16; 3/31/00 for August 22; 9/30/00 for October 3, November 15, and December 19.
[b]Measured annually, as of 12/31/99.
[c]A 38% drop in the Nasdaq over the time period.
[d]A 4% drop in the Dow over the time period.

The 36-Day Election

The question is: Why didn't the Fed cut rates when economic conditions indicated it should have? Did it not see the signs of trouble—or did it choose to ignore them as political events gripped the nation with the 36-day legal battle for the 2000 presidential election? A loud chorus of political disunion was in effect at the time. Was it enough to paralyze the Fed into inaction?

Specifically, on November 7, 2000, the presidential election was contested, creating a bitter political battle between George W. Bush and Al Gore. Thirty-six days later, on December 12, 2000, the U.S. Supreme Court essentially ruled five to four in favor of Bush by stopping a recount in the State of Florida.[9]

On December 18, 2000 (one day prior to the Fed's December meeting), Alan Greenspan, then chairman of the Fed, went to the White House to congratulate Bush on his victory. It had to have been a tough conversation. Bush had been unhappy with Greenspan for not cutting rates in 1992, causing another weak economy. During this political turmoil, a cut in rates may have been interpreted as a show of support for the incumbent Democratic administration. The Fed did not choose sides and rates were left unchanged.

Greenspan Who?

President Ronald Reagan first appointed Alan Greenspan as Federal Reserve chairman in August 1987. He was reappointed at successive four-year intervals until retiring on January 31, 2006. His tenure was the second-longest tenure in history. He received favorable media coverage, and was often referred to as a "rock star." However, he also received much criticism for being too deferential to President George W. Bush. Economist Paul Krugman, for example, once wrote that Greenspan possessed a "lack of sincerity" by "repeatedly shilling for whatever the Bush administration wants" and "has betrayed the trust placed in the Fed chairman."

Greenspan wrote in *The Age of Turbulence* of his 2000 meeting with Bush, "In this instance, I was obliged to report that the short-term outlook was not good. For the first time in years, we seemed to be faced with the real possibility of recession." In other words, on Monday, December 18, 2000, Greenspan told the president-elect the country faced the real possibility of recession, and yet on Tuesday, December 19, when the Fed met, Greenspan did nothing.

Was this a reaction to uncertainty in the economy or was the decision effected by political events?

"Famously, the Fed sat on its hands heading into the 1992 and 2000 elections. I do not foresee any difference this year, which means the Fed needs to act early and often at the beginning of this year. However, this may cause an overreaction. This 'overreaction' may be the most important economic event of the year. If the Fed cuts too much and too soon, they could stimulate an already bubbling inflation pot. This would almost ensure a (future) recession."

—*Mark Grimaldi,* The Navigator, *January 2008*

Table 2.2 shows the changes in the effective federal funds rate from January 1, 2000, to March 3, 2012.[10] It can be seen that it has been a bumpy ride for the rate. The darker areas in the table represent two recessionary periods. When Ben Bernanke became Federal Reserve Board chairman in February 2006, the rates were on the way up again and reached a plateau of slightly 5.5 percent just before the beginning of the 2008 Great Recession. It was around August 24, 2007, when the credit markets froze in the United States. In the last few months of 2007, the depth of the business slowdown began to be realized, and that realization can be seen in Table 2.1 as the federal fund rates began to shoot downward. Figure 2.1 vividly illustrates the reduction in the federal funds rate as the bottom dropped out of the economy. In any case, what happened next was the collapse of the 2001–2007 housing bubble.

Can You Say Bubble?

In 2006, the policymakers at the Federal Reserve seemed oblivious to the impending collapse that was coming in a few months. This perspective can be seen in the minutes of the FOMC on January 31 and December 31, 2006. The FOMC exhibits a jovial, clubhouse atmosphere of collegial members who seem to genuinely enjoy their meetings as they congratulate each other for various activities. Before Greenspan left in January 2006, this was the assessment of the economy by the FOMC:

> I would say that the overall outlook is quite positive. The economy
> is near full employment with real GDP tending toward trend-like

(Continued)

(Continued)

growth. Core inflation is within a reasonable range but a bit on the high side. Needless to say, it's fitting for Chairman Greenspan to leave office with the economy in such solid shape. And if I might torture a simile, I would say, Mr. Chairman, that the situation you're handing off to your successor is a lot like a tennis racquet with a gigantic sweet spot.

In December 2006 that jovial demure still continued as the economy was showing mixed signs of positive and negative growth.[11] After the December meeting, the recent increases in federal fund rates were left unchanged.

Builders in my region report that the ability of potential homebuyers to qualify for home mortgages is becoming an issue. One homebuilder from Columbus told me that he is giving away new cars as well, but his motivation provides a twist on the Lexus story. Some of his customers are struggling to qualify for mortgage loans. So he's giving them new cars so that they can get rid of their current cars and the payment obligations that go along with them. [Laughter] He's not giving them a Lexus; he's giving them a Kia. [Laughter] Now, if we could get these homebuilders to adopt a Buy American strategy, we might also be able to solve our domestic auto problem.

Figure 2.1 also shows the rates since 2009 have been essentially zero. For individual savers, today's rates are so low that they are negative—that is, the more you save, the more you go into the hole. In other words, if you are saving money, you are losing money because the inflation rate is higher than the interest rate earned on your savings.

The Fed's rapid rate cuts from 2001 to the middle of 2004 had created a demand for homes unlike anything the country had ever seen. Prior to the 2000 presidential election, the average 8.50 percent interest rate on a $200,000 mortgage required a monthly payment of $1,537.83, which could be supported by an annual income of $65,907. As a result of the Fed's rate cuts, interest rates on 30-year mortgages fell below 3.00 percent, and the same payment of $1,537.83 could cover a $364,756 mortgage. That represented an

82 percent increase in the mortgage an American with a $65,000 income could carry. The country began buying houses, the bubble expanded, and the selling price of homes shot up.

Legislative efforts—such as the American Dream Down Payment Initiative, signed into law on December 15, 2003—only exacerbated the problem. The Act was funded with an annual appropriation of $200 million. Suddenly, first-time homebuyers had up to $10,000 of free money to be used for down payments, closing costs, or renovations. The act—which pumped up to $200 million per year into the already bubbling housing market during fiscal years 2004 through 2007—allowed an estimated 80,000 more Americans to buy homes. In other periods, these homeowners would not have qualified to purchase a home, and mortgages began to be approved as fast as they could be signed.

All of those mortgages and government programs drove up demand for homes, which in turn drove up housing prices. According to the Office of Federal Housing Enterprise Oversight (OFHEO), the average U.S. home price climbed 12.95 percent in 2005, about double the historical average of 6.4 percent. By March 2006, home prices were at record highs.

Ever wonder how all those new SUVs going down the interstates were financed? Homeowners used the increasing bubble value in their homes to finance RVs, SUVs, exotic vacations, vacation homes, and expensive boats. If you wanted it, you just refinanced your house every time the value of the home increased.

Americans, as they did in 1999, thought the rally would last forever. This time, however, the Fed wanted to curtail any chances of an inflationary cycle. Between 2004 and 2006, it raised the federal funds rate 17 times to 5.25 percent. The FOMC noted in its December 13, 2005, press release that "possible increases in resource utilization as well as elevated energy prices have the potential to add to inflation pressures."[12]

As interest rates rose, so did the rates on adjustable-rate mortgages. Normally, borrowers who couldn't make their mortgage payment would refinance or sell their home—but this time, they couldn't refinance because interest rates were rising, and many had taken out all the equity in their homes. Homeowners couldn't sell because the housing market was plummeting. Troubled borrowers had only one choice, and foreclosures started to rise. A double whammy occurred as the consumer economy started to sputter because homeowners could no longer use the increasing value of the homes as an ATM.

"A recession can be a self-fulfilling prophecy. If consumers act like a recession is coming, it will only increase the odds of one. My best guess is that we are already in a recession, or that one will start very soon."

—*Mark Grimaldi*, The Navigator, *January 2008*

Often, government efforts to stimulate the economy have effects that are not fully anticipated—in part because the effect of the stimulation is often seen well after that effect is desirable. As Greenspan notes in *The Age of Turbulence* (2008, p. 212), "recessions are tricky to forecast" because "sentiment about the economic outlook usually does not shift smoothly from optimism to neutrality to gloom; it's like the bursting of a dam, in which a flood backs up until cracks appear and the dam is breached." In this case, however, the recession could have been predicted—and prevented. But it wasn't.

Greenspan has provided selfless service to our country that shows he is a true patriot—but in regard to the financial events of 2000 to 2005 he lacked the vision needed to react to the changes in the economy that had taken place during this period. Recessions don't just appear; there are signals, such as stock market meltdowns. If you saw it coming Mr. Greenspan, you ignored it.

My Takeaway Is More than Fries

Every intervention of the federal government into the economy has long-range and lasting consequences that are often unanticipated. One aspect is a constant in these interventions; it changes the way we act. Just think about what we are willing to do to reduce our taxes.

Although it may seem complicated, it is important to consider what the Fed or congressional laws may have on our actions. Back in 2005, as everyone was experiencing the rise in housing prices, I remember sitting in a coffee shop and hearing a mother tell her friend as they shared coffee:

> "I told Todd to buy a house. He doesn't even need to make a down payment with an interest-only loan. All he has to do is buy a house and then in three years he can sell it for more than he paid for it," she said. Apparently, Todd was her son who had just started working after graduating from college.

And her friend listened thoughtfully, nodding her head.

I wondered if her son followed her advice and tried to sell his house in 2008. The conversation between them reminded me of the story where J. P. Morgan recalled how he had heard elevator operators giving stock tips before the 1929 stock crash, and it made him think it was time to sell stocks.

There is a herd instinct when it comes to financial investments, whether it is houses, stocks, or tulip bulbs. When everyone is running after the same imaginary value, it is important to stop and consider what is really occurring. Whether it is a Madoff or Sanford interest pyramid or just a general run on an asset such as gold, it is necessary to control the investment excitement that is generated and consider what is actually occurring.

Where is the next bubble? How about the lemming excitement of crowd funding for soliciting investment funds? Crowd funding is built for bubbles and rumors. With crowd funding, entrepreneurs with an idea for a new company are underwritten by small investors who make investments over the Internet. The funds are received in return for securities from start-up companies. The Jobs Bill signed into law in April 2012 makes it easier for startups to use crowd funding to solicit up to $1 million in annual funding without registering as an initial public offering (IPO) with the Securities and Exchange Commission (SEC) and providing a swath of financial disclosures. These offerings are also exempt from state securities commission reviews. This is another legislative step in the dismantling of the New Deal legislation of the 1930s when protections were initiated to protect investors against the excesses that led to the 1929 stock market crash.[13] Small capitalized organizations can solicit monies for nonregistered securities without disclosing audited financial information required by the SEC for other IPOs. It is more of a buyer beware attitude managed by the Internet site where the donations are made.[14] So get ready for the "easy money" sales pitches and potential investment fraud.

Summary

In *The Age of Turbulence* (2008), Greenspan acknowledges there were signs of trouble in 2000, including a precipitous decline in the Nasdaq Composite Index, but argues that two major concerns were the disappearing national debt and disinflation.

The national debt is a legitimate concern. The national debt is created when the U.S. Treasury sells bonds and notes to investors. If the Fed wants to increase demand and spur growth, it buys U.S. Treasury securities from the public, thus increasing the amount of money in the economy. If there are no U.S. Treasury securities to buy (i.e., no debt), the Fed has one less monetary tool in its arsenal, and that was Greenspan's concern.

Disinflation, which is an inflation rate that grows more slowly than it has in the past, is always a concern. While lower prices are usually good, disinflation can easily become deflation, which is a sustained decline in prices. If prices fall for an extended period of time, your debts get larger. For example, if you use a credit card to buy a TV for $3,000, and it costs $2,000 a few months later, you owe an extra $1,000. Consumers thus cut back on spending. Because two-thirds of the nation's gross domestic product comes from consumer spending, that's bad.

Neither the national debt nor disinflation was a problem in 2000, however. The national debt had declined due to record-setting budget surpluses that would be short lived. And the average inflation rate in the third quarter of 2000 was 3.44 percent, which doesn't seem indicative of disinflation. The Fed and Congress set the stage for a bubble, so what happened to us? The next chapter deals with the housing market and the additional mistakes and myopic behavior that caused millions of U.S. citizens to lose their homes and their wealth.

Reference

Greenspan, A. 2008. *Age of Turbulence.* New York: Penguin Books.

Notes

1. See "The Dutch Tulip Bubble of 1637," Dam Interesting, www.damninteresting .com/the-dutch-tulip-bubble-of-1637.

2. In 1999, Cisneros pleed guilty to a single misdemeanor charge of lying to the FBI about $250,000 he paid to a former mistress. Cisneros had originally been indicted in December 1997.

3. Pub. L. 95-128, title VIII, 91 Stat. 1147, 12 U.S.C. §2901 et seq. The law was revised in 1995 and has been revised almost every two years since then.

4. As a matter of practice, however, banks generally do not subject CRA-related loans and investments to the same standards for profit and loss as their other lines of business. CRA investments tend to be viewed as *de facto* grants or as "soft" money with significantly higher risk and lower return expectations than other lines of business activity. (Financial Issues Subcommittee Recommendation to the Federal Communications Commission's Advisory Committee on Diversity for Communications in the Digital Age, December 10, 2004, Recommendation on the Community Reinvestment Act.)

5. Countrywide Financial has been implicated in mortgage fraud, and in 2011 paid $108 million to settle its mortgage fraud claims.

6. Bear Stearns was founded in 1923 and ceased to exist in May 2008 due to its trading activities in the securitization of mortgages.

7. In 2009, Forbes.com called the CRA a "poisonous cocktail." (www.forbes .com/2009/10/03/community-reinvestment-act-mortgages-housing-opinions contributors-peter-schweizer.html.)

8. Although federal funds are considered "borrowings," technically they are not. They are purchases of funds from one bank by another, usually on an overnight basis. These borrowings are made because of the reserves a bank is required to hold. The rate at which the funds are loaned is called the federal funds rate, and that rate determines the interest rates charged on other credit instruments (i.e., mortgage rates).

9. The U.S. Supreme Court overturned the Florida Supreme Court ruling that called for manual recounts. The court's unsigned "per curiam" decision carried the opinion of seven justices and says that the recounts as ordered by the Florida court suffered from constitutional problems. However, four justices wrote dissenting opinions regarding possible remedies in the case. The court said in the 7–2 per curiam, "Because it is evident that any recount seeking to meet the Dec. 12 date will be unconstitutional . . . we reverse the judgment of the Supreme Court of Florida ordering the recount to proceed." For a complete timeline of the events of the election, see www.uselectionatlas.org/INFORMATION/ARTICLES/pe2000timeline.php.

10. On occasion there may be a difference between the effective and target federal funds rate. The target rate is set by the U.S. Federal Reserve Bank. The effective rate may drift away from the target rate. It is computed as the weighted average rate across all negotiated interest rates among banks' overnight borrowings. It should also be noted that since 2003, the federal funds rate has been divided into a primary and a secondary borrowing rate based on the creditworthiness of the banking institution seeking federal funds.

11. The jovial attitude is present in the most recently released minutes of the FOMC from the 2007–2010 period. These documents were released prior to

the Fed's five-year schedule under a Freedom of Information request, and they have been redacted.

12. www.federalreserve.gov/boarddocs/press/monetary/2005/20051213/default .htm.

13. Remember, banks were led into financial distress within a short time after the Glass-Steagall Act, passed during the New Deal, was repealed.

14. The IPO issuer has a choice between selecting a broker-dealer registration or Internet portal registration. The latter is more lightly regulated.

CHAPTER

Drop the "U" Out of "Housing" and You Get What America Got

The only real mistake is the one from which we learn nothing.

John Powell

We had a bubble in housing. I really didn't get it until very late in 2005 and 2006.

—Alan Greenspan

I remember a morning in early March 2006 as if it were yesterday—because my first thought of the day was that if I lost my home, I couldn't afford to buy it back.

By now, many U.S. homeowners have experienced that fear and seen it become a reality. The number of "underwater" homeowners grew by about 400,000 during the fourth quarter of 2011, to 11.1 million, as home prices fell as a result of seasonal declines and a slowdown in processing homes through the foreclosure process. According to data aggregator CoreLogic, 22.8 percent of all residential properties with a mortgage had negative equity.

Back in 2006, however, the U.S. housing market was on a tear. President George W. Bush's 2004 campaign slogan "the ownership society" encouraged Americans to own homes. That became easier in the wake of the recession caused by the dot-come bubble bursting in 2000. The U.S. Federal Reserve Board (Fed) dramatically

33

lowered the federal funds rate, from about 6.5 percent to 1 percent over a three-year period, spurring easy credit for banks and low-interest mortgage rates.

As more and more Americans entered the housing market, home prices skyrocketed, peaking in March 2006. Americans, meanwhile, just couldn't conceive of the possibility that the housing market would not continue its rally. As a result, Americans lined up for loans at any cost, even those they could not afford. Beyond the rush to buy, the number of suspicious activity reports (SARs) filed by depository institutions indicating the level of mortgage loan fraud increased by 1,411 percent between 1997 and 2005, as reported by the U.S. Treasury.[1]

Then the Fed stepped in. Between 2004 and 2006, the policy-makers raised interest rates 17 times, ultimately stopping when the federal funds rate hit 5.25 percent in 2006. That increased the monthly payments for adjustable-rate mortgages and lowered demand for homes. As a result, homeowners who had adjustable-rate mortgages could no longer make their payments. At the same time, they couldn't sell their homes, because the housing market had stalled. Most home buyers had been told not to worry about the affordability of a home, as the value of the home would continue to increase. That was false, and the housing crash started.

In March 2006, of course, that process had only just begun, so my fear that morning was speculative.

Mark's Perspective

It was frightening enough, however, that I wrote about it in the March 2006 issue of *The Navigator*. "Inflation since 1997 is roughly 21 percent. That means to calculate the value of your house in 2011, take the 1997 value and add 21 percent. For most of us, that is quite an adjustment from 2006 values."

We can't change what has happened in the past, but we can learn from our mistakes in order to hopefully avoid making similar ones in the future. In that vein, this chapter is not an economist's guide to the housing market meltdown; it is intended to explain how the housing market declined, how we could have foreseen it, what we can learn from it, and if we can take advantage of it now.

In early August 2007, the Dow Jones Industrial Average enjoyed its biggest one-day point gain in four years, rising by 286 points to 13468. Just a year later, the U.S. economy was shaken to its core by a credit crunch stemming from a lack of confidence in subprime mortgages, leading the U.S. government to implement a sweeping bailout package unlike anything seen since the Great Depression.[2] At the time, trying to pinpoint the significance of a world-shattering event such as this was tricky.

Now, however, we have a better perspective. Looking back, it's easy to see that a convergence of factors created the housing market bubble. The markets had been deregulated. In the years leading up to the bubble, the federal government did everything possible to make the dream of homeownership available to every American. To bail out the U.S. economy, the Fed cut the federal funds rate from 6.5 percent in May 2000 to 1 percent in June 2003, and as lending standards declined, more and more risky loans were written.

2000 to 2006: The Perfect Storm

In the early 2000s, as the Internet boom ended and the September 11 terrorist attacks shocked the nation, the Fed tried to combat an economic slowdown by lowering the federal funds rate. From August 2001 to the middle of 2003, the federal funds rate fell from 3.5 percent to 1 percent.

At the same time, the American Dream Down Payment Initiative, which was signed into law on December 15, 2003, provided to first-time home buyers with up to $10,000 for a down payment, closing costs, or home rehabilitation. With $200 million per year authorized for fiscal years 2004 through 2007, $800 million was pumped into the housing market, putting 80,000 Americans on the road to homeownership for the first time.

These steps certainly stimulated the economy—but they also led the nation to gorge on real estate. Free down payments and lower interest rates cut monthly mortgage payments, encouraging consumers to take out loans. If you want a $200,000 mortgage at 8.50 percent, you'd need an annual income of $65,907 to support the monthly payment of $1,537.83. If you can get an adjustable-rate mortgage at 3.00 percent, however, you get a mortgage of $364,756 and still keep your monthly payment at $1,537.83. Americans went crazy buying houses based on the monthly payments. They didn't stop to think what would happen if interest rates rose and their mortgages got adjusted back up.

As demand for mortgages increased, lenders began offering two new products—subprime mortgages, which were made to individuals with questionable credit histories, and Alt-A mortgages, which were made to individuals *without documented income*—many of which had adjustable interest rates. Borrowers with poor credit histories made up 21 percent of mortgagees during 2005 and 2006, up from 9 percent between 1996 and 2000.

The availability of these loans encouraged individuals to buy more real estate, which fueled home-price appreciation. By 2004 and 2005, the housing market boom had begun to take on a life of its own. In July 2005, for example, the president of a small local bank sat in my office and crowed about how well the bank's mortgage department was doing thanks to a new product called a reverse-amortization mortgage, which arises when the payment made by the borrower is less than the accrued interest and the difference is added to the loan balance. A $500,000 reverse-amortization mortgage would require only a monthly payment of only $416.67, he said. Of course, the amount owed would increase, but it didn't create any difficulties as housing prices continued to increase.

Soon, institutions were getting on the bandwagon. The Federal National Mortgage Association (FNMA), which is usually referred to as Fannie Mae, and the Federal Home Mortgage Corporation (FHMC), which is usually referred to as Freddie Mac, took these new types of mortgages and with them created mortgage-backed securities, as they did with all mortgages.

There was one problem, however; these mortgage-backed securities had different "tranches," each with different streams of income and risk.[3] For example, the first tranche's income stream might be relatively secure, the second tranche's income stream less so, and third tranche's income stream even less so. The idea was to reduce the overall risk in the security. Losses were allocated from the bottom up, as shown in Figure 3.1. Figure 3.1 also shows various tranches that could be combined into one securitized investment. With this structure, billions of dollars of mortgage-backed securi-

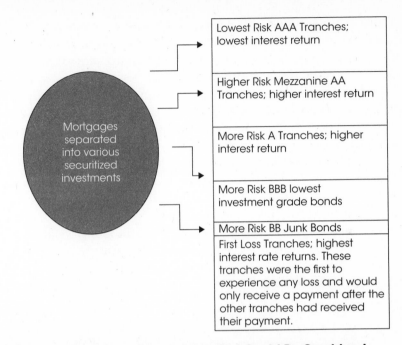

Lowest Risk AAA Tranches; lowest interest return

Higher Risk Mezzanine AA Tranches; higher interest return

More Risk A Tranches; higher interest return

More Risk BBB lowest investment grade bonds

More Risk BB Junk Bonds

First Loss Tranches; highest interest rate returns. These tranches were the first to experience any loss and would only receive a payment after the other tranches had received their payment.

Mortgages separated into various securitized investments

Figure 3.1   Example of the Tranches That Could Be Combined into One Collateralized Debt Obligation (CDO), Repackaged from Numerous Mortgages
The CDO would have a paper value in the hundreds of millions of dollars.

ties that had subprime mortgages as underlying collateral received investment-grade ratings from the bond rating agencies and were considered secure investments.

At the same time, investors—mostly big financial institutions— had money to spare, thanks to low interest rates, which made it more profitable to borrow money and invest it in financial assets. These financial institutions didn't want to invest that extra money in historically safe investments, such as government and corporate bonds, because low interest rates had reduced the returns on those vehicles. Instead, they took advantage of the Fed's easy money and bought mortgage-backed securities just like everyone else. Overall debt grew at an alarming rate, just as it did at other times when the Fed held interest rates too low for too long, such as the 1970s. The financial institutions that bought mortgage-backed debt securities generally had no expertise evaluating their underlying collateral, and instead made decisions solely by the rating, which was deceiving. This strategy soon turned into a problem.

It was a vicious circle. The proliferation of mortgage-backed securities created even more demand for subprime mortgages. The subprime mortgage market grew from $35 billion in 1994 to $140 billion in 2000, an average annual growth rate of 26 percent, according to the Federal Reserve. Former pizza delivery boys got jobs writing mortgages.

All of these mortgages drove up demand for homes, which continued to drive up housing prices. According to the Office of Federal Housing Enterprise Oversight (OFHEO), the average U.S. home price climbed 12.95 percent in 2005 (despite rising mortgage rates in the second half of the year). This rate of appreciation was about double the historical average of 6.4 percent.

Oops, Almost Made It

Americans thought the rally would last forever, but by then the Fed changed course. As we've noted, between 2004 and 2006, the policymakers raised interest rates 17 times to 5.25 percent. It was expected that the rate for mortgages would increase and cool the housing market. But as can be seen in Figure 3.2, 15-year and 30-year fixed mortgage rates did not reach a higher interest rate

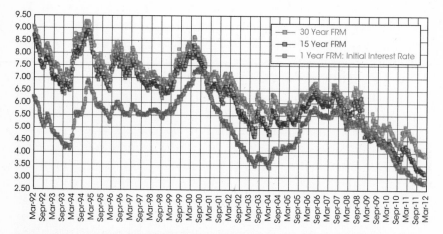

Figure 3.2   Home Mortgage Interest Rates from March 1992 to March 2012
Source: Mortgage-X.com. Copyright © 2012.

plateau until 2006, and even so, home buyers could still switch to adjustable-rate mortgages (ARMs), which continued to stay below 4 percent until the middle of 2005. Although the Fed raised interest rates and expected mortgage rates to increase, other events occurred to prevent mortgage rates from increasing in unison with the Fed's increases as they had in the past. Huge amounts of money were flowing into the United States from overseas locations such as China. As the booming U.S. economy ran trade deficits with other countries, these countries poured their surplus cash into the United States. The effect was to stop mortgage rates from increasing as overseas cash flows were used to finance triple-A securitized mortgages.[4]

So, subprime home buyers still bought homes and the boom continued. After an initial period of low interest rates, the rates on ARMs increased as the Fed's monetary tightening effects finally started to take hold. The increased monthly payments meant all those homeowners who had purchased homes they couldn't afford without the teaser rates on ARMs could no longer make their payments. In a normal situation, they would simply sell their homes, but this time they couldn't because the housing market had stalled. Two whammies at once started to bring the house down.

By March 2006, the housing market had peaked and was slowly declining. By the end of 2006, 13.3 percent of subprime borrowers were behind in their payments, the highest level since 2002, according to the Mortgage Bankers Association. At the same time, 4.5 percent of subprime mortgages were in the process of being foreclosed, up from just 3.3 percent a year earlier. Initially considered a problem in a limited segment of the market, it began expanding, and foreclosures in the mortgage market as a whole also hit a record high.

Countrywide Financial was a major player in the subprime mortgage market until the mortgage lender collapsed and was purchased by Bank of America. The collapse was surrounded in cries of mortgage fraud. Figure 3.3 shows Countrywide's home page on February 1, 2005. Notice that in the lower right-hand corner of the home page, the bank is touting no-money-down and interest-only loans. Both of these practices contributed to the housing meltdown. Countrywide made a practice of encouraging homeowners to refinance their mortgages when interest rates increased. Once these loans were made, they were securitized and sold around the world.

Figure 3.3   Countrywide Financial's Home Page from February 1, 2005
Note: Countrywide Financial is a fraudulent company that has gone bankrupt and dissolved. The CEO has been prosecuted and has paid massive fines. There is no one left at the company.

2007: All Fall Down

> A new wave of mortgage defaults is imminent—a situation which would flood the housing market with an even greater supply of unsold homes and potentially weakens the U.S. economy as a whole. . . . Home prices will continue to fall.
> —*Mark Grimaldi*, The Navigator, *January 2007*

The housing market fell apart as two economic situations combined to create what many economists consider the perfect storm. First, interest rates began to rise, and second, housing prices began to weaken. Troubled borrowers had only one choice, and foreclosures on subprime loans started to rise.

Initially, the federal government insisted that the problem was contained. On June 5, 2007, Fed president Ben Bernanke told a South African audience that "troubles in the subprime sector seem unlikely to seriously spill over to the broader economy or the financial system."

That clearly wasn't true, however. As early as March 2007, the entire housing market was suffering, with national home sales and prices seeing dramatic declines. Existing-home sales were down 13 percent of their peak of 554,000 in March 2006 to 482,000 a year later, the steepest since 1989. Meanwhile, the national median price of existing homes had fallen 6 percent from a peak of $230,200 in July 2006 to $217,000 a year later.

If the problem had been limited just to the housing market, there might have been a quick resolution. But this housing market correction was like no other in that it led to a crisis of confidence in the global banking system.

Other events in 2007 highlighted the depth of the financial crisis. For example, in July Bear Stearns & Co. disclosed that two of its hedge funds, which had bet heavily on securities tied to subprime mortgages, had lost nearly all of their value. When Germany's IKB Deutsche Industriebank announced major subprime losses as well, forcing the German government to organize a €3.5 billion bailout in August 2007, the world began to worry.

Then, on August 9, 2007, French bank BNP Paribas announced that it would not allow investors to withdraw money from three funds because it couldn't determine the market for their holdings. "The complete evaporation of liquidity in certain market segments of the U.S. securitization market has made it impossible to value certain assets fairly regardless of their quality or credit rating," the bank said. In other words, banks didn't know what mortgage-backed securities holding subprime mortgages were worth, due to the tranches, and since no one was buying them, there was no market price.

As fear paralyzed the world credit markets, the world's central bankers responded. The European Central Bank (ECB) was the first to act, with an injection of €94.8 billion into European money markets, a larger infusion than the one that came after the September 11 terrorist attacks. Other central banks followed with similar but smaller steps. The Fed, for example, injected $38 billion into the money markets, but not in a traditional fashion. The Fed usually buys U.S. Treasuries, but this time it bought bonds backed by subprime mortgages, because there were so few buyers for them. The Fed became the buyer of last resort.

On August 31, 2007, President Bush tried to intervene, outlining a plan that would help troubled subprime borrowers keep their homes. The changes to the Federal Housing Administration (FHA) mortgage insurance program would allow more people to refinance with FHA insurance if they fell behind on ARMs, which offer low introductory rates that can later rise, sometimes doubling a monthly payment. White House officials estimated the initiative could help as many as 80,000 new homeowners—which, interestingly, is the exact number that were able to initially buy new homes thanks to the earlier passed American Dream Down Payment Initiative. Thanks for that!

The Fed, for its part, also followed the traditional playbook to some extent. On August 17, 2007, one week after the credit crunch first surfaced, the Fed lowered its discount rate (which it charges qualified lenders for temporary loans) from 6.25 percent to 5.75 percent. In a slightly more unusual move, the Fed also extended the duration on loans banks took out under the discount window, which is the facility through which the Fed makes loans to commercial banks (that pledge a variety of financial instruments as collateral), from overnight to 30 days.

Where Was the Fed?

Out killing inflation: The following is a quote from the Federal Open Market Committee (FOMC) meeting on August 7, 2007 (p. 113):

> The Federal Open Market Committee seeks monetary and financial conditions that will foster price stability and promote sustainable growth in output. To further its long-run objectives, the Committee in the immediate future seeks conditions in reserve markets consistent with maintaining the federal funds rate at an average of around 5.25 percent. Although the downside risks to growth have increased somewhat, the Committee's predominant policy concern remains the risk that inflation will fail to moderate as expected.

At first, these moves were well received, with the U.S. equity markets rallying to new highs in the following weeks. Still, tight credit conditions would not abate, so the Fed persisted, and soon showed it was willing to get aggressive if necessary. On September 18, the central bank cut both the discount rate and the federal funds rate, to 5.25 percent and 4.75 percent, respectively.

By the end of 2007, the discount rate was at 4.75 percent and the federal funds rate was at 4.25 percent, but it was clear these low interest rates wouldn't be the easy fix they were in the past. Some analysts said this was because the Fed hadn't responded quickly enough, but the medicine still didn't match the illness. It was impossible to value—and thus trade—banks' assets. By December 2007, the Fed understood and, in coordination with other world central banks, announced a surprise two-part plan to combat the credit crunch by pumping money into the global banking system.

First, the Fed, along with the ECB, Bank of Canada, Bank of England, and Swiss National Bank, created a new lending facility called a *term auction facility*. This was a hybrid of the Fed's two normal funding methods of auctioning of funds to 21 primary dealers via a system of repurchase agreements, and the discount window available to commercial banks.[5] Under the term auction facility, the Fed auctioned off funds, but any commercial bank deemed to be in generally sound financial condition by its local Fed bank could participate (anonymously, and by pledging a wider variety of financial instruments as collateral).

Second, the Fed set up $20 billion swap lines with the ECB and $4 billion swap lines with the Swiss National Bank. Under these swap lines, the Fed agreed to loan the central banks a total of $24 billion, which the banks could in turn lend to commercial banks in Europe.[6] This, it reasoned, would help large commercial banks in foreign countries gain access to U.S. dollars.

By then, the housing market was in dire straits. Sales of existing single-family homes fell in 2007 by 13 percent, the largest amount in 25 years. At the same time, the median home price dropped 1.8 percent to $217,000, the first annual price decline on record, which goes back to 1968. Lawrence Yuan, the chief economist at the National Association of Realtors, said it was likely that the country had not experienced such a decline in housing prices since the Great Depression.

We didn't know it then, but by the end of the year, the U.S. economy was already in a recession that came to be called the Great Recession.

2008: The Year of Reckoning

> "I believe the worst is yet to come," I wrote. "Why? Because unlike many other corrections (1987, 1997, 1998, 2001, and 2002), this time American homeowners have their biggest assets on the table, their houses."
>
> —*Mark Grimaldi*, The Navigator, *February 2008*

Despite the confidence of many economists, Americans were scared, and their fears showed up in the world equity markets. January 2008 was particularly volatile, with some members of the news media even referring to January 21 as "Black Monday."

At this time, the government was insisting we weren't in a recession. Former Fed Chairman Alan Greenspan, for example, said in January that data showing a recession "is by no means conclusive" because "you don't gradually fall into recession, you jump."

Meanwhile, the Fed kept trying. On January 22, it announced a surprise intermeeting rate cut, this time reducing the discount rate and federal funds rate to 4.00 percent and 3.50 percent, respectively. At its regularly scheduled January 30 meeting, the Fed acted again, reducing the discount rate and federal funds rate to 3.50 percent and 3.00 percent, respectively.

Unfortunately, the Fed's moves weren't enough to make financial institutions increase their borrowing from one another. There was still a crisis of confidence, often referred to as "counterparty risk" or default risk. Counterparty risk is a fear that a financial institution will default on its obligations. As a result of these risk concerns, lending dried up, and an unexpected failure shook the global financial system when Bear Stearns collapsed.

Like many financial firms, Bear Stearns had invested, through its hedge funds, in bundles of subprime mortgages. In July 2007, the firm disclosed that two of its hedge funds had lost nearly all of their value amid a rapid decline in the market for subprime mortgages. To prevent the market crash that it believed would result from Bear Stearns becoming insolvent, in an emergency unscheduled meeting on March 16, the Fed cut the discount rate to 3.25 percent (but left the federal funds rate at 3.00 percent). The policymakers quickly realized that wasn't enough. So, just two days later, on March 18, cut the discount rate to 2.50 percent and the federal funds rate to 2.25 percent. Still not enough. So the Fed next engineered the controversial takeover of Bear Stearns by JPMorgan Chase. The U.S. government (i.e., the taxpayers) assumed the risk of Bear Stearns's less liquid assets—bundles of subprime mortgages.

Fed chairman Ben Bernanke defended the bailout by stating that a Bear Stearns bankruptcy could have caused a "chaotic unwinding" of investments across the U.S. markets and thereby threatened the entire U.S. economy. Former Fed chairman Alan Greenspan criticized the Fed for allowing itself to exceed its mandate of promoting growth and stable prices. His reasoning was that the Fed's actions would have unintended consequences on the economy as a whole.

Greenspan, it turns out, was on target, as the fallout from the subprime mess had by then started to show up throughout the U.S. economy. Employers were cutting more jobs. Consumers weren't spending. They couldn't even repay their loans. By March 2008, nearly 30 million homeowners, 25 percent of them, were under water—more than four times the amount that were just five years earlier. By the summer of 2008, the situation was dire, and RealtyTrac reported that foreclosure filings rose 48 percent year-over-year in May 2008, meaning that one in every 483 U.S. households received a foreclosure filing. A record 9 percent of American homeowners were either behind on their mortgage payments or in foreclosure at the end of June 2008, according to the Mortgage Bankers Association. Moreover, that was only the beginning, since the number of adjustable-rate loans scheduled to reset to higher rates peaked in May and June, pushing more homeowners into default and foreclosure in the third and fourth quarters of 2008.

By this time, even mortgage giants Fannie Mae and Freddie Mac were struggling, and the Fed felt it had no choice but to assist the Treasury Department in preventing their collapse. The multipart plan to take over Fannie Mae and Freddie Mac and the $5 trillion in home loans they backed was announced on September 7. It was one of the most sweeping interventions in the financial markets since the Great Depression.

The Fat Lady Sings: "It's Not Over"

On September 15, 2008, one of Wall Street's most venerable financial institutions—the 158-year-old investment bank Lehman Brothers Holdings—finally succumbed after losing billions in bad real estate–related loans. Adding salt to the wound, Merrill Lynch & Co. sold itself to Bank of America, and Goldman Sachs Group posted its sharpest decline in earnings since going public in 1999. The announcements led to one of the biggest declines in stock market history, with the Dow falling 504 points on Monday, September 15, 2008—its largest drop since the September 2001 terrorist attacks. Other world markets followed suit.

Central banks around the world moved quickly to reassure the markets, with the Fed announcing that it would loosen lending restrictions by accepting, for the first time ever, stocks owned by banks as collateral for discount window loans. Meanwhile, the U.S. federal government tried to assuage the world, with U.S. Treasury Secretary Henry Paulson insisting that the American banking system remained "safe and sound." Those were words he likely later regretted, as the week of September 14 was one of most stunning in world financial history.

On September 16, shares of Reserve Primary Fund, a money market fund, fell below $1 per share, due to losses on debt issued by Lehman Brothers. The decline in a money market fund's value below $1 per share—which is referred to as breaking the buck—has happened only once before in history.[7]

In response, on September 18, the Fed injected $280 billion to the world financial markets through swap lines with world central banks, and the Securities and Exchange Commission (SEC) temporarily banned short-selling on 799 financial stocks.[8]

Despite these actions, on September 19, the markets were still in a panic, and a run on money funds seemed imminent. In just one week, assets in money funds serving institutions dropped $173 billion to $2.17 trillion, according to the Investment Company Institute.

In response, the Treasury Department and the Fed announced separate plans to bolster the nation's $2 trillion of money market fund assets. The Fed also took a second step, agreeing to buy up to $69 billion of discount notes, or short-term debt, issued by Fannie Mae, Freddie Mac, and the federal home loan banks. In doing so, it hoped to provide additional liquidity to money market funds, since discount notes reportedly amount to about 5 percent of money market assets.

The global markets shuddered. Clearly, the patchwork approach to the financial crisis—putting out fires as they arose—wasn't working. Ultimately, the federal government began to think the unthinkable, and as the week came to a close, Paulson proposed a bailout plan that would allow the Treasury Department to spend up to $700 billion of taxpayer money to buy distressed assets from struggling institutions.

What Dropped in 2008?

- Some 3.6 million jobs were lost—the highest job loss since record keeping began in 1940.
- Gross domestic product (GDP) dropped at an annual rate of 6.8 percent.
- Of the $17.8 trillion of household net worth lost from 2007 to 2009, $5.8 trillion was from falling house prices.
- Home prices dropped on average 32 percent from 2006 to 2009 and in some markets the drop was steeper.
- Standard & Poor's 500 Index fell by one third in 2008.
- Retirement accounts also lost one third of their value, or $2.8 trillion.
- Between 2008 and 2010, credit card debt fell by 19 percent or about $187 billon.
- From 2008 to 2009, 2.5 million households declared bankruptcy.

Source: "The Financial Crisis Inquiry Report," 2011, pp. 390–394.

On October 2, a bailout bill was approved, and President Bush signed it into law.

Just before the congressional vote on the bill, the Dow was up almost 300 points, but by mid-afternoon trading, it had cut its lead by about 200 points. That was because despite the government's efforts to prevent a total collapse of the global banking system little was done to address the subprime mortgage mess, which was a key ingredient in the financial meltdown.

The subprime crisis had taken on a life of its own, and the housing market correction remained firmly entrenched. On December 30, 2008, the S&P/Case-Shiller Home Price Index reported its largest price drop in its history, 18 percent year-over-year ending in October.

2009 to 2012: The Road to Recovery?

Most of us know what happened from October 2008. After the passage of the bailout bill in October of 2008, the government kept pushing more money into the economy via additional bailout packages and programs that encouraged home buying. The recession ended in June of 2009, and the melee of the financial bank crisis died down. The housing market, however, never recovered.

In fact, as of this writing, the housing market has continued to collapse to what were once unimaginable levels. The latest numbers from the S&P/Case-Shiller Home Price Index show that home prices fell in 18 of 20 markets in December 2011. The index, which is normalized to have a value of 100 in January 2000, attained its all-time high of 189.93 in the second quarter of 2006. It declined a record 18.9 percent from then until the first quarter of 2009, when it reached 129.2. After a gradual climb, it began declining again, however, and as of the end of 2011, was at 125.67.

"The past two years has been a story of a housing market that is bottoming out but has not yet stabilized," wrote S&P/Case-Shiller in its report on the December 2011 data. "Up until today's report we had believed the crisis lows . . . were behind us. Now it looks like neither was the case, as both hit new record lows in December 2011. The national composite fell by 3.8 percent in the fourth quarter alone, and is down 33.8 percent from its second-quarter 2006 peak."

As of this writing, we're also looking at a new wave of foreclosures. The number of homes entering foreclosure dropped in February 2012, but I'm expecting an increase for the remainder of the year. The reason is because five major banks and state attorneys general recently reached a $26 billion settlement over past foreclosure practices. Banks will now be able to move forward and foreclose on delinquent owners who have been squatting on the properties for months, even years. "The pig is starting to move through the python," said RealtyTrac when it released its foreclosure report for February 2012.

Looking Ahead

More people get it today, but maybe not enough of us. The problem with the ongoing housing market depression is that it affects the entire U.S. economy. In reducing home prices, the housing market collapse wiped out massive sums of American wealth, destroying the buying power of consumers. Declining consumer spending led to reduced demand for goods and services, and that, in turn, led to the loss of millions of jobs. With so many Americans without jobs, fewer people are buying homes, causing housing prices to fall even more. It's a vicious economic cycle.

Politicians have lots of dreams about fixing the problem. President Obama's latest idea: Eliminate the mortgage interest tax deduction for upper-income taxpayers. In other words, his plan to save the U.S. economy from the ongoing housing market collapse is to severely limit the tax benefit that makes it advantageous to own a home.

Whether you make $50,000 or $500,000 a year, when you bought your home, you factored in the mortgage interest deduction. That deduction makes your mortgage a little cheaper, and you depend on it to pay your mortgage. If the government takes it away, overnight, those of us who are impacted will be unable to afford our homes. If you think the housing market is troubled now, wait until that happens. All over the country, prices in upscale neighborhoods will drop—and if foreclosures are a problem now, what will happen when housing prices drop even further.

May 10, 2012: JPMorgan Suffers $2 Billion Loss in Six Weeks Trading Derivatives

Today is yesterday, again.

The Financial Crisis Inquiry Commission concluded that "AIG failed and was rescued by the government primarily because of its enormous sales of *credit default swaps* were made without putting up initial collateral, setting aside capital reserves or hedging its exposure . . ." (Financial Crisis Inquiry Commission, 2011, p. 352).

JPMorgan sold "insurance" in the CDX IG9 market which is based on an index of 125 U.S. companies' ability to repay their debt. Credit default swaps or derivatives were provided by JPMorgan in this market, which tracked corporate default risk. The index had a valuation of $150 billion.

(Continued)

(Continued)

JPMorgan was providing insurance with the assumption that improving credit conditions would lower the cost of insurance and not require any payments by the bank as there would be no defaults. Essentially, they were betting the economy would improve. It didn't and they lost $2 billion. These bank transactions are similar to those made with the credit default swaps made in the housing market and that were instrumental in the 2006 meltdown. The derivatives in the JPMorgan case were made against a different index. JPMorgan was able to take this position without collateral because since 2008 the Federal Reserve has shown it will bail out any "too-big-to-fail" bank with taxpayer money.[9]

50-Year Mortgages

One change that could be an immediate fix to the housing market, without involving Congress, would be to extend the payment period on a home purchase. Mortgage terms should be extended to 50 years. Nowhere is it written that mortgages must have a maximum life of 30 years, and two individuals earning the national minimum wage 40 hours a week can afford the average-size mortgage fixed at a 5 percent interest rate if it's amortized over 50 years. If we make this adjustment—which doesn't require any new government spending or principle forgiveness—it is estimated that foreclosures will decline by 30 percent in nine months and 50 percent in 18 months. Then, as the economy improves, homeowners can, themselves, change their mortgage terms back to 30 years by simply paying more than they owe (assuming the mortgage doesn't have prepayment penalties). It's that simple.

With an outstanding mortgage of $200,000 at an interest of 5 percent, a change in the payment period from 30 years to 50 years would reduce the monthly payment from $1,073.64 to $908.28. The result is about $165 reduction in monthly mortgage payments. It should be remembered that the total cost of the house will increase due to the additional 20 years in increase payments. Consequently, the cost of the home to the homeowner will increase from $386,511.57 to $554,966. Therefore, it is important for the homeowner to begin making higher monthly payments as soon as they are financially able.

What to Do Next? Let's Buy a House

With all the events described in the chapter, it may seem incredulous, but now may be the time to take advantage of the downturn in the housing market to purchase real estate. With the housing market still in the doldrums and interest rates likely remain low until 2014, the timing couldn't be better. There are two ways to make these purchases. One approach is with self-directed individual retirement accounts (IRAs) and the other is to purchase foreclosed real estate.

Self-Directed IRAs

Self-directed IRAs are purchased within an IRA. In order to purchase real estate within an IRA, you'll need a specific type of IRA called a self-directed IRA. Today, only about 2 percent of all IRAs are self-directed IRAs.

These IRAs work like a traditional IRA except that a custodian holds the assets in the IRA and maintains all records pertaining to them. Unlike a traditional IRA, a self-directed IRA can be used to purchase nontraditional assets, including real estate. Virtually any type of real estate may be purchased, such as land, commercial property, single-family homes, multifamily dwellings, condominiums and co-ops, for example. The only major rule is that you can't engage in what's called "self-dealing." In other words, you or your family members cannot derive any current benefit from the property. Neither you nor your family members (other than siblings) may have owned the property prior to its purchase in an IRA; the property must be an investment property; neither you nor your family members (other than siblings) may live in the property while it's in the IRA, and your business may not be located in the property.

If you can adhere to those restrictions, you buy the property using IRA funds, with the assistance of your custodian. All expenses associated with the property, such as property taxes, homeowners' association fees, and maintenance expenses, are also paid from the IRA. Income from the property then flows back into the IRA. Because IRA investments grow tax deferred until they are withdrawn, that income, as well as the property's capital appreciation, is taxed as regular income only when withdrawn from the IRA.[10]

A benefit of purchasing real estate in a self-directed IRA is getting into the housing market when it's at its lowest point and diversifying a retirement portfolio that primarily holds traditional standard securities and mutual funds. If you're interested in estate planning, it also gives you a way to pass certain assets on to beneficiaries upon your death.

Other than making the limited yearly $5,000 limited contributions to a self-directed IRA, it is possible to rollover a traditional IRA containing securities investments into a self-directed IRA. The rollover of the traditional IRA into a self-directed IRA allows for the immediate investment into real estate when the market is down. The withdrawal rules for a traditional IRA are all applicable to a self-directed IRA. For example, the funds need to begin to be withdrawn at the age of 70½. Should the investor have their IRA monies invested in nonsaleable real estate when they reach that milestone? Unfortunately, it may be difficult for the investor to make the necessary withdrawals in a timely manner as their investments are in illiquid real estate.

Buying Foreclosed Homes

Another choice is to buy foreclosed properties as an investment. Web sites and some TV ads tout the ability of companies to provide their viewers with special access to foreclosed homes for a fee. Figure 3.4 is an example of a web site that provides "free" access for an initial time period to foreclosed properties. It is not necessary to pay a fee to get a listing of foreclosed homes.

If you do not have a traditional IRA that can be rolled over into a self-directed IRA, but you do have cash for a down payment that you can invest into housing, then foreclosed houses may be another alternative for entering the housing market as a first-time buyer or an investor. As the number of foreclosed homes being sold has increased, the asking price for those homes has dropped to bargain prices that may never be seen again.

Foreclosed houses are being held by local banks and a number of lending institutions such as Fannie Mae, Freddie Mac, and the Housing and Urban Development (HUD) agency. These institutions hold valuable real estate located all over the United States and they are trying to sell them as quickly as possible. In many cases, these houses or apartment units have been well maintained. In other cases, the homeowners who were evicted from the house damaged the home before leaving by using markers on the walls, removing hot tubs, and cutting up cabinets. Depending on the neighborhoods in which these homes are located, vandals may have ransacked the home looking for anything they could sell. Therefore, it is important to visit the foreclosed property. The prices on these homes range from $1,000 to over $1 million, and some of properties listed by Fannie Mae can be purchased with as little as 3.5 percent down.[11] The listings range from New York City condos to Nevada ranch land.

The home maintenance costs incurred with a self-directed IRA invested in real estate are also incurred with a foreclosed home. For an investor, the tax deductions in both plans are similar. With a purchase, the investment objective is to rent the property until home prices increase and then sell the property for a profit. Apartments with multiple units are for sale on these web sites, allowing the investor to purchase these properties at bargain prices. Once the units are rented, an immediate positive cash flow can be obtained. With rental units, the objective is to have a tax-deductible loss on the properties while at the same time obtaining positive cash inflows. Expenses incurred in maintaining the property, property taxes, realtor or property management fees, and other fees can be used to reduce wage income received by the investor, thus reducing the investor's overall income tax obligation.

Table 3.1 provides the web sites where foreclosed and IRS-confiscated homes are listed. At some of the sites, it is necessary to register and place a deposit prior to being able to make a bid on the property. For example, the General Services Administration (GSA) requires deposits in order to make a property bid. The

Table 3.1   Government Web Sites Listing Foreclosed and Confiscated Homes

---

HUD Homes: www.hudhomestore.com/HudHome/Index.aspx

Fannie Mae Home Path: www.homepath.com/

Freddie Mac Home Steps: www.homesteps.com/featuresearch.html

U.S. Marshals Service: www.justice.gov/marshals/assets/nsl.htm

U.S. General Services Administration: http://gsaauctions.gov/gsaauctions/gsaauctions/

U.S. Internal Revenue Service: www.treasury.gov/auctions/irs/cat_Real7.htm

U.S. Department of Agriculture: www.resales.usda.gov/

U.S. Treasury: www.treasury.gov/auctions/treasury/rp/

---

deposit can be sent in as a cashier's check or as a charge on a credit card. The amount of the deposit varies with the valuation of the property. At the end of the auction, the deposit is returned to all bidders. It should be noted that if the winning bidder is unable to get the financing to complete the purchase, the second highest bidder must make good on their bid.

With other properties, it is not necessary to register. For example, Fannie Mae and HUD properties require no registration. Once a property is identified, the name of a realtor familiar with the property can be found on the web site, and an offer can be made through that realtor. Fannie Mae's Home Path properties contain a wealth of information about the property, but sites such as the GSA web site, provide only sketchy information and little in the way of "successful" contact information. Unlike the GSA site, which is an active auction site with bidders trying to outbid each other, the Fannie Mae site is more of a listing of properties handled by real estate firms, such as Century 21. After contacting the real estate agency and making an offer, the property is handled like any other sale. If Fannie Mae accepts the offer, the buyer goes to a bank to obtain financing.

Summary

My two barometers, my ears, tell me what's going on in the world. They provide me with data that doesn't show up on most economic reports—information from family, friends, clients, and even strangers.

I trust my ears completely, because often, what people are saying about the economy tells us something government reports don't, at least not clearly. Economists talk about macroeconomics and microeconomics, but there is another level of economics at work: our personal budgets. If you take the total of every American's budget, you end up with the country's gross domestic product (GDP).

That's why, when my ears tell me that budgets are tight, I believe the economy is troubled. I don't always know why. Maybe interest rates have increased; maybe work is hard to find; maybe energy costs are very high; maybe all of these things are true. I know, however, that something is wrong, and I can usually get to the bottom of it by looking a little deeper.

In 2006, for example, when the housing market first showed signs of trouble, I started writing about neighborhoods littered with "for-sale" signs. Later, I began writing about how people couldn't get loans. Now, I'm writing about why and how we should buy real estate.

Reference

Financial Crisis Inquiry Commission. 2011. "The Financial Crisis Inquiry Report," Final Report of the National Commission of the Causes of the Financial and Economic Crisis (New York: Public Affairs).

Notes

1. Suspicious activity reports are required to be filed with the U.S. Treasury Department by financial institutions when they suspect criminal activity, such as money laundering, may be involved in cash deposits received by the banking institution.
2. Subprime mortgages are loans given to borrowers with less than good credit. They are more risky and consequently carry a higher interest rate premium.
3. Tranches are the portions in one investment security that is composed of a variety of investments, all with different levels of risk and maturity. The objective of developing such a security is to reduce the overall risk to the buyer. *Tranche* is a French word meaning slice.
4. "The Financial Crisis Inquiry Report," 2011, p. 104.
5. Repurchase agreements, or repos, occur when securities are sold with the stipulation that they will be repurchased at a later date at a higher price. The increase is the interest paid by the seller of the securities to the purchaser of the securities. The purpose of such an agreement is to provide the seller with cash, and it is essentially a loan initiated by the seller. In the case of the Fed, the repurchasing plan was an attempt to put more cash into the economy as credit was drying up during the meltdown.
6. Swap lines are used to increase U.S. dollars available to foreign central banks. It is a swap between the U.S. dollar and foreign currencies. The foreign central banks use the dollars to ease credit restrictions (i.e. increase liquidity) in their countries to help prevent financial problems from occurring in these regions.
7. The Community Bankers U.S. Government Fund broke the buck in 1994, paying investors 96 cents per share.
8. Short selling is the selling of stocks that you don't own, for a contracted time period, and betting that the price of the stock is going to fall. If the stock price falls, you can buy back the stocks at the lower price and use them to terminate the contract. You make the difference between the lower price and the price on the day the contract was initially executed.
9. A hedge is made to prevent a future loss. For example, a farmer can buy a futures contract to guarantee the delivery price of a corn crop in three

months at $3 a bushel. The hedge allows the farmer to sell corn crop at $3 a bushel after the corn is harvested. The farmer has protected his selling price. This is not a bet. A bet is a credit default swap, which is based on the risk associated with the debt issued by a third party or the movement of prices in market. One side bets the risk of default is low or market prices are going up and the other side bets the risk is high or market prices are going down.

10. Fractional ownership is also possible, meaning IRA funds can be used to purchase less than 100 percent of the property within the IRA. The other investors in the property are also listed on the deed. So, for example, let's say you purchase a property for $200,000, with $100,000 coming from your IRA and $100,000 coming from your spouse. Each of you would contribute half of the purchase price. Each of you would own 50 percent of the property, so the deed would list the retirement plan as one owner (you) and your spouse as another. The expenses and income would be split 50/50 between the retirement plan and your spouse. When the property is sold, the proceeds would also be distributed 50/50.

11. If that interest rate is available, a $5,000 down payment will support a home purchase price of a $143,857. In addition, the investor will have to pay various closing costs.

CHAPTER 4

Credit Cards

LET ME HAVE IT NOW! AND THEY DID

Credit is a system whereby a person who can not pay gets another person who can not pay to guarantee that he can pay.
—Charles Dickens[1]

At one time, only the very rich used credit cards and the best the rest of us could hope for was to have a gas station credit card. Gas station credit cards allowed you to buy gas at your favorite service station. What a privilege! But times do change. Now everyone who can get a credit card has one or two, or four of them, and banks have a stronger revenue stream. Many consumers get sucked into using credit cards without thinking of the financial consequences. The credit card companies' (i.e., banks) direct mail make it enticingly easy to apply for credit cards, and it is even easier to apply online. College campuses have students hawking credit cards on campus streets along with a free T-shirt for signing up for a card. Of course, universities also get a "kickback" for allowing these activities on their campuses. Everyone wins—well, not quite.

Pay to Play

The CARD Act requires credit card companies to disclose the details on how much they pay to colleges for the rights to market their cards to students and alumni. The Federal Reserve's first Report on College Credit Card Agreements was released Monday, showing that credit card issuers paid over $83 million to colleges and their related alumni organizations in 2009. The University of Illinois Alumni Association received the highest payment of $3,272,657 in 2009.

Source: Bill Hardekopf, "This Week in Credit Card News," *Forbes*, November 1, 2010, www.forbes.com/sites/moneybuilder/2010/11/01/this-week-in-credit-card-news-18

Creditcards.com reports that credit card debt in the United States was $15,799 per household in 2011.[2] As of the end of 2008, each household had an average 3.5 credit cards. Ninety-eight percent of total U.S. revolving debt is credit card debt, and it was about $777 billion in 2011. The average rate of interest on this debt is 14.89 percent but that rate can reach up to 30 percent. Many credit card holders do not even know the interest rate (APR) they are paying on their cards, as they are focused on meeting the minimum monthly payment. Most Americans are in debt to their banks for billions. Is there any way to fight back? Well, first you have to understand what you signed up for when you got your credit card. This chapter will explain some of the details in your credit card agreement as well as tell you how to get back at credit card companies and get free money from them.

The New Law

The Credit Accountability and Disclosure (CARD) Act of 2009 was phased in over a 15-month period and changed many of the recent abuses of credit card companies. The law implemented restrictions on interest rate hikes and the reasons for raising those rates; universal default practices where your interest rates are raised due to unrelated credit issues with other organizations has been curtailed; now the decision of card holders to pay off their balances and opt out of credit card agreements requires banks to hold the terms unchanged; credit cards issued to those under 21 must be cosigned by an adult; campus credit charge booths giving away pizzas and so on must stay off college campuses; payments are allowed 21 days of grace before late fees are charged; over-limit fees can be rejected by the card holder, but you can still be charged a "rejection" fee; highest interest balances (rather than the lowest rate) are paid off first if more than the monthly minimum payment is received by the bank; "occasional" late fees are capped at $25; if rates go up, card holders have 45 days to opt out of the card, and then the bank can charge whatever rate they want; minimum payment disclosures are required regarding how long it would take to pay off the balance when only minimum payments are made; and the practice of two-cycle billing, where you are charged for previous paid-off debt, has been eliminated.

Once a new law such as this one is passed, the objective of the organizations subjected to the new regulations is to find a way around the rules or to get their lobbyists to change the law. For example, variable interest rates allow banks to get around the 45-day notification rule. In response to the new law, banks have increased fees and imposed new fees such as an annual fee; foreign transaction fees for any online retailers outside the United States, even purchases from your U.S. home paid with U.S dollars; $1 paper statement fee; and a nonuse fee for not using a credit card. The use of low teaser interest rates has expanded. These rates go up to 30 percent after the expiration period and can be charged on your *entire* balance. This billing procedure allows a bank to charge you for your balance plus the interest you owe on the balance (even if you pay it off), thus creating a credit balance on your card. New "professional" credit cards are being advertised to everyone, such as *Chase Ink*. As these professional cards are for small businesses, the new credit card law does not apply to them. It can be expected that other practices will be implemented as creative bankers find other ways to extract money from credit card users.

Let's Skip a Payment

Credit card companies may allow their credit card holders to skip a minimum payment after the Christmas holidays—for free. Using the online calculator at CreditCards.com shows how much this free service will cost the consumer. Remember, the payment can be skipped, but interest continues to accumulate on the card's balance. In this example, it is assumed the card holder will continue to make the minimum payment after skipping one payment.

In the following example, it is assumed there is a $4,000 balance on a card with a 15 percent interest rate and 4 percent of the balance or $30, whichever is higher, is the minimum payment. The column on the right shows the total interest if no payment is skipped and the column on the left shows the results if the first $160 payment (.04 × $4,000) is skipped. The illustration assumes no additional purchases are placed on the card.

	Skipping a Payment	Not Skipping a Payment
Balance	$4,000	$3,840
Minimum monthly payment is $30 or 4% of the balance, whichever is higher. The 4% minimum payment will decrease as the balance goes down.	Skip payment	$160
Months to pay off initial balance	97	96
Total interest	$1,663	$1,590

The increase in interest paid is $73. This "freebie" costs the consumer $73 in additional interest. It is not free, and this additional charge should be disclosed by the card company. In addition, the card company may charge a minimum fee for this consumer service that needs to be added to the interest charges. The card customers who are likely to skip a payment are those with the least amount of family income.

The Contract

The last credit contract I received had about 30 pages of eight-point font. Wow! What did I sign up for? Do you understand terms like revolving credit limit, balance transfers, variable rates based on prime, penalty APR, small claims court procedures, arbitration, the state laws applicable to my agreement, overseas transaction fees, when interest charges begin, miscellaneous fees, and grace periods? *Well, if you want to know who took your money, you better understand your contract.*

Let's take a look at some of the more important terms.

Interest Varieties

Interest rates on your credit card are going to be different depending on whether you are making a purchase, getting a cash advance, or making a balance transfer from one credit card to another. In addition, the rate can vary based on the interest rate peg that is being used by the bank. Credit card companies use these different rates to make you pay more interest. In the past, a monthly payment above the minimum on your card would be applied to the outstanding balance with the lowest interest. The credit card company's objective is to keep you paying the highest interest rate while they earn the most interest revenue. If the interest rate that you pay is important to a billion-dollar bank, maybe it should be important to you. Why should a bank reduce your balance on a cash advance that pays them 25 percent interest when they can apply the payment to the monthly balance where the interest rate is only 13 percent? Although this practice is currently outlawed, it shows the prevailing attitude of the banking industry toward its customers.

APR

APR stands for the annual percentage rate of interest. In your credit card contract, the APR has to be stated. APR is a standardized way to compute annual interest charges and allows you to make reliable comparisons from one credit card company to another. Banks have 15 days to let you know they are raising their rates, and you have 45 days to cancel the card. Now if you are carrying the average credit balance of $15,799 per year and your interest rate is 13 percent, you are paying $2,054 in interest expense during the year; at 18 percent, it is $2,845 in interest charges every year. Add various bank fees to determine the actual amount you pay out when you carry a balance. The interest paid on credit cards is not tax deductible, like mortgage interest, so these charges are very expensive. There goes the money for that vacation. Of course, you can charge the vacation—imagine the possibilities.

Let's Move to South Dakota

Why are credit card companies such as Citi located in South Dakota? If you thought it was the climate, you are wrong. The South Dakota legislature eliminated its usury laws allowing for a high rate of interest to be charged on credit cards issued by banks chartered in South Dakota. If a financial institution is located in that state, they can charge the maximum interest to all their credit card holders throughout the United States. For example, if the State of Michigan allows credit card companies to charge a rate of only 10 percent, a credit card issued by a bank chartered in South Dakota can still charge 30 percent. So, a 30 percent rate of interest in South Dakota trumps a 10 percent usury law in Michigan. The Supreme Court decided this in *Marquette National Bank of Minnesota vs. First Omaha Services* back in 1978 whereby it was not necessary for a bank to follow the usury laws of the state where it issued its credit cards, only those laws of the state where the bank was incorporated.[3] Delaware soon followed South Dakota's lead, and other banks moved their credit card operations there.

How Is That Interest Rate Figured?

In order to squeeze the most out of credit card holders, banks have come up with innovative ways to compute interest charges. They include average daily balance, daily balance, two-cycle balance, and previous balance methods.

Average Daily Balance

When a bank uses this method, the interest charges are based on the daily balance on your card. The following example illustrates how these charges are computed on a credit card with a 30-day cycle and APR of 15 percent.

APR = 15 percent

		Running Balance	Days Outstanding
Balance Day 1–3	$250	$250	3
Purchase Day 4	$1,000	$1,250	17
Credit on card from a Return Day 20	$200	$1,050	10*
			Cycle 30

*Count from Day 21.

Calculate the average daily balance:

$$\$250 \times 3 = \quad \$750$$
$$\$1,250 \times 17 = \$21,250$$
$$\$1,050 \times 10 = \underline{\$10,500}$$
$$\$32,500/30 = \$1,083.33 \text{ average daily balance}$$

Interest charge:

$$(\$1{,}083.33 \times .15) \times 30/365 = \$13.35 \text{ for the 30 day}$$
$$\text{period based on 15 percent APR}$$

If there were no more charges against this card (an unlikely event), and the minimum balance was paid each month, the annual interest would be $160.20.[4] The computations become more complicated as more purchases are made during the month, and it becomes necessary to use a computer program to make the calculations. Banks may use variations on the average daily balance method such as the average daily balance excluding new purchases. The latter method does not allow the banks to charge more interest, so it is not widely used by national banks, but average daily balance with compounding is a method that is widely used.[5]

Hey, Didn't They Get a Bailout?

And then there's Sallie Mae's pilot program offering a credit card to parents who cosign their children's private loans that provides cash-back rewards for making payments on the loans. Basically, parents who cosign a line of credit (the loan) can get another line of credit (the card). They are then encouraged (with cash rewards) to use the credit card to pay off student loans. This seems to encourage a vicious cycle of spiraling debt and higher interest charges.

Source: "Think Twice before Using Credit Cards to Repay Student Loans," *Student Loan Ranger*, Equal Justice Works, December 21, 2011, www.usnews.com/education/blogs/student-loan-ranger/2011/12/21/think-twice-before-using-credit-cards-to-repay-student-loans.

Average Daily Balance with Compounding

A variation on the average daily balance is called the average daily balance with monthly compounding. In this approach, interest is charged against interest you have already been charged. The interest charged at the end of one day is added to the outstanding balance and then the next day, the new interest charge is based on the old balance and any previously added interest. A short example illustrates this approach.[6]

APR = 15%

The daily interest rate is .15/365 =.0004109

	Running Balance	Days Outstanding
Balance Day 1–3 $250	$250	3

Interest Day 1 $250 × .0004109 = .1027
*Interest Day 2 $250.1027 × .0004109 = .1028
**Interest Day 3 $250.2055 × .0004109 = .1028

*Day 2 = Balance + interest from Day 1.
**Day 3 = Balance + interest from Day 1 and Day 2.

It should be clear that a daily charge for interest results in higher annual interest expense for the credit card holder. In the case of the $250 balance on this credit card, there is a 31-cent charge for interest over a three-day period. For our example, we would have to do the math for the entire 30 days. A better way is to compare the APR with the effective rate of interest on the card. To determine the real interest rate on a credit card with daily compounding, go to Ultimate Calculators (www.ultimatecalculators.com/effective_annual_rate_calculator.html) and fill in the APR to determine your rate for 365 days. With a 15 percent APR and daily compounding the actual rate of interest is 16.18 percent. As the bankers say, "every little bit counts."

The theme of this book is identifying where your money went. Without some concern about the interest rates on your credit cards, you can assume some banker is taking it in their million-dollar bonus. Or some K Street lobbyist is using it to try to make sure no one takes these privileges away from the banks. If you want to be knowledgeable about your finances, there are ways to fight back and these methods will be discussed before the end of this chapter.

Previous Balance Method

Now let's look at another way to get more money out of you. It is called the previous balance method of interest calculation. The previous balance method uses the balance at the beginning of the billing cycle. The payments received during the current billing cycle are not subtracted from the balance and additional charges' are not added to the balance. In the last example, the beginning balance was $250 and the interest on that amount was 31 cents.

With a previous balance method, the beginning balance is multiplied times the monthly interest rate ($250 × (15 percent/12)) and the interest on the $250 is $3.125. The effect of new purchases and reductions in the account are not considered in the calculation. Next month, assume the beginning balance is $1,050, and the interest will be calculated on that amount. It may be possible to plan your purchases around this cycle so that your lowest balance occurs at the end of each month. In order to ensure that your lowest balance is at the end of the month, online payments would have to be made and received by the bank before the end of the month and before your actual statement was received—a tricky feat. The last method that will be considered is the two-cycle method.

Two-Cycle Method

Although this method has been eliminated in the CARD Act of 2009, it is still worth a look because it demonstrates bankers' attitudes toward the public. This method allowed banks to charge interest on amounts that you have already paid off. "Every little bit counts." To illustrate how these calculations are made, it is necessary to run through a two-month payment period. Interest is computed on the average daily balance of the previous month even though those amounts have been paid off at the beginning of the second month.

Month 1

		Running Balance	Days Outstanding
Balance Day 1–3	$250	$250	3
Purchase Day 4	$1,000	$1,250	17
Credit on Card from a Return			
Day 20	($200)	$1,050	9
Credit Card Payment	($1050)	$0	1
			Cycle 30

Calculate the average daily balance Month 1:

$$\$250 \times 3 = \$ \quad 750$$
$$\$1,250 \times 17 = \$21,250$$
$$\$1,050 \times 9 = \$ \ 9,450$$
$$0 \times 1 = \underline{\$ \qquad 0}$$
$$\$31,450/30 = \$1,048.33 \text{ average daily balance}$$

Month 2: Paid $1,050 at the end of the Month 1

	Running Balance		Days Outstanding
Balance Day 1–10	$0	$0	10
Purchase Day 11	$1,800	$1,800	19
Credit Card Payment	$25	$1,725	1*
			Cycle 30

Calculate the average daily balance Month 2:

$$\$0 = 10 = \$\quad 0$$
$$\$1,800 \times 19 = \$34,200$$
$$\$1,725 \times 1 = \underline{\$\ 1,725}$$
$$\$35,925/30 = \$1,197.50 \text{ average daily balance}$$

Interest charge on **two-month** average daily balance:

$$[(\$1,048.33 + \$1,197.50)/2] \times .15) \times 30/365 = \$13.84 \text{ for}$$
the 60-day period based on 15 percent APR

Jacking the Interest Rate

Banks use a number of different methods for setting their credit card rates. The two basic methods use either a fixed rate or a variable rate. As the variable rates can change monthly, it is unlikely a bank will provide an unchangeable fixed rate of interest on their cards. Instead of a fixed rate, your credit card is most likely to have a variable rate, which allows for the jacking up of already high interest rates when the underlying basis for determining the rate increases. Variable rates are pegged to a premium above the prime rate or rate on T-bills and any of the time periods for which T-bills are issued by the federal government.[7] Thus, if you have a card rate of prime plus 5 percent and the prime rate is 10 percent the rate you will be charged is 15 percent on your card. In addition to the interest rate peg, there is a multiplier that can be used. For example, your card's rate may be pegged to the 90-day Treasury bill rate multiplied by 2.[8] Of course, if you pay late, all bets are off because you broke the credit card agreement, and the bank can raise your rates by 20 percent. It is called the penalty rate of interest. With first-class mail in the United States taking longer and longer to deliver, it is more likely that millions of credit card customers will be making late payments in the future.

When variable rates decrease, it would be expected the rate on your card would decrease. Not necessarily so. In your card agreement, it may state the rate is variable but it will not decrease below a 10 percent APR. Welcome to the world of finance. Further, the rate may be fixed to an average index of interest rates or any interest rate over a quarterly period, thus allowing the bank to pick the highest rate during that quarter instead of the rate on a specific date.

The interest rate charged by a credit card company also depends on the transaction. For example, you can expect to pay a higher rate for cash advances.

The Credit Card Tax

There is a tax that everyone pays whether they use credit cards or not. It is a fee charged to merchants by credit card companies for using credit cards. The interchange fee is a merchant cost that is passed on to consumers in the form of higher product prices. This interchange fees range from 2 percent to 3 percent of the purchase price. Disclosures about these fees are found in the *Master Card Manual for Merchants*. The *Manual* is composed of over 200 pages, and its companion *Chargeback Guide* consists of over 600 pages. Both are available at www.mastercard.com/ca/merchant/en/getstarted/rules .html. Credit card companies argue that these fees cover fraud losses on their cards, nonpayment of balances, 30-day interest free periods, processing, marketing campaigns, and the issuance of cards that do not charge an annual fee.

Even if you only use cash, you still pay this fee because it is incorporated into the higher cost of the product you are purchasing. It is interesting to note that a portion of this fee is for electronic processing; maybe if paper was processed by clerks, the cost would be justified, but with electronic processing, it is not. Another portion of the fee is used to pay for awards programs on cards. You didn't think the card company was paying for these flight and gift awards, did you? The consumers who buy products are paying for it themselves. This fee was not considered in the CARD Act of 2009, and it is still an area of contention.

If the demand for the product is strong, consumers will pay this hidden cost without a thought. If the demand for the product is weak, the merchant may have to recognize the fee as an operating cost and reduce their profits.

Who Took My Money?

The Foreign Currency Conversion Fee antitrust class action lawsuit, filed in 2001, alleged that Visa, MasterCard, Diners Club, and a handful of credit card–issuing banks concealed credit and debit card fees on foreign currency transactions or sales by foreign merchants, which the plaintiffs said added up to 3 percent per transaction. The lawsuit further alleged that Visa and MasterCard boosted their base exchange rate before applying the fees. A decade later, after years of appeals and an initial settlement reached in 2006, the court in October ordered the settlement administrator to disburse the $336 million in settlement funds.

Source: Dawn Kawamoto, "The Foreign Currency Conversion Settlement Check Is Finally in the Mail," *Daily Finance*, December 22, 2011, www.dailyfinance .com/2011/12/22/the-foreign-currency-conversion-settlement-check-is-finally-in-t.

Tipping a Hat to Debit Cards

There are always debit cards. Debit cards were hawked as a means to keep consumers from incurring credit card debt; that is, you could spend only the money that you had in your account. There are some differences between debit cards and credit cards that should be noted. First, theft loss on a credit card for which the consumer is liable is limited to $50 of the unauthorized purchases, but the same loss on a debit card is $500 if you do not notify the bank within 48 hours. In the latter case, the thief is draining your checking account, which could result in a number of bounced checks and further late penalty fees.

The debit card transaction is a withdrawal from your checking account balance. It is taking money that you could have had in the form of cash and using it as an electronic payment. It's your money, but because an electronic transaction is made, someone has to *pay*. Prior to the Durbin Amendment to the Dodd-Frank Wall Street Reform and Consumer Protection Act of 2010, the interchange fee to merchants was about 2 percent of every transaction or an average of 44 cents for accepting a debit card. This fee was less than the credit card fee charged to merchants, but still a significant source of bank revenues.

After the Durbin Amendment, a cap was placed on these debit card transactions fees of between 7 to 12 cents, on average, per transaction resulting in close to an 80 percent decrease in fee charges to the merchant. The reduction to the banks was in billions of dollars of revenues. Merchants were also allowed to give discounts to customers who paid in cash or with debit cards, a practice that was not allowed before the Amendment. The reduction of the debit fees could provide for a significant wealth transfer from the banks to consumers as the prices of products could be reduced and the merchant would make the same amount of profit—only it didn't happen.

The retail cost of merchandise in the stores did not decrease when transaction costs on debit cards decreased. The wealth transfer was from the banks to the merchants, not to the consumer. The Electronics Payment Coalition determined that based on a basket of goods purchased before and after the Durbin Amendment, there was no effect.[9] Further, most merchants have not differentiated the price of their merchandise between credit and cash (debit) purchases.

In response to these debit fee decreases and to make up for lost revenue, Bank of America (BOA) decided to initiate a $5 per month debit card fee. This fee is charged by the bank to use your own money in your own checking account. The difficulty was that this fee was an "in-your-face" charge to the consumer whereas in the past the card charges had been largely hidden from the consumer—even though they still paid it with higher priced merchandise. The response from BOA's depositors was outrage. Eventually, BOA's executives decided to drop the $5 monthly charge.

Most consumers are not aware of the fees they pay in higher prices and transaction fees as most of these fees are "hidden" charges within the 30 pages of 8-point font in their credit card agreements. But those fees add up to billions of dollars to the banks and a transfer of wealth from consumers to bank executives who continually enjoy million-dollar bonuses.

Is there a way a consumer can avoid transferring their wealth to banks. Most consumers think, "We just have to endure it." This is not true, and the next section tells you how to get around some of these bank practices.

Getting Back

All the suggestions for getting back at credit card companies are effective only if you pay your monthly credit card balance in full each month. Fifty-four percent of Americans pay their balance off each month.[10] If you cannot make this commitment, you need to continue as you are and keep asking the question: "Where is my money?"

The first step in this process is to determine your credit score. If you do not have a credit score high enough to apply for new credit cards, you cannot take the following steps to get back some of your money. If you already know you have a high credit score, you can skip this step.

Your credit score is based on your payment history; amounts owed and your available credit; length of credit history, which is an age factor; amount of new credit in new accounts; and types of credit used, from credit card purchases to loans. There are online services that will provide your credit score totally free. You do not want to sign up for a 30-day trial on these web sites. You want a totally free credit report. Any web site is going to ask you for some personal information, but they should not ask you for your credit card number. With a higher credit score, the remaining steps in this process become easier to implement.

One such credit score web site is CreditSesame.com.[11] The web site will report your credit score from Experian without asking for a credit card. Experian is one of three credit bureaus that calculate credit scores for consumers.[12] CreditSesame does ask for your name, Social Security number, address, homeownership status, annual salary, information about your birth date, e-mail address, and some other information. Once you provide the information, the site reports your credit card score. Credit scores range from 300 to 900, and scores above 720 are considered good. Today, someone with a credit score of 520 is more likely to pay higher interest on loans and have difficulty obtaining new credit cards. The score identifies credit risk to a bank or other loan agency and how likely you are to repay your loan.

Knowing your credit score allows you to determine how successful you can be in the next step. The next step is to earn the highest level of awards on credit cards that you can possibly get. In my case, I have earned $14,000 toward the purchase price of automobiles over the years, flights across the United States for $10, and $1,000 worth of gift cards at leading stores. And, I say, "Thank you, Mr. Credit Card Company." One source of information for determining credit card rewards is mymoneyblog.com. The site provides information about credit card deals, investment advice, and other methods to save money for the average consumer. The site has an RSS feed where the financial updates are sent directly to an e-mail account.

The easiest method to get rewards from your credit card is to run payments through your card for which you don't have to shell out your own cash. Does it sound like a crime? Not really. If you have employer-reimbursed travel expenditures, make sure as much of these expenditures go through your credit card as possible, not your employer's credit card. You employer may not allow you to put these charges on your credit card, but if it is possible, make sure they go through your credit card. If your employer is slow in reimbursing your travel expenditures, it will become necessary for you to have a cash reserve to pay off the balance before you are charged interest by the credit card company. There is no reward plan that can make up for the interest paid by carrying balances on your credit card.

Another technique to run charges up on your credit card without shelling out your own money is to buy cash. Yes, cash. These opportunities come up every once in a while. The most recent example occurred when the U.S. Treasury started selling dollar coins to the public. The U.S. Treasury has wanted to replace dollar bills with dollar coins. Such an objective is impossible without the withdrawal from circulation of dollar bills, but this is the government. Up until recently, the U.S. Treasury allowed consumers to buy the dollar coins online with their credit cards. There were no shipping charges. Going to the U.S. Treasury web site, you could buy $50,000 of dollar coins that's a $1,000 award on a 2 percent credit card or $2,500 on a 5 percent credit card. Once the coins were delivered to your address for free, you lug the coins to your bank and deposit them. Thus, you don't spend anything. When the credit card statement came, you paid it without reducing your account balance below your original balance before making the purchase. Thus, you wind up with a minimum $1,000 award from your credit card company without really purchasing anything. Anyone could implement this plan, as it required no cash balance reserve.

The federal government makes these types of opportunities available occasionally. At another time, it was possible to purchase Treasury I-bonds online. These bonds must be held for one year before they can be cashed in, unlike the dollar coins. After the one-year period, they could be cashed in (with the loss of three months interest), but the purpose of this plan was to obtain reward points on a credit card, not the accumulation of interest on I-bonds. Unlike the purchase of dollar coins, these purchases would require a cash reserve to make up for the one-year time period until the I-bonds could be cashed. It is worthwhile to keep track of the U.S. Treasury to see if its future plans will allow another method for us to get reward points without using our own cash.

Another plan is to get flight miles from an airline credit card. Of course, those awards can be used for hotel rooms or car rentals, so you do not have to fly anywhere. Simply applying for an airline card can give you 50,000 flight points, which will allow you to fly roundtrip across the United States for around $10. Once you have received the points and taken the flight, you can cancel the credit card without paying any annual fee. In many cases, there is no annual fee for the first year. In most cases, as long as you cancel the card within the first year, the flights are basically free. Even with a $99 annual fee on the card that needs to be paid up front, you are still receiving a $500 airline ticket.

If you don't have any place to go or do not want to visit relatives, you can still use these credit card points to buy a $500 LCD TV from Walmart or BestBuy. Again, these points are given to you for simply signing up for a card and meeting the minimum requirements, which may be just buying a cup of coffee, to get the award points and then canceling the card before the first year and an annual fee is due.

An example of one of these credit card plans comes from Citibank. The bank provides $500 in gift cards or $655 in airfares if you sign up for the card and spend $2,500 on the card in the first three months. If you spend $833 per month on anything, you can put it on this credit card and you will receive a gift or free airfare. Other banks have had similar offers except they might include a $99 annual fee to be paid up front and then make one purchase to receive the awards.

A question may be asked as to how banks pay for these awards? The question is fairly easy to answer. Anybody who does not take advantage of the award points pays for them. For example, those people with low credit card scores who cannot apply for one credit card after another to take advantage of these programs pay for these programs. The bank passes these costs on to merchants and credit card holders either with interchange fees, interest, annual fees, or other charges. The bank or credit card company is not paying for these programs by reducing their profits.

Any Negative Effects

Some business journalists state that continually applying for and canceling credit card plans will reduce an individual's credit score. Bah! Humbug. The more important measure is your utilization rate or how much open and available credit you have compared to the balance on your credit cards. A rate of 10 percent is much better than a rate of 75 percent. For example, if you have a credit limit of $12,000 on a card and you have a balance of $1,800 on that card, your utilization rate is 15 percent. So it is not the canceling of the card, per se, that is the important factor. Rather, it is how the canceled card affects your overall utilization rate on all your credit cards. As you cancel a card, it reduces the overall credit available to you and it raises your utilization rate. Another consideration with the opening and closing of credit cards is the average age of your accounts. Lowering the average age of your accounts lowers your credit score. To get around this issue, do not close your old accounts as you open and close new accounts. By keeping old accounts open, the average age of your accounts will not be significantly reduced and your credit score will be protected. You should follow this procedure even if your old accounts are inactive— providing the bank is not charging you a fee for being inactive on the card account. Of course, you can always buy a cup of coffee with that credit card and keep the bank happy. For someone with a long credit history, applying for new credit cards is not going to have much of an effect on their credit score.

Finally, one other factor that may affect your credit score is credit inquiries by third parties. There are two types of inquiries: (1) hard and (2) soft inquiries. Hard inquiries are those queries about your credit that come from auto loans, mobile phone plans, apartment leases, and mortgage applications. Soft inquiries occur when you, your employer, or credit card companies check your credit score. Hard inquiries have more of an effect on your credit score because this indicates you are incurring more obligations and consequently there is an increased risk of repayment on these debts. These inquiries can affect a credit score by 1 to 5 points, so the other factors are usually more important.

Summary

Unfortunately, the main point in this chapter is that credit cards are being used to transfer resources from one group in society to another. In most cases, the group losing resources is composed of all consumers, and the group that is gaining resources is financial institutions. It is not unreasonable to expect financial institutions to earn a profit on their credit card services, but the methods by which those profits are earned need to be clearly disclosed and not be abusive. As long as the methods used to extract resources from the public are hidden with nebulous fees and mysterious interest rate calculations, the fairness of these methods will continue to be questioned. The average credit card user also needs to make a serious effort to understand his financial obligation when he signs a credit card agreement in this environment. Some methods have been suggested in the chapter to stem the outflow of resources from consumers, but these suggestions are only pennies in a bucket compared with the billions of dollars consumers continue to pay for these financial services.

Notes

1. See www.brainyquote.com/quotes/keywords/credit_2.html#ixzz1hOLDYwEP.
2. The total revolving debt in the United States ($793.1 billion as of May 2011 data, as listed in the Federal Reserve's July 2011 report on consumer credit) divided by the estimated number of households carrying credit card debt (50.2 million).
3. *Marquette Nat. Bank v. First of Omaha Corp.*, 439 U.S. 299 (1978) 439 U.S. 299 *Marquette National Bank of Minneapolis v. First of Omaha Service Corp. et al.* Certiorari to the Supreme Court of Minnesota No. 77-1265. Argued October 31, 1978. Decided December 18, 1978.
4. $\$13.35 \times 12 = \$160.20$.
5. The term *compounding* refers to the practice of calculating interest on an account balance as well as the previously earned interest accumulated in the

account. Without compounding, consumers would not earn interest on their previously earned interest.

6. The example skips the use of present values and the time value of money, which would make the calculation easier but less informative.

7. The prime rate is the rate that banks used for loaning money to each other, and it is largely set by the Federal Reserve Bank in Washington, DC.

8. For information about current credit card interest rates at Bankrate.com, see www.bankrate.com/funnel/credit-cards/credit-card-results.aspx.

9. See www.cutimes.com; D. Morrison, "New Research Charges Retailers with Pocketing Interchange," *Credit Union Times*, December 9, 2011.

10. www.hoffmanbrinker.com/credit-card-debt-statistics.html.

11. Other credit reporting services such as AnnualCreditReport.com require your exact birth date.

12. The other credit bureaus are Equifax and Transunion.

CHAPTER

Who Are Target-Date Retirement Funds Targeting?

Y ou, that's who.

Let me tell you a story about Jane, who wrote to me in 2013 about an experience she had investing in target-date retirement funds, also called target-date funds, which automatically rebalance their assets to become more conservative as an investor gets closer to retirement.

In 2005, Jane Doe, as I'll call her to protect her privacy, received a large inheritance from her parent's estate. Having no experience managing a six-figure portfolio, Jane asked for recommendations, and friends suggested she call one of the large national investment firms. Jane did so, speaking to a client service representative who asked questions designed to determine Jane's investment experience, investment horizon, and tolerance for risk—much what you'd expect of any financial professional.

"At the time, I was 57 years old and I thought that this inheritance would put me on pace to retire at age 65," recalls Jane, a single mother and the sole breadwinner in her family, who had previously handled all of her own retirement planning, placing other investments in very conservative mutual funds.

The client service representative Jane spoke to told her that a target-date fund would be a fantastic choice, and explained why. The "target date," the client service representative explained, refers to a target retirement date, and often is part of the name of the fund. For example, you might see target-date funds with names such as Retirement 2030 Fund or Target 2030 Fund, which would be designed for individuals who intend to retire during or near the year 2030. The client service representative told Jane that target-date funds offer a long-term investment strategy based on holding a mix of stocks, bonds, and other investments that automatically shifts as the participant ages. For example, a fund's initial asset allocation, when the target date is years away, might consist primarily of stocks, which have greater return potential but also greater volatility. As the target date approaches, the fund's asset allocation might shift to include a higher proportion of more conservative investments, such as bonds and cash, which generally are less volatile. "As a novice, I thought that this was a very prudent approach," says Jane.

That's a thought echoed by other purveyors of target-date funds. "They're an excellent investment solution for most people in most situations," said one financial planner at T. Rowe Price, which offers a full menu of target-date funds, quoted in the media. "I liken them to being the automatic transmission of the investing world—and 95 percent of cars sold in North America have automatic transmission."

Since Jane's desired retirement date was 2013, when she turned 65, the client service representative recommended that Jane split the assets between two funds, one with a target retirement date of 2010 and with a target retirement date of 2015. Jane agreed and was thrilled with her decision. "When the call was finished, I was filled with confidence and was very proud of myself for selecting a combination of two funds that would be managed in accordance with my risk and retirement in mind," she says.

Jane's investment strategy worked well for a few years, but then the financial crisis hit. In 2008, the fund with a target retirement date of 2010 lost 20.67 percent, and the fund with a target retirement date of 2015 lost 24.06 percent. Jane was devastated and flabbergasted. "I couldn't believe that these funds did not do what they were advertised to do," she says. "I couldn't sleep."

When Jane called the mutual fund company for an explanation (several times), the client service representatives she spoke with simply told her to stay the course. Jane, however, wanted answers. "How could a fund with a retirement date of 2010 lose 20 percent just two years before its maturity date?" she asks. "I want to know because I'm forced to postpone my retirement for at least two years as a result."

Understanding the Glide Path

Different mutual-fund companies take different approaches when their target-date funds reach their target dates. Some companies convert the assets into a retirement-income fund (either at the target year or later); others keep the assets in the original fund and keep the same name. For example, Vanguard Target Retirement 2010 is still around, even though 2010 has long since passed.

Either way, however, what happens to the fund's asset allocation when the target date is reached depends on its "glide path." A glide path is simply the shift in a target-date fund's asset allocation over time. There are two different approaches to glide paths. A "to-retirement" approach reduces the fund's equity exposure over time, reaching its most conservative point *at* the target date. A "through-retirement" approach also reduces the fund's equity exposure over time, but does so through the target date, so the fund reaches its most conservative point years after the target date.

According to a recent research paper published by Morningstar, one of the key differences between target-date funds with to-retirement glide paths and target-date funds with through-retirement glide paths is the speed with which allocation to stocks decreases. The average fund with a to-retirement glide path reaches its target retirement year with a 33 percent allocation to equities. Meanwhile, the average fund with a through-retirement glide path reaches its target retirement year with a 49 percent allocation to equities, then lowers its equity exposure over the next 20 to 30 years before reaching a final equity allocation of 28 percent.

The reason? Funds with through-retirement glide paths are designed to provide greater protection against longevity risk (since stocks tend to outperform other asset classes over time). The problem? You could end up a few years into retirement with a significant allocation to equities.

You may think Jane's experience is a one-time incident. After all, target-date funds are very popular. Assets in target-date funds totaled approximately $485 billion at the end of 2012, up 29 percent over the previous year, according to *Pensions & Investments*. That's a lot of money, when you consider that it took the entire mutual-fund industry more than 50 years to reach $2 trillion in assets. And Boston-based research firm Cerulli says the growth looks sustainable, and assets in target-date funds will more than double to $1.1 trillion by 2017. That's impressive growth for a fund category that didn't even exist until the mid-2000s.

Despite this popularity, however, Jane isn't alone in her experience. In 2008, Fidelity Freedom 2010 Fund and Vanguard Target Retirement 2010 Fund—some of the biggest names in the business—both lost more than 20 percent. I've heard worse, though. Also in 2006, Fidelity Freedom Fund 2005—a fund targeting people *who had already retired*—lost 24 percent. I know the stock market plunged in 2008, but assets in a fund with a 2008 or 2010 target date should have been almost completely out of the stock market by then.

In fact, the markets hit an all-time high of 14,000 in October 2007, so why didn't the fund managers sell then? It seems obvious to me that a retirement fund with a target date of 2008 or 2010 should reduce its exposure to equities one to three years before the target date—especially if stocks reach an all-time high then.

In some cases, target-date funds are designed to stay significantly allocated to equities after the target retirement date, as I explained in "Understanding the Glide Path." But there are other explanations for what happened in 2008. One that's bandied about is greed: Holding more assets in stocks means more profit for the companies that manage target-date funds, because actively managed stock funds generally charge higher expenses than bond funds. Or consider this as an explanation for what happened in 2008: The fund managers just didn't have the control you would expect them to have. That's because many target-date funds are simply composed of other funds in the same fund family. For example, a Fidelity target-date fund invests in other Fidelity funds, just like a Vanguard target-date invests in other Vanguard funds. As a result, the target-date fund managers, not managing the underlying assets themselves, don't keep on top of the overall asset allocation.

Here's the proof. According to the Fidelity Freedom Fund 2005 prospectus dated May 30, 2009, the fund's principal investing strategy is "investing in a combination of underlying Fidelity equity, fixed-income, and short-term funds using a moderate asset-allocation strategy designed for investors expected to have retired around the year 2005."

The fund, the prospectus said, works by "allocating assets among underlying Fidelity Funds according to an asset-allocation strategy that becomes increasingly conservative until it reaches 20 percent in domestic equity funds, 35 percent in investment-grade fixed-income funds, 5 percent in high-yield fixed-income funds, and 40 percent in short-term funds (approximately 10 to 15 years after the year 2005)." But, according to Value Line Mutual Fund Analysis, Fidelity Freedom Fund 2005 had almost 40 percent in equities as of June 30, 2009. That's twice the amount suggested by the prospectus, a full four and a half years after the retirement date. The fund also had almost 8 percent of its assets invested in international equities, including the emerging markets. Looking through the prospectus, I couldn't find anything that explained how international equities could make up 8 percent of the fund.

You might think that mutual fund companies changed after the debacle that was 2008. No to that, too. According to Brightscope, a company that ranks 401 (k) plans, from 2007 to 2010, the targeted percentage of stocks in target-date funds rose from an average of 40 percent in 2007 to 43 percent in 2010. "Many fund companies failed to learn from the 2008 debacle, which failure will surely hurt participants again," Brightscope concluded.

Who's the Biggest Offender?

According to Morningstar, some target-date fund providers have stable ratios of stocks to conservative investments over time, while others (notably Fidelity, the market leader) have more fluctuations.

Separate research by Morningstar in 2013 found that 13 of Fidelity's 14 target-date funds performed worse than three fourths of their competitors. Also in 2013, the Center for Due Diligence, an independent information and strategic services firm serving retirement plan advisers, posted an analysis of Fidelity's target-date funds compared to similar offerings from the company's major competitors. When it came to funds with target retirement

(Continued)

(Continued)

dates from 2010 to 2055, 79 percent of the Fidelity Freedom funds, 74 percent of the Fidelity Freedom K funds, and 68 percent of the Fidelity Advisor Freedom funds landed in the bottom half of category rankings.

Of course, stronger returns aren't everything: Phil Chiricotti, president of the Center for Due Diligence, said that Fidelity's more conservative glide path is one of the primary reasons its funds were underperforming, and a conservative glide path may be a good thing for risk-averse investors. But anecdotal evidence doesn't support that, as I've explained with my discussion of what happened to some Fidelity target-date funds in 2008.

Well, you might say, that's just a problem with Fidelity. Other mutual-fund companies might do a better job. Nope—because there just aren't that many other mutual-fund companies heavily into the target-date fund business. According to an April report by the Securities and Exchange Commission's (SEC's) investor advisory committee, "there is a high degree of saver concentration among just a few target date funds. According to Morningstar, the top 3 fund families had 75 percent of the market share in 2011, and the top 10 fund families had 90 percent of the 2011 market share. As a result, large numbers of investors, including individuals approaching retirement at the same time, will be affected by the approaches these companies adopt." Who are those three fund families? Well, Fidelity, T. Rowe Price, and Vanguard captured 69 percent of net inflows during the fourth quarter of 2012. That should give you an idea.

The Retirement Plan's Role

Much of the growth in target-date funds is due to defined-contribution retirement plan assets invested in target-date strategies. They rose nearly 29 percent to $96.5 billion in year ending September 30, 2012, according to the *Pensions & Investments'* annual survey of the largest retirement plans. All told, as of that date, target-date funds represented 11.6 percent of aggregate assets among the top 200 defined-contribution plans, up from 9.6 percent the year before.

That, in part, is because more and more defined-contribution retirement plans, such as 401 (k) plans, are offering automatic enrollment. Roughly 70 percent of U.S. employers report offering target date funds as their default investment option for company sponsored defined contribution plans, according to an SEC survey entitled *Investment Company Advertising: Target Date Retirement Fund Names and Marketing* (File No. S7-12-10, June 23, 2010). In other words, if you don't specify how you want your 401 (k) plan assets invested, they'll be invested in a target-date fund.

Here's another problem with target-date funds in retirement plans: The domination of the large 401 (k) plan managers crowds out smaller (and possibly better) target-date funds. Think about it. If Vanguard manages your 401 (k) plan, you're likely to be offered only Vanguard target-date funds (not American Century LIVESTRONG, which Brightscope ranked better than Vanguard in a 2010 report). It's like going to Walmart and only being able to buy Walmart-brand paper towels.

I discussed the problem with target-date funds years ago, in the February 2010 *Navigator Newsletter,* writing, "Do the funds live up to the hype? Let's see. To me the biggest attraction these funds would have is if they did indeed proactively reallocate the portfolio to reduce the risk as you got within 10 years of retirement and eliminated nearly all of it by five years out." Target-date funds didn't do that then, and they don't do it now.

The unfortunate thing is, these funds are designed to appeal to investors such as Jane who just don't know any better. They're packaged as a turnkey approach to retirement, or, as Fidelity describes its Fidelity Freedom® Funds, they're "all-in-one investment strategies that can help take the guesswork out of building and maintaining an age-based retirement portfolio." In other words, "It's easy! Just pick a fund with a date that matches your projected retirement, and we'll take care of the rest!" Sadly, many of these funds don't take care of the rest, and investors don't know it.

According to the aforementioned April 2013 SEC report, "evidence suggests that individual investors are ill-equipped to identify those risk disparities among similar seeming funds. For example, on a survey commissioned by the SEC, only 36 percent of respondents (including 48 percent of target-date fund owners and 26 percent of nonowners) correctly answered a true-false question regarding whether target date funds provide guaranteed income after retirement. Thirty percent (including 25 percent of owners and 34 percent of nonowners) answered incorrectly that target-date funds do provide guaranteed income. Fifteen percent of respondents said whether there is a guarantee depends on the fund, and 20 percent said they didn't know."

Moreover, investors can't even rely on the professionals to help them with target-date funds, because the professionals don't understand them either. According to the aforementioned April 2013 SEC report, many professional pension fund consultants—those are the people who help select retirement plan fund options—underestimate the risk of target-date funds. One unpublished study, conducted for PIMCO in 2010, found that, although the average target-date fund exposed investors nearing retirement to a significantly higher maximum potential loss than most consultants surveyed deemed appropriate, only about 35 percent of those consultants viewed the glide paths as somewhat to highly inappropriate (i.e., too aggressive). "In other words, almost two-thirds of these pension consultants assumed that funds were invested more conservatively than was in fact the case," says the report.

The Baffling Fees of Target-Date Funds

If you need another reason to avoid target-date funds, consider this: Their expense ratios can vary dramatically. The average expense ratio across all target-date funds, according to a 2010 Brightscope report, is 0.75 percent. But, as of May 2013, Vanguard target-date funds had an average expense ratio of 0.18 percent (pretty low) vs. 0.60 percent for Fidelity target-date funds and 0.70 percent for T. Rowe Price target-date funds. In other words, a T. Rowe Price fund is 250 percent more expensive than a Vanguard fund. How will that affect your portfolio? Well, if you have $100,000 in assets, saving 50 basis points in expenses annually means you're saving $500 annually. Add that $500 to your portfolio and compound it annually, and you'd have $28,118 after 30 years, assuming a relatively modest 3.5 percent return.

A Ticking Time Bomb

Now, here's the really bad news about target-date funds (as if what I haven't already written isn't bad enough): Today's macroeconomic conditions are making the problem even worse.

Even if target-date funds work exactly as they're supposed to—which I've already shown they don't—there's a problem given their heavy allocation to bonds. What, you may ask? Aren't bonds safer than stocks? In theory, yes; more bonds should make a fund safer because bonds tend to be less risky than stocks.

Right now, however, the bond market is close to an all-time high, as gauged by the all-time low yield of the 10-year U.S. Treasury. (Remember, bond prices and bond yields are inversely correlated: as the price goes up, the yield goes down.)

The first problem with the bond market today is that in moving assets from stocks to bonds as the retirement date approaches, a fund manager is forced to sell stocks and buy bonds, and those bonds are, simply explained, expensive. So by buying bonds at today's level, a portfolio manager is actually adding risk to a fund instead of reducing it, as you would expect in a target-date fund.

Additionally, should interest rates revert to their historic norms (which they will), bond prices will fall. The historic norm of the 10-year U.S. Treasury yield is roughly 4 percent compared to. 1.37 percent, its all-time low reached in July 2012. And, the increase in a bond's yield is always proportional to the decrease in a bond's price. If a 10-year bond yield increases by 1 percent, there would be a 5 percent drop in its price. So, when the bond market normalizes, there could be a 10 percent to 15 percent percent drop in bond prices. This drop may be a fatal blow to retirees who've been thinking that as time marches on, their target-date funds will take on less risk.

These misunderstandings may be a ticking time bomb to the next generation of American retirees. Most target-date funds with target retirement dates of 2015 and 2020 hold somewhere between one-third and one-half of their assets in bonds, according to the *Wall Street Journal*—much greater than the 10 percent to 20 percent of assets in some 2040 funds.

How to Hedge against Rising Rates

Rising interest rates aren't just a problem for target-date investors; they're a problem for all bond investors. Thus, if what I've written about their affect on bond funds worries you, I suggest you start using inverse bond funds as a way to hedge your risk. When interest rates rise, inverse bond funds increase in price, making them essentially the mirror image of a traditional bond fund.

The Dawdling SEC

The good news, if there is any, is that the Securities and Exchange Commission (SEC) got wind of this problem, and 2010 proposed a rule that, if adopted, would require any target-date fund that includes the target date in its name to disclose its allocation at the projected retirement date "immediately adjacent to" the first use of the fund's name in marketing materials. The rule would also require more disclosure about a fund's asset allocation and glide path. The SEC invited comments from the public, but for whatever reason, nothing came of this review in 2010.

Then, in 2013, the SEC's investor advisory committee adopted recommendations asking the agency to rewrite its proposed rule on target-date retirement funds. The recommendations would expand the 2010 SEC proposal with five recommendations: Mutual fund companies, the committee said, should (1) develop a glide path illustration for target-date funds based on risk rather than asset allocation alone; (2) adopt a standard methodology to be used in the risk-based and asset-allocation glide path illustrations; (3) clearly explain the assumptions used to design and manage the fund to attain the target risk level over the life of the fund; (4) warn that target-date fund returns are not guaranteed and that losses are possible, including at or after the target date; and (5) amend fee disclosure requirements to show the impact of those costs over the lifetime of the investment.

"In making this change in disclosure, we are actually going to teach investors something really important that most of them don't understand," said James Glassman, a committee member and founding executive director of the George W. Bush Institute, at a hearing. "There is more to risk than asset allocation."

I thought that was a good sign that something—finally!—would be done about target-date funds. Investors needed to be informed that these funds have better marketing strategies than investment strategies. But guess what? We're still waiting for a final rule. And if you think government always works that slowly, consider this: In the spring of 2013, it took the SEC only weeks to declare that public companies could announce vital information via social media. Let's hope that they move as fast on a matter that affects most Americans' 401 (k) accounts.

What Can You Do?

We've established that target-date funds are riskier investments than they're widely considered, and that the SEC isn't acting promptly to correct those misperceptions. That being the case, what can you do?

It's simple: Don't invest in target-date funds. Ever.

It just doesn't make sense. Putting everyone of the same age into the same asset allocation defeats the entire purpose of financial planning, which is supposed to construct a portfolio appropriate to an individual investor's investment goals and risk tolerance, and change it over time based on changes in that an individual investor's circumstances. Target-date funds are like asking a doctor to write every 50-year-old a prescription for blood pressure medication, because that's what all 50-year-olds needs, then switching the prescription to cholesterol-lowering medication in five years, because that's what all 55-year-olds need.

Remember Jane, whose target-date retirement fund lost 20.67 percent just two years before its maturity date? She gets it. "I've always been told if something seems too good to be true, it probably is, and these funds were that," she says. "Somebody was sleeping at the wheel, and I hope what you're writing helps avoid another person making the same mistake that I did. People have to understand that these funds have disappointed in the past, and will most likely disappoint in the future."

Protecting Your Purchasing Power

I've told you that you shouldn't invest in target-date funds, and I've scared you away from the bond market. How, then, can you protect your purchasing power?

Protecting your purchasing power involves more than making sure your disposable income stays ahead of inflation.

Inflation, the traditional wisdom holds, occurs when the price of goods and services increases over time. Well, that's not really true. Inflation really occurs when the value of the dollar decreases, forcing you to spend more of them to buy the same goods or service.

There are many reasons that the value of the dollar would decline. The government's quantitative easing efforts, for example, have diluted the value

(Continued)

(Continued)

of the dollar. This book, however, is not the place to have this discussion in detail. It's more important that I help you position yourself to mitigate the effects of inflation.

Historically, many investors have used gold to hedge against inflation. There are problems with gold, however. It generates no income. It can come with a high holding cost. And physical gold is illiquid. Think about it: If you need to fix a broken pipe, how do you break just enough gold off your gold bar to pay your plumber?

Dividend-paying stocks can be used to offset inflation, but as we all learned in 1987, 2002, and 2008, even dividend-paying stocks can at any time lose up to half their value.

In my models, I like to use Treasury Inflation Protected Securities (TIPS). These securities are issued by the U.S. Treasury and backed by the full faith and credit of the U.S. government. But they are indexed so they keep pace with the inflation as measured by the consumer price index (CPI).

CHAPTER

Four-Oh-One-Kay Tales

Why aren't you signed up for the 401K? I'd never be able to run that far.

Scott Adams, *Dilbert*, May 2, 2001

A lot of people become pessimists from financing optimists.

—C. T. Jones

Technically, a 401(k) is a defined-contribution plan for retirement that allows wage earners to reduce their taxes by having deductions taken from their pay and reducing their taxable income. There are other tax-deductible plans like 401(k)s for non-profit organizations, but all are designed to reduce the wage earners current income taxes and create an incentive for retirement saving. All earnings from the investment plan are tax deferred until the retiree begins to receive them. The saver is pushing his tax payments into a future period when he hopes he will be in a lower tax bracket and consequently get to keep more of his earnings. In 2006, Roth 401(k)s became available allowing wage earners to contribute after tax monies into a retirement plan. These contributions had already been taxed so at retirement their previous contributions are received tax free along with the possibly that investment earnings could qualify for a nontaxable distribution. The funds are invested in the stock of companies or some combination of bonds and stocks. Many financial advisers, company managers, and financial institutions tout the advantages of these plans for employees or investors. In addition, there are the management fees.

Wish I Had Thought about That . . .

I thought I was smart until I got my Fidelity 401(k) materials in the mail. It turns out that Fidelity Cash Reserves, the $118 billion money market fund where my cash is held, charges annual expenses of 0.31 percent. That's more than three times the 0.10 percent expense ratio Fidelity charges for its S&P 500 index fund, which also happens to have yielded 1.9 percent during the past year compared to a 0.01 percent yield for cash reserves.

Source: Scott Cendrowski, "Your Cash Is Costing You," CNN Money, February 20, 2012, http://money.cnn.com/2012/02/17/retirement/401k_cash_expenses.fortune/index.htm.

The Truth about Your 401(hey)!

Hey—brace yourself, because the advice I'm about to give you may seem like financial heresy:

Stop contributing to your 401(k) plan immediately!

You read that right—and the reason is that investing in your 401(k) plan is a mistake that could cost you and your loved ones hundreds of thousands of dollars in taxes.

I've studied this topic extensively. So far, however, my theory hasn't gained any traction. I've spoken to clients, certified public accountants (CPAs), and even an Internal Revenue Service (IRS) agent about it. One CPA looked me square in the eye and said, "You're nuts!"

Am I nuts or just not brainwashed?

Throughout our working lives, we've all been taught to save money for retirement via a 401(k) plan. The pitch goes something like this: You get a tax deduction today, and the money grows tax deferred. Then, when you withdraw the money in retirement, you'll likely be in a lower tax bracket. In the end, then, you reduce how much you pay in taxes.

What do I think about that argument? It's wrong! The problem with the traditional logic is that it doesn't tell you how things will work out in the end. It's like Evel Knievel telling you how easy it is to jump a motorcycle over 50 buses. The jumping is easy; it's the landing that can be very painful.

Similarly, when it comes to 401(k) plans, people generally talk about only the accumulation phase (the jump); no one is willing to talk about the distribution phase (the landing). I, however, am going to present you with both the jump and the landing—proving in the process that a 401(k) plan will generate more tax revenue for the IRS than an investment in a properly tax managed account. Hold on tight, because you're in for quite a ride.

The primary purpose of a tax-managed fund is to reduce the taxes paid by investors. Such funds avoid dividend paying stocks that would create an income tax liability; they hold stocks for long periods to avoid short-term capital gains; purchase tax free municipal bonds; make investments in Treasury securities that do not require the payment of state taxes; and sell stocks to capture losses in order to reduce taxes, for example.

Meet Mr. Uninformed and Mrs. Navigator

To make my point, I ran two different scenarios, one for Mr. Uninformed and one for Mrs. Navigator. Both invested $1,000 per month from August 1979 until August 2009. Both invested in Vanguard 500 Index Fund (VFINX), a mutual fund that tracks the S&P 500 Index, so investment performance was identical. Both ended up with $1,781,538 in their accounts.

However, Mr. Uninformed invested his money in a traditional 401(k) plan, and Mrs. Navigator invested her money in a tax-managed account, which is a mutual fund that is managed to limit the amount of income and capital gain distributions.

Mr. Uninformed received a tax deduction (because his contribution was made with pretax dollars), so he was able to invest his monthly tax savings of $200 each month. He chose to place it in a traditional after-tax account, not a tax-managed after-tax account. Ultimately, that after-tax account grew to $356,308.

Although Mrs. Navigator paid no taxes on her tax-managed account after 30 years (because it was managed with that goal in mind), and Mr. Uninformed paid $20,349 in taxes on his tradi-

Table 6.1   Mr. Uninformed Meets Mrs. Navigator

	Mr. Uninformed	Mrs. Navigator
401(k) plan	$1,781,538	$0
Traditional after-tax account	$356,308	$0
Tax-managed after-tax account	$0	$ 1,781,358
Taxes paid	$20,349	$0
Net value at retirement	$2,117,497	$1,781,538

Table 6.2   Mr. Uninformed's Tax Bill

	401(k) Plan	After-Tax Account	Total
Withdrawal	$71,147	$13,552	$84,699
Taxes	$17,273	$2,711	$19,984
Net income	$53,874	$10,841	$64,715

tional after-tax account, Mr. Uninformed ended up with $335,959 in addition to the money in his 401(k) plan, so it seems as if he did well, doesn't it? Table 6.1 illustrates.

So the winner is Mr. Uninformed, right? So far, it certainly looks that way, because Mr. Uniformed has more money, and this is where the story ends for most investors. If, by the time you retire, you have accumulated more money in a 401(k) plan than you would in an after-tax account, the 401(k) plan must be the best option, most people would say.

But wait a moment. Let's look what happens as Mr. Uninformed and Mrs. Navigator progress into retirement (Table 6.2). Both investors start a systematic withdrawal program taking 4 percent from their nest eggs annually.

Mr. Uninformed receives $84,699 taking money from each of his accounts in the same proportion of total assets. Thus, 84 percent ($71,147) comes from Mr. Uninformed's 401(k) plan, and 16 percent ($13,552) comes from his after-tax account. Mr. Uninformed's tax bracket is 25 percent. I also assumed he was taxed 5 percent at the state level (although each state's income tax rate is different, so please consult your home state for rates that apply to you). With these assumptions in place, Mr. Uninformed nets $53,874 on his 401(k) plan distribution (which

Table 6.3 Mrs. Navigator's Tax Bill

	Tax-Managed Account
Withdrawal	$71,261
Taxes	$3,885 (federal), $3,563 (state)
Net income	$63,813

is taxed as income) and $10,841 on his after-tax-account distribution (which is taxed at the capital-gains rate of 15%). Ultimately, Mr. Uninformed's total net income is $64,715, and his total one-year tax bill is $19,984.

Meanwhile, Mrs. Navigator withdraws the same 4 percent from her tax-managed account ($71,261), but she pays much less in taxes, just 15 percent (Table 6.3). Why? Her income was considered a capital gain. As a result, her annual tax bill (federal and state combined) is $7,448, so her net income is $63,813.

Although Mr. Uninformed's tax rate is double Mrs. Navigator's, again, Mr. Uninformed comes out ahead, netting $64,715 in income to Mrs. Navigator's $63,813. Maybe Mr. Uninformed is really Mr. Informed. Did Mrs. Navigator go down the wrong path? It looks that way—until we ask if Mrs. Navigator did a better job protecting her heirs.

Mr. Uninformed and Mrs. Navigator, 10 Years Later

Ten years into retirement, both Mr. Uninformed and Mrs. Navigator still have exactly the same amount of money with which they started, because even in today's crazy economy, a 4 percent distribution rate can be compensated for by appreciation of the assets remaining in the account.

Then tragedy strikes, and both Mr. Uninformed and Mrs. Navigator pass away—and here is where the rubber meets the road.

Upon Mr. Uninformed's death, his funds are distributed to his beneficiary. Let's assume his sole beneficiaries are his surviving children, and they pay no estate taxes. This distribution is considered income to Mr. Uninformed's children, and that distribution is a taxable event. As a result, Mr. Uninformed's children are hit with a tax bill of $747,630 (assuming a tax bracket of 39.6 percent at the federal level and 5 percent at the state level). In the end, the IRS

Table 6.4   The Big Picture

	Mr. Uninformed	Mrs. Navigator
Taxes paid during accumulation phase	$20,349	$72,000
Taxes paid during distribution phase	$199,840	$74,480
Taxes paid at death	$747,630	$0
Total taxes paid	$967,819	$146,480
After-tax account	$335,959	$1,635,058
Net value at death	$1,149,678	$1,635,058

receives $967,819 in taxes, and Mr. Uninformed's children's net inheritance is only $1,149,678.

Now, let's look at what happens to Mrs. Navigator's beneficiary, who we will assume is her husband (Table 6.4). He did not receive a 1099R and gets to keep all of the $1,635,058 in Mrs. Navigator's account. Why? Because upon Mrs. Navigator's death, her husband gets what is called a "step-up" in cost basis to the value of the account at the date of death—a provision that does not apply to retirement accounts such as Mr. Uninformed's. That may sound complicated, but it simply refers to the adjustment of the cost of an appreciated asset, upon inheritance, for tax purposes. With a step-up in cost basis, the value of the asset is the market value of the asset at the time of inheritance, not the market value at which the asset was purchased—and the former is usually higher. As a result, Mrs. Navigator's tax bill at death is $0, and her husband nets $1,635,058.

So, Mrs. Navigator's beneficiary netted $485,380 more than Mr. Uninformed's beneficiary. You must be saying to yourself, "How can this be? This is not what I was told all these years." But there's a reason Mrs. Navigator came out ahead. It's not because she possessed an incredible ability to manage the stock market, but because she was an expert at managing the tax code—simply by investing in a tax-managed account. In other words, Mrs. Navigator's fund manager tried to match capital gains and losses so the net tax effect of the trading would be zero. In essence, that allowed Mrs. Navigator to create her very own tax-deferred investment account that, upon distribution, would be taxed as capital gains, not income.

■ 20% Vanguard Tax-Managed Balanced Fund
■ 20% Vanguard Tax-Managed Small Cap Fund
■ 20% DFA Tax-Managed U.S. Targeted Value Fund
■ 20% Vanguard Tax-Managed International Fund
■ 20% Schwab 1000 Index Fund

Figure 6.1   A Simple Tax-Managed Portfolio

Figure 6.1 is an example of a tax-managed model, which invests 20 percent of assets in each of five funds: Vanguard Tax-Managed Balanced Fund, Vanguard Tax-Managed Small Cap Fund, DFA Tax-Managed U.S. Targeted Value Fund, Vanguard Tax-Managed International Fund, and Schwab 1000 Index Fund. Of course, other tax-managed investments could also be used.

A Little More Sizzle

If that's not enough to convince you that investing in a 401(k) plan isn't a good idea, let's add some more sizzle to this steak. During both the accumulation and distribution phases—meaning before and after retirement—Mrs. Navigator can withdraw money at any time from her account without paying a penny in income taxes, penalties, or excise taxes. So, if Mrs. Navigator needs to make a big purchase, or encounters some kind of financial hardship, such as significant medical bills, she can easily get to her money. Whether she needs $500 or $50,000, she can touch it at *any time* for *any reason.* Mr. Uninformed, however, has to jump through government-created hoops—which include claiming hardship, making in-service withdrawals and taking loans—to touch the smallest amount of his money.

But what about loans, you may ask. Mr. Uninformed could easily, if necessary, take a loan from his 401(k) plan to access his money. Moreover, traditional wisdom holds that taking a loan from your own 401(k) plan is a good idea—because in doing so, you are actually paying yourself back with interest. And the interest rate is typically low, usually around the prime rate plus 1 percent. There are some difficulties with 401(k) plan loans, however. You typically have to borrow at least $1,000, and you usually can't borrow more than 50 percent of your account balance (to a maximum of $50,000). You can borrow only the vested amount, meaning your unvested company contributions are off limits. The maximum loan term is five years. You generally cannot have more than one loan at a time, meaning you must borrow what you need the first time. If you can overcome all of those obstacles, there will likely be a loan origination fee and annual administration fee. And, if you are unable to pay back your loan, the IRS will view the unpaid balance as an early withdrawal and hit you with a 10 percent penalty.

You may also wonder about catch-up contributions. Do they make investing in 401(k) plans more appealing? Just to ensure we're on the same page, a 401(k) plan may permit participants who are age 50 or over at the end of a calendar year to make an elective contribution beyond the general limits that apply to 401(k) plans. These contributions are commonly referred to as catch-up contributions. You may be able to make a catch-up contribution or you may not because an employer is not required to provide for catch-up contributions in any of its plans. However, if your plan does allow for catch-up contributions, here are the general rules: If you participate in a traditional or so-called "safe harbor" 401(k) plan, and you are age 50 or older, the catch-up contribution is $5,500 as of 2013. If you participate in a Savings Incentive Match Plan for Employees of Small Employers (SIMPLE) 401(k) plan, and you are age 50 or older, the catch-up contribution is $2,500 as of 2013. For both types of plans, those amounts will be subject to cost-of-living increases after 2013. Assuming you can make such contributions, is investing in a 401(k) plan still a bad idea? Yes, and for the same reasons I've already stated. Being able to contribute more money doesn't make a difference. A tax-managed account has no limits on contributions or on catch-up contributions. If you win the lottery, you can put as much as 100 percent of the windfall in a tax-managed account and multiply the benefits.

One Exception

Now, you may have one more question. What if your company matches 401(k) plan contributions? Does that still mean investing in a 401(k) plan is a bad idea? First, fewer and fewer companies are matching 401(k) plan contributions these days. But if you're one of the lucky few employees who receives a match, the answer is that investing in a 401(k) plan isn't *quite* such a bad idea. But you should invest only up to the level of the company match. In other words, if your company matches up to 4 percent, contribute 4 percent and not a penny more.

Four Reasons to Invest in After-Tax Accounts

In summary, here's why you should invest in a tax-advantaged after-tax account instead of a 401(k) plan.

> *You're taxed at the capital gains level.* When the government established 401(k) plans in 1980, it ran projections showing that if you get a tax deduction at the time of investment, if the assets grow tax-deferred, and if you withdraw the money at a lower tax rate, you end up with more money. The government was right in those projections. However—and this is a huge "however"—the government changed the rules along the way. It lowered the capital gains tax rate. When 401(k) plans were established, income and capital gains were taxed at the same rate. Today and for the foreseeable future, federal income is taxed at a maximum of 39.6 percent, and capital gains are taxed at a maximum of 20 percent. So at the time of distribution and death, the money in your 401(k) plan will always be taxed at the higher income rate, and not at the lower capital gains rate.
>
> *It allows for a step-up in cost basis.* To recap, a step-up in cost basis is a tax code provision that allows the cost of an appreciated asset, upon inheritance, to be adjusted for tax purposes. With a step-up in cost basis, the value of the asset is the market value of the asset at the time of inheritance, not the market value at which the asset was purchased—and the former is usually higher. The step-up in cost basis is the single

biggest tax break the IRS gives us, and it does not apply to retirement accounts.

You get to choose exactly what you want to sell. You probably know what cost basis is: essentially, the original value of an investment (usually the purchase price). The difference between the cost basis of an investment and its current market value is your capital gain. Often, when selling an investment, investors will choose which "lot" to sell based on cost basis. For example, let's say you have 100 shares of stock. You purchased 50 shares at $50 a share, and 50 shares at $100 a share. Now, you want to sell 50 shares at the market price of $125 per share. Chances are you'd choose to sell the lot of shares you purchased at $100, because then your capital gain would be only $25 per share. But that matters only in an after-tax account. With a 401(k) plan, all before-tax contributions have a cost basis of zero. As a result, it doesn't matter which ones you withdraw, and every dollar withdrawn is taxed as income. You lose an important means of managing your investments for tax efficiency.

You have total access to your money. Tax-managed accounts have none of the withdrawal restrictions that 401(k) plans do. You can access any amount of money you want, at any time.

Source: Photo by Stevenson Smith

In conclusion, your long-term investments must navigate not only the markets but also the tax code—and as long as the tax code is structured so that income is taxed at a higher rate than capital gains, and there's a step-up in cost basis for after-tax accounts, your 401(k) plan will likely be the most taxed of all your assets. Now that you know better, don't invest in a 401(k) plan. In avoiding this tax trap, you'll be joining every member of Congress. They don't have 401(k) plans, either. Maybe that should tell you something.

Summary

Finally, it should be noted that investing strategies should seek a well-diversified portfolio to decrease portfolio risks before an individual's exertions turn to the reduction of taxes. Another consideration must also be a focus on the management service fees that are charged by the fund managers. With those two considerations in mind, the value of a tax-managed fund needs to be evaluated along with the tax effects for inheritors of the portfolio.

CHAPTER 7

Exchange-Traded Funds

Thanks to a deal finalized in 2008, Chicago's parking meters will be operated for the next 75 years by a group of investors put together by Morgan Stanley, including the sovereign wealth fund of Abu Dhabi.
> —Thomas Frank, "The Real Chicago Way," *Wall Street Journal,* October 8, 2009, http://online.wsj.com

By the time I have money to burn, my fire will have burnt out.
> —Unknown

Is Mr. Bogle "Indexing" the Problem?

Are exchange-traded funds (ETFs) a good way to invest? Not if you ask Wall Street legend John Bogle, founder of the Vanguard Group.

"For all [their] popularity and allure, not to mention the disproportionate share of new money that's being invested into ETFs, Bogle says the temptation to trade is their ultimate shortcoming," reads a February 2011 Yahoo! Finance article expressing John Bogle's view of ETF trading versus indexing.

The article goes on to state:

> "The growth has been much more than I would have ever expected," Bogle says of this fast-growing, $1.4 trillion dollar

industry that still faces "a lot of misunderstanding." Generally speaking, Bogle says most broad index ETFs are just fine, but he warns investors that individual sector and country funds are probably "too narrow for most." As for leveraged and inverse ETFs, Bogle says this is where the "fruitcakes, nut cases, and lunatic fringe" can be found. "There's just no possibility or any realistic way that you're going to win that bet," he says about leveraged ETFs. And finally, when you factor in the reality that about 75 percent of ETF assets are held and whipped around by institutions, and therefore subject to high turnover, Bogle says it's not the place for the weak of heart. "That's no way to invest," says this octogenarian creator of the index fund, before reiterating his preference for indexing.

—Matt Nesto, "ETF Trading: It's 'No Way to Invest'
Says Bogle"[1]

I disagree with Bogle, but before I explain why, let's talk a little about indexing, which is his preferred method of investing.

What Is an Index Fund?

An index fund is a mutual fund that mimics an index in the way it invests its assets. For example, a Standard & Poor's (S&P) 500 Index fund (such as VFINX, Vanguard's S&P 500 Index fund) would invest in the same stocks in the same percentages as the S&P 500 Index, which is the most commonly used benchmark for the performance of equity funds. Designed to be a broad indicator of stock price movement, the index consists of 500 leading companies in major industries chosen to represent the American economy. So, by buying an index fund, you are buying a sliver of these 500 leading companies.

There are dozens of index funds from which to choose—those that track the technology-heavy Nasdaq Composite Index, the international MSCI EAFE Index, and even the fixed-income-based Barclays U.S. Aggregate Index. Whatever the index, one thing remains constant: The fund owns a representative collection of securities in exactly the same ratios as the target index. Holdings are modified only when companies enter or leave the target index, which occurs only periodically.

I like to refer to index funds as "access" funds because that's really what they are. They give you access to a particular index. Of course, as a do-it-yourself investor, you have to know which index best matches your investment objectives, given how many you have to choose from. There are well more than 1,000 index funds in the database of Morningstar, the financial reporting analysis company, as of the end of 2012.

Why Invest in an Index Fund?

Now, why invest in an index fund instead of a mutual fund? To start, you get instant diversification: You are automatically invested in a number of different companies. Second, you don't face the risk that your portfolio manager will choose stocks poorly, because there's no choice to be made. Third, if your fund invests only in the stocks in which an index invests and following the same percentages, your fund will likely provide a return similar to the index's return. To the extent that you consider the index "the market," then, when you invest in an index fund, you will never significantly underperform the market (or outperform it). Finally, because there is no management required of index funds, the expenses are usually much lower than those of traditional managed funds.

It is the latter benefit—this lower expense ratio—that our friend Bogle likes. Essentially, Bogle thinks buying and holding index funds, a strategy called indexing, is the best way to invest. He uses it as his sales pitch.

Yes, every investment has a sales pitch—and as is the case with all sales pitches, it's important, when listening, to look beyond the surface.

To help you do so, it's a good idea to remember one constant theory of economics: Every time you get something, you give something up. I use that philosophy when making life choices. For example, if I buy a sports car, I'm likely getting speed in exchange for less room in the backseat and poor gas mileage. I also use that philosophy when analyzing investment options, including index funds. You see, I like what you get in an index fund: instant diversification into a particular index, limited potential for underperforming the market, virtually no management risk, and low expenses. But what do you give up for those benefits? Bogle will never tell you the costs of indexing, but I will. Indexing—again, buying and holding an index fund—does cost something. In exchange for the benefits I described earlier, you give up true downside protection and the ability to take profits.

Giving Up Downside Protection

First, consider downside protection. As noted, an index fund invests all of your money in the same stocks that an index tracks. As a result, you gain or lose money based on how that index performs. Sometimes that is good; sometimes that is not so good. In 1999, for example, the height of the technology boom, everyone loved their index fund. In 2002, however, you probably hated it. That was when stocks, after recovering from lows reached after the September 11 attacks, slid steadily, with dramatic declines in July and September leading to lows previously reached in 1997 and 1998. Ah, but markets are fickle. In 2007, love bloomed again (that is when the Dow Jones Industrial Average reached 14,100), and in 2008 you hated it again (I probably do not need to bring up the financial crisis). Do you see a pattern? Investing in index funds necessitates a love-hate relationship—and the hate part really matters.

Sure, index funds have low expenses, and that is great. But it is hard to imagine, after the bloodbath of 2008, when the S&P 500 Index fell 37 percent, that many people who were indexing looked at their spouses and said, "I know we lost 37 percent of our life savings, honey, but it's okay because our expense ratio was low!"

Bogle, however, seduces investors into thinking the most important aspect of an investment is its cost. I do concede that smart investors should "monitor their investment expenses," as Bogle suggests, but *people get rich based on total returns, not low expenses.*

Think about it this way: Do you hire your doctor, plumber, landscaper, or dentist based on who gives you the lowest bid? Probably not. So why would you trust your life savings to an investment that charges the least?

To make my point, Bogle is often pontificating about the value of indexing when the markets are performing well, but he's nowhere to be found when the markets are performing poorly. Where was Bogle, for example, during the aforementioned bloodbath of 2008? Where was he when the markets hit a postrecession low in March 2009?

He's Back!

Jack Bogle is back! He was on CNBC April 1, 2013, and April 8, 2013, hawking his same old sales pitch: "stay the course," "buy and hold," "think 10 years out," "have a stiff upper lip," blah, blah, blah. During both "interviews" (I use that word lightly because he was barely challenged by the host), he said that the market will grow by 5 percent capital appreciation and 2 percent dividend yield over the next 10 years. This rate of growth will basically double your assets in 10 years. He also said that the markets could go down 20, 30, or as much as 50 percent (maybe twice) during that time period. His advice: "Stay the course." Oh brother!

In sum, then, Bogle's theory of indexing—that it is an inexpensive way to gain access to a market—offers no downside risk protection. As with other things in life, the benefit comes with a cost.

Giving Up the Ability to Lock In Profits

The other cost of indexing is the fact that it does not allow you to lock in profits easily. For example, sophisticated, wealthy investors will get into a stock early, and thereby start a market rally. The rest of us will not jump onboard until the rally is well underway. In other words, the sophisticated, wealthy investors get the glass to the half-pull point; the rest of us fill it all the way. Then what happens? The sophisticated, wealthy investors sell first. The rest of us—with paper gains—sit on the sidelines and watch as the values of our portfolios plummet. Then we sell, when the market is on the downswing. This is a pattern that repeats itself over and over. The little guy has a habit of buying late and selling late.

This is a particular problem with indexing. Remember, earlier, when I said that an index fund will not sell a stock unless its underlying index does so? As a result, when you own shares of an index fund, it is an all-or-nothing choice; you cannot move out of an individual stock you dislike. You could move out of the index fund entirely, but you would need to make the decision yourself—and most noninstitutional investors just do not have the skill to time the market in that way. That is why people invest in traditional, actively managed mutual funds: they get the guidance of professional management.

Table 7.1 **Stock Picking: Sometimes Good, Sometimes Bad**

Stock	Starting Value	Starting Price (March 1, 2004)	Ending Price (March 2, 2009)	Return	Loss	Ending Value
Citigroup	$100,000.00	$50.46	$1.20	-97.62%	-$97,621.88	$2,378.12
AIG	$100,000.00	$74.09	$0.42	-99.43%	-$99,433.12	$566.88
Bank of America	$100,000.00	$82.13	$3.59	-95.63%	-$95,628.88	$4,371.12
GM	$100,000.00	Bankrupt	Bankrupt	-100.00%	-$100,000.00	$0.00
Ford	$100,000.00	$13.99	$1.88	-86.56%	-$86,561.83	$13,438.17
	$500,000.00					$20,754.29
% loss	95.85%					

Do you think you are a better decision maker than that? If so, think back to the housing market boom and bust. The housing market peaked at the end of 2006 and started declining in 2007. In 2010, there were more than 1 million foreclosures in America. Then, the final blow hit: the stock market meltdown of 2008 and 2009. Yes, the stock market eventually recovered to reach its 2007 levels, but how many investors got that timing right? Had you divided $500,000 between five stalwarts of the prefinancial crisis era—Citigroup, AIG, Bank of America, GM, and Ford—you would have lost more than 90 percent from March 2004 to March 2009 (see Table 7.1). Had you included Bear Stearns, Lehman Brothers, Merrill Lynch, Countrywide, and Washington Mutual (three of which went bankrupt and two of which were sold at a huge discount to Bank of America), your losses would have been even greater. We are not even including Enron, Global Crossing, or Tyco International. You would have done better giving your money to Bernie Madoff. Because the losses in his fund were due to theft, they were insured up to $500,000.

In sum, indexing is not a good way to take profits from an investment. In fact, indexing is Wall Street's way of saying, "Let it ride!" The longer you let it ride, the greater the chance the rich will take your money. Here's what I say: Take your profits before someone else does.

Why Not Buy and Hold?

Some of you may understand the points I am making but respond with a counterargument: Doesn't buying and holding for longer periods eliminate downside risk? After all, Warren Buffet, who may be the greatest investor of all time, likes to say his favorite holding period is forever.

I agree with you—if you have Buffet's talent for finding, valuing, and overseeing portfolios of individual stocks. In that case, you should stop reading and start investing. However, if you're like the rest of us, a buy-and-hold policy is just stupid.

To illustrate why, think about the technology boom of the 1990s. We all know how that worked out. On March 10, 2000, the Nasdaq Composite Index closed at an all-time high of 5048.62. The index declined to half its value within a year, and finally hit the bottom of the bear market on October 10, 2002, when it settled at an intraday low of 1108.49. What if you bought in March of 2000 and held? Would that buy-and-hold strategy have worked? I supposed it depends on what your holding period is. In March 2013, 13 years after it peaked, the Nasdaq Composite Index has yet to recover fully. It closed on March 22 at 3245. So keep on holding. I hope you don't need your money soon.

Another example: the housing market boom and bust, which I earlier used as an example of why it's so hard to time the market. It's also an example of why buy-and-hold isn't a good strategy. Let's say you indexed using a fund that invested in blue-chip companies, which was advice of the talking heads on television. How many of the 10 stalwarts of the era—Citigroup, AIG, Bank of America, GM, Ford, Bear Stearns, Lehman Brothers, Merrill Lynch, Countrywide, and Washington Mutual—are around today? If you had bought and held those stocks, where would you be now?

So I disagree with Bogle's claim that the "temptation to trade ETFs is their ultimate shortcoming." In my opinion, Bogle's unrelenting belief in a buy-and-hold strategy has harmed many small investors. If your plan is to hold, you will never take a profit—and that profit (your profit) will be realized by someone else.

So What's Wrong with ETFs?

Bogle says ETFs are no way to invest, and I agree—in part. Investing in ETFs is not simple and is best done with professional navigation.

But I don't dismiss ETFs altogether, and I certainly think they're a better option than indexing.

Before I explain why, let's review what an ETF is. Essentially, it's an index fund—a pool of stocks that tracks an index. Unlike a mutual fund, however, an ETF trades on an exchange much like a stock does.

Their genesis was Index Participation Shares, a proxy for the S&P 500 Index that began trading on the American Stock Exchange and the Philadelphia Stock Exchange in 1989, but stopped shortly thereafter as a result of a lawsuit by the Chicago Mercantile Exchange. In 1990, the Canadians beat us to the punch and began trading Toronto Index Participation Shares, which tracked the Toronto Stock Exchange (TSE) 35 and later the TSE 100 stocks, on the Toronto Stock Exchange in 1990. That ETF was so popular, the Americans tried again, and succeeded when Nathan Most and Steven Bloom launched Standard & Poor's Depositary Receipts (SPY), an ETF that tracks the S&P 500 Index, in January 1993.

There's no way around it: Investors love ETFs. Just as digital downloads have revolutionized music, ETFs ended 2012 with more than $1.3 trillion in assets, nearly 30 percent higher from a year earlier. Management consulting firm McKinsey & Co. has said that "no other significant segment of the U.S. asset-management industry has grown as quickly."

So why are ETFs so popular? The upside to investing in ETFs is similar to the upside of investing in index funds. You get instant diversification into different stocks, to the extent that the index the ETF tracks is diversified. You also get low fees, because ETFs aren't actively managed: as is the case with index funds, they tend to change their holdings only when their underlying indices do so. The 10 largest and most liquid ETFs in the United States charged an average fee of 0.26 percent, according to Morningstar as of March 2013, competing well against the 1.5 percent charged by the average actively managed mutual fund.

Additionally, and unlike index funds, ETF shares trade on exchanges, so they can be bought or sold at any time the stock market is open. Index funds, when bought or sold, provide you with the price at the next daily market close.

The downside of investing in ETFs is similar to the downside of investing in index funds: You give up true downside protection and the ability to take profits because ETFs do not offer active management, which puts most of the responsibility on you, the individual investor, to decide when to buy and sell.

ETFs also offer some risks that index funds do not. For example, ETFs can be priced to a discount to their net asset value, while index funds are always priced according to their net asset value.

Net asset value is the total value of all of a fund's assets minus its liabilities divided by the number of outstanding shares for that fund. Mutual fund price is determined by the fund's holdings rather than the perceived value of that fund.

An ETF is priced by supply and demand. If buy demand exceeds the sell supply, a premium is created. Conversely, if the sell demand outnumbers buy supply, a discount results. This means that until a balance is reached, the underlying ETF will be priced at a discount or premium, its net asset value (NAV).

Another unique and significant risk with ETFs is that they are also subject to vagaries of supply and demand. For example, as safety-seeking investors have been funneling cash into fixed-income ETFs during the past year, their numbers and prices have risen. As a result, many fixed-income ETFs are now worth more than the bonds they hold.

How could this happen, given that ETFs, like index funds, are designed to track an index and perform in line with it? ETFs work well as vehicles for trading baskets of stocks designed to track the performance of equity benchmarks ranging from the broad-based S&P 500 Index to sector-specific indices such as those that track health care or telecommunications. Because these ETFs own equities that trade widely on public exchanges, the values of the ETF's holdings is never in doubt, and the ETF's price—its NAV seldom deviates from the value of its underlying holdings. But its traded market price may differ from its NAV.

There is a caution with fixed-income ETFs. Non-Treasury fixed-income markets tend to be much less liquid than equity markets. That means fixed-income ETFs are often subject to price distortions. That could lead to difficulties if bond prices enter a long slump: Investors who bought ETFs at a premium could end up selling them at a discount.

In sum, unlike Bogle, I like ETFs—with caveats. As is the case with index funds, in order to invest in ETFs, you must know which index aligns with your investment objectives and risk tolerance (and should not be fooled into thinking one index is all you need).

And you need to have a plan for taking gains. Don't just buy and hope that a low expense ratio will get you the return you need.

That's why I advise professional management when investing in ETFs—because, as is the case with everything else, you get what you pay for. Money managers also use ETFs differently than investors who index as described in the next section.

How Much Should You Pay for an ETF Trade?

Trading ETFs is much like trading stocks: You buy and sell from a broker, which will charge a trading commission. We have researched the marketplace to determine the typical commission on an ETF transaction, and it is $8.95. Large discount brokerage firms may offer up to 100 ETF trades free of charge, but these offers usually come with a minimum holding period, which is typically 30 days.

The Benefits of Professionally Managed ETFs

ETFs have been a boon for money managers, who are increasingly running mutual fund portfolios solely with ETFs.

Portfolio managers who invest solely in stocks take on company risk. That simply means they run the risk of one of their holdings being mismanaged. For that reason, I tend to use no-load mutual funds in my models: they provide for instant diversification.

However, adding ETFs allows me to seek growth of capital by buying a wide range of sectors, not just asset classes. For example, with a mutual fund, it is possible to invest in a continent or region (such as Europe); but with an ETF, it is possible to isolate a country, not just a continent. ETFs also allow for the investing in the price of gold or silver without holding precious metals or buying the stocks of precious metals companies.

It is possible to rotate in and out of sectors with ETFs. Unlike indexing, sector rotation is fundamentally designed to move from sector to sector. This means that profits can be harvested and losses can be trimmed. It's a dramatically different strategy than indexing.

So why don't I use index funds for sector rotation instead of ETFs? Good question. Index funds tend to be very broad based—that is, they track an entire index of stocks, such as 500 in the case of the S&P 500 Index. There are mutual funds and ETFs that invest in particular sectors, however, which focus on very narrow market segments. An index fund invests in an entire shopping mall. An actively managed mutual fund invests in several stores in a shop-ping mall. But ETFs invest in a single product in a single store. Rotating between stores and/or products can create an opportu-nity to catch the next Tickle-Me Elmo or Wii. But rotating between malls only ensures you are stuck with all the John Carter (Disney's huge box office flop) and Lance Armstrong (disgraced seven time Tour-de-France winner) merchandise.

Holding a well-diversified portfolio of ETFs will be more focused, less expensive, and more tax-efficient than one consisting solely of no-load mutual funds or index funds (because it is possible to offset a realized gain with a realized loss to keep taxes to a minimum). It will also allow for the taking of profits in a way that indexing does not.

Ranking ETFs the Grimaldi Way*

In 2005 I assumed the role of publisher for a newsletter called *The Sector Navigator* that recommends model portfolios of ETFs. Launched in September 2002, when ETFs had not found wide rec-ognition, it has now gained a following, thanks to a fantastic track record. *You can receive a free subscription to this newsletter. Information is provided at the end of this chapter.*

To analyze ETFs, a proprietary ranking system is used to iden-tify the sectors showing the greatest relative strength. Essentially, the model's "secret recipe" is to rank ETFs based on eight criteria.

1. First, the ETF's 52-week high and low prices are evaluated to gauge where it is in the business cycle. For example, the ETF known as Consumer Staples Select Sector SPDR (XLP) was get-ting close to its 52-week high of $32.46 on November 1, 2012. That was a positive sign, suggesting it could break out above its 52-week high, continue to rise, and establish a new high.
2. Next, the ETFs' one-month, three-month, and one-year per-centage returns are gauged to help spot price trends.
3. The ETF's relative strength index (RSI), which is a techni-cal indicator intended to chart the current and historical strength or weakness of a stock or market based on the clos-ing prices of a recent trading period, is taken into consider-ation. An ETF's RSI shows if the herd is moving in or out of the ETF, and whether it is overvalued (in the case of an RSI

---

*The Grimaldi Way is a creation of Mark A. Grimaldi, patent pending.

greater than 70) or undervalued (in the case of an RSI under 30). Typically, we like a reading at the midpoint, as was the case with XLP on November 1, 2012, when its RSI was 54.38.

4. The ETF's three-year standard deviation, which allows us to track its volatility or its tendency to move up and down, is reviewed.

5. Now for the ulcer index. The ETF's ulcer index is a technical indicator that measures volatility, but only downward volatility. Essentially, the ulcer index measures short-term risk. It helps determine if the herd should start selling, how low the price can drop. An ulcer index reading greater than five indicates the ETF is risky; an ulcer index reading lower than 5 implies the ETF is only moderately risky. On November 1, 2012, XLP's ulcer index reading as 3.41, indicating a low to moderate level of risk.

6. Dividend yield on the ETF is evaluated.

7. The ETF's Sharpe ratio, which measures the excess return (or risk premium) per unit of deviation, is measured. The ratio helps determine whether an ETF's high returns are due to good investment decisions (which is good) or high risk taking (which is bad).

8. Trading volume is the last indicator. The strength of its market move is evaluated with trading volume. If the market moves up with a high volume of transactions, the move is more significant.

Using those factors, ETFs are ranked on a monthly basis. During volatile times, the ranking can be done twice monthly. The top four domestic and top international ETF will be added to the model. If any of the current holdings drop out of these levels they are sold.

Summary

Comparisons of purchasing ETFs that have been highlighted in the chapter. There are differences of opinion as to the best investment policy to follow when it comes to mutual funds, index funds, and ETFs. Although the cost of fund management is not the only issue that should be considered when selecting an investment fund, clearly an increase in management fees will lower the investor's return. If that is a concern, those costs can be mitigated by using discount brokers such as E-Trade, TD Ameritrade, Charles Schwab, or Fidelity.

Finally, ETFs provide the investor with little money to invest an opportunity to get into the market. A mutual fund may require an initial $2,000 investment, but with an ETF the investment equals the purchase price of the stock. This lets a small investor into the market with a minimum investment, but it must be remembered that the trading cost of purchasing individual shares may significantly reduce any returns.

Our Sector Rotation Model at a Glance

Indexing or ETFs?

I've told you how I feel about indexing and ETFs, and it should be clear to you that I prefer ETFs, when professionally managed. Amateurs manage expenses; professionals manage total return, risk, and profit taking. Indexing does none of these things. However, ETFs—used within the confines of our proprietary ranking system—has allowed us to successfully identify where the money flows are and help us position ourselves ahead of the market.

Free one year subscription to the top-ranked sector rotation newsletter!!!

Go to *www.grimaldieconomics.com* and enter the code SECTOR to receive your free one-year subscription.

ETF SECTORS
SECTOR ROTATION MODEL AS OF 9/30/2013

Name & Purchase Date	Buy Price	Symbol	Shares	NAV	Value	Pct	MTD Return
Consumer Staples Select Sector - 12/31/12	$34.90	XLP	2763.241	$39.80	$109,976.97	33.86%	0.73%
Market Vectors Pharmaceuticals - 8/30/13	$46.48	PPH	1538.053	$47.84	$73,580.44	22.65%	2.93%
iShares DJ US Health Care - 2/28/13	$90.93	IYH	717.248	$106.92	$76,688.10	23.61%	3.17%
iShares DJ US Consumer Goods - 8/30/13	$87.42	IYK	432.434	$89.30	$38,616.36	11.89%	2.66%
iShares MSCI Malaysia - 7/31/13	$15.11	EWM	1724.100	$15.04	$25,930.47	7.98%	4.16%
					$324,792.34		

2002 Return -0.51% **	2005 Return 10.74%	2007 Return 9.45%	2009 Return 2.95%	2011 Return 7.11%	Monthly Model Return	2.29%
2003 Return 29.17%	2006 Return 14.56%	2008 Return -4.23%	2010 Return 17.84%	2012 Return 8.14%	Year To Date Return	18.74%
2004 Return 13.90%	** Inception date - 9/1/2002	* Return percentages for individual securities in the model are month-to-date for the security.				

PROFUNDS/RYDEX SECTOR FUNDS
PROFUNDS/RYDEX SECTOR ROTATION MODEL AS OF 9/30/2013

Name & Purchase Date	Buy Price	Symbol	Shares	NAV	Value	Pct	MTD Return
Rydex Consumer Products - 12/31/12	$41.42	RYCIX	1137.669	$49.71	$56,553.54	17.73%	1.84%
Rydex Health Care - 8/30/13	$24.52	RYHIX	3531.057	$25.50	$90,041.95	28.23%	4.00%
Rydex Utilities - 5/31/13	$31.83	RYUIX	2050.741	$31.94	$65,500.66	20.53%	1.59%
Rydex Retailing - 6/28/13	$20.97	RYRIX	3205.514	$22.35	$71,643.25	22.46%	4.34%
ProFunds Pharmaceuticals - 11/30/12	$12.67	PHPIX	2147.679	$16.41	$35,243.41	11.05%	2.88%
					$318,982.81		

2002 Return 4.92% **	2005 Return 12.24%	2007 Return 5.61%	2009 Return -8.97%	2011 Return 0.44%	Monthly Model Return	3.06%
2003 Return 20.46%	2006 Return 14.37%	2008 Return -1.79%	2010 Return 11.44%	2012 Return 15.92%	Year To Date Return	29.74%
2004 Return 23.71%	** Inception date - 9/1/2002	* Return percentages for individual securities in the model are month-to-date for the security.				

FIDELITY SELECT FUNDS

FIDELITY SELECT SECTOR ROTATION MODEL AS OF 9/30/2013

Name & Purchase Date	Pur. Price	Symbol	Shares	NAV	Value	Model Pct	Return*
FS Health Care - 8/30/13	$171.96	FSPHX	452.548	$180.98	$81,902.09	27.32%	5.25%
FS Consumer Staples - 12/31/12	$80.02	FDFAX	690.229	$89.02	$61,444.17	20.49%	2.24%
FS Pharmaceuticals - 8/30/13	$17.99	FPHAX	3358.487	$18.62	$62,535.03	20.86%	3.50%
FS Med Systems & Equip - 8/30/13	$33.62	FSMEX	1472.363	$34.93	$51,429.63	17.15%	3.90%
FS Air Transport - 8/30/13	$48.61	FSAIX	809.272	$52.55	$42,527.24	14.18%	8.11%
					$299,838.15		

2002 Return 1.64% **	2005 Return 11.54%	2007 Return 5.20%%	2009 Return 27.83%
2003 Return 30.59%	2006 Return 11.36%	2008 Return -34.45	2010 Return 21.91%
2004 Return 25.79%			

2011 Return -2.71% Monthly Model Return 4.41%
2012 Return 14.87% Year To Date Return 20.38%

**Inception date - 9/1/2002 * Return percentages for individual securities in the model are month-to-date for the security.

Note

1. Yahoo! Finance, "ETF Trading: It's 'No Way to Invest' Says Bogle," February 11, 2013, http://finance.yahoo.com/blogs/breakout/etf-trading-no-way-invest-says -bogle-140924616.html.

CHAPTER

Who Took My Money Now?

THE COLLAPSING EDUCATION SYSTEM

I have never let my schooling interfere with my education.
—Mark Twain

Under the United States Constitution, the federal government has no authority to hold states "accountable" for their education performance. . . . In the free society envisioned by the founders, schools are held accountable to parents, not federal bureaucrats.
—Ron Paul, Statement on the Congressional
Education Plan, May 23, 2001[1]

Investment in education is similar to an investment in stocks. With the right choices, a gain is earned. Future riches can arise from those choices. Yet today's K–12 educational system takes more away from families than would a stock market crash. For a family's future generations, it reduces their ability to earn a living and shrinks their levels of success while, at the same time, keeping them in the dark as to why this is occurring. Unlike an investment loss on a stock, losses created by a collapsing educational system create a spiraling generational loss that cannot be rectified. Where to start in this quagmire and bring to light how these losses occur?

Maybe the best place to begin is to identify the players or the stakeholders involved in our educational system. K–12 education is a local community operation in the United States . . . well, that's the first lie.

The Feds and State Government

Stakeholder number one in our schools is the federal government because they put up a lot more money than parents pay with their property taxes or sales taxes to support local schools. The federal government provides monies to local schools if these schools do what the federal government tells them to do. A big player in secondary education is the federal government acting as the overseer in public education through the U.S. Department of Education (DoE) in Washington, D.C. The DoE annual budget request for 2013 is almost $70 billion, including Pell grants, which are transfer payments that do not have to be repaid, to low-income undergraduates. Without the Pell grants, the 2013 budget is a little less than $50 billion. What does $50 billion buy? In the two-volume 2013 education budget bill, there are a total of 30 programs with various uplifting names such as Supporting Student Success, Innovation and Instructional Teams, English Learner Education, and Accelerating Achievement and Ensuring Equity. The guidelines, inclusions, and exclusions in this budget bill cannot be covered here.

In the Ensuring Equity program, the federal government requires that low-achieving students be provided with accelerated programs to develop their reading and mathematical abilities. The funding for these programs is usually given to teachers currently employed in the systems as "overtime" pay. Regular classroom teachers continue in their classroom duties after the end of the regular school period, and this extended school time is considered acceleration for low-achieving students. How acceleration takes place is a mystery, but paychecks get fatter.

Several of the groups targeted for remedial assistance are migrant, neglected, delinquent, and homeless students.

None of the federal monies come without some stipulation of conduct for the school system. The rush to student assessment is based on the requirements under federal education funding regulations. Teachers have gamed this system to show "adequate yearly progress" improvements in their students' scores. One such game is to identify as many students as possible as students with "cognitive disabilities." These students are allowed to take assessment tests based on alternate achievement standards ("easy ones"), thus raising overall school assessment scores. As more regulations are issued, more games are played by school officials to get their federal and state funding. Definitions are twisted, counts are miscalculated, the efforts of successful administrators are concentrated on replenishing grants, integrity is lost by everyone, and, oh yeah, education success may be a myth because Johnny still can't read.

With $50 billion up for grabs, the approximately 16,000 school systems in the United States are going to do what they need to do meet the formula requirements and collect their share of federal funding.[2] These funding games don't consider the other set of regulations coming in the *School Meals Eligibility Manual* from the Department of Agriculture and its $11.1 billion budget in 2011. Local control is a myth. Local control is about gaming the system to make sure the cash keeps flowing. These dollars do not include the $14.5 billion in 2012 funding and additional school regulations for federal mandated testing and other "quality" improvements from No Child Left Behind legislation. Most of these monies sent by the federal government to the states are used to force local school systems to follow national guidelines for teaching, testing, and political correctness learning, and the regulations even travel down to what students should eat.

In my own experience as a high school teacher, I remember asking our high school principal why some of better high school students who seemed to be treading water in their senior year could not graduate early. My principal started pounding his fist on the table to emphasize his point: "No one is graduating early. We get state funds for each student, and they are not leaving until we get all the state funds for each of them." Although these students would have been better served by leaving school one year early, the principal did not want to lose a dollar's worth of state funding. Their parents were unaware of why their sons and daughters were so bored in their last year of high school, but they completely supported their local school system and their dollar-grubbing principal.

The Vendors

Another important stakeholder, let's call them number two in our list of interested parties, is the local vendors and suppliers who provide various services to the school systems. The students are a basic money source for vendors. Vendors can be suppliers of goods or professional services from contract employees such as psychologists. It always made me wonder what would happen to the fees a school psychologist received if they cured everyone. Is that a conflict of interest or not? Don't worry; it is a mild ethical issue compared with outright fraud.

Vendors supplying goods to the schools receive their contracts on open bid, right? As we all know, many of these vendors have inside relationships with school officials, and they received their service contracts because of those relationships or because of outright bribes taken from the school's budget in excess service charges and paid back to school officials. You don't think vendors would take bribes out of their own pockets? The scenario goes like this: "Let me charge you more now, and I will kick it back to you later."

Why Do We Have to Pay for Our Own Textbooks?

The former insurance broker for the Toms River Regional School District in New Jersey today admitted his role in a scheme to pay bribes and other benefits to the then-superintendent of schools to get and maintain a contract to provide insurance services for the district, U.S. Attorney Paul J. Fishman announced. From 2002 to 2010, Gartland and coconspirators Frank D'Alonzo, 54, a former administrator at the Toms River Regional School District; Frank Cotroneo, 61, an insurance broker; and others paid $1 million to $2 million in bribes and other benefits to Michael J. Ritacco, 65, who was then superintendent. The payments were made to allow Gartland to obtain and keep the insurance contract with the district.

Gartland admitted that in 2002, he, Ritacco, Cotroneo, and D'Alonzo agreed to have Ritacco approve a workers' compensation insurance contract between Gartland and the school district in which the contract fee would yield $500,000 to $600,000 per year in excess fees, which would be used to pay bribes and kickbacks to Ritacco.

Source: United States District Attorney's Office, District of New Jersey, "Broker Pleads Guilty in Bribery, Kickback, Fraud and Perjury Scheme Involving Toms River Schools," April 2, 2012, www.justice.gov.

Beyond these issues are the questions of the quality of services provided by the vendors. Are vendors maintaining school bus safety or cutting costs to increase their profits? Are bus routes scheduled in a manner that allows the highest reimbursement to the service provider? Are corners cut on school construction as in China, where hundreds of young children are killed when these buildings collapse? Shoddy supplies? Maintenance of outside playgrounds? And, finally, food quality provided to the students is another vendor issue.

The level of vendor fraud or abuse that occurs in funding for U.S. school systems is rampant. With such a high level of theft and unethical behavior, it is small wonder that little attention is paid to other aspects of education. These frauds steal money from an already crippled education system. The DoE maintains a web page with lists of millions of dollars in fraud that have been identified by the DoE's Office of Inspector General. These are only the cases that have been prosecuted by that agency.

Even Charter Schools Can Fail

Dorothy June Brown, 75, of Haverford, Pennsylvania, was charged today by indictment with defrauding three charter schools of more than $6.5 million between 2007 and April 2011. Charged with Brown in a 62-count indictment are four current and former charter school executives. The indictment alleges that Brown used her private management companies, Cynwyd and AcademicQuest, to defraud the Agora Cyber Charter School ("Agora") and the Planet Abacus Charter School ("Planet Abacus") soon after she founded the schools in 2005 and 2007, respectively. Brown caused Agora to make fraudulent payments to Cynwyd totaling more than $5.6 million under a fabricated management contract. Brown caused the creation of false documents, including false board meeting minutes, and fabricated contracts to falsely make it appear as if the boards of the schools had held meetings to discuss and authorize contracts.

Source: "Charter School Founder Charged in $6 Million Fraud Scheme," Office of the Inspector General, U.S. Department of Education, July 24, 2012.[3]

School Administrators, Relatives, and Cronies

So who are our next stakeholders? Let's consider school administrators and, of course, their relatives and cronies as one single group of stakeholders. Nepotism and cronyism runs rampant in our local school systems. Many hiring, promotion, and firing decisions in these schools are based on nepotism or cronyism rather than the merit of individuals. Examples of such behavior are continually documented. These events decrease the value of the education received by students.

When I lived in rural Maryland, one school superintendent was an administrator over the entire county school system, which may include numerous towns. There was one superintendent at one central administrative building. After moving to rural Oklahoma, I discovered that there is a superintendent for each high school in each small town in every county. In addition, there is a principal, vice principal, and staff for each of these administrators. Some of the towns in these counties have a population of only 2,000 people. I often wonder whose relative or friend is filling all these administrative positions. The main reason there are so many administrators in all our K–12 schools today is that teachers do not want to be in the classroom with the students and because the salaries are better once a teacher "moves on up" to become an administrator.

Such practices destroy the public's trust in the school system; rob the students of a quality education; create a cynical group of teachers and employees prepared to be as unethical as the next person; increase disharmony and in-fighting among teachers; cause the development of unfair employment procedures; cause professionalism to disappear; increase the personnel costs of replacing employees who leave due to intolerable working conditions; and, finally, cause the inevitable result of the school system's expending millions of dollars of its limited resources to legally defend itself.

Thanks for the Job, Mommy

Instead of hiring based upon qualifications, staff members were hired based upon who they were related to or who they knew. When hiring teachers, the teacher who was leaving would decide whom his or her replacement would be, and the two of them would approach the local political boss, who in turn would contact the superintendent or personnel director, and the person was hired. Whether or not a person was certified [in a subject] or qualified for the position was irrelevant.

Source: Chester Brookover, "An Examination of State Takeover as a School Reform Strategy in a Small Rural School District," (dissertation), May 2010, p. 123.

K–12 students have purchasing power that textbook publishers and other vendors recognize and want to tap into by having exclusive rights to sell to those students. Administrators also recognize that they have a financial asset in their students' purchasing power. Administrators can sell the student's purchasing power to certain companies for returned "benefits." Such practices may not be illegal but they certainly are unethical. Selling students for profit to textbook publishers after accepting a junket to the Florida Keys is not illegal as the decision was not directly tied to the trip, right? Giving soft drink distributors the exclusive rights to sell their sodas for bribes . . . well, that's illegal.

Are We Related? Really!

Reid was charged in June with accepting a bribe from a tutoring vendor for special treatment. The contract with the vendor was for supplemental education services, which is for underachieving, low-income students in schools that don't make adequate yearly progress. The vendor also is her brother-in-law. It is unclear if he is under investigation. Reid allegedly sent a letter to parents in the district in August 2010 for ninth-grade math and reading supplemental services that would be run by Brian Flaggs, her brother-in-law. In the letter, she allegedly said it was mandatory for all SES students and didn't offer any other vendors besides Flaggs.

Source: Alan Burdziak, "New Court Dates Set for Rouge School Official Accused of Accepting Bribe," *The New-Herald*, October 12, 2012.

The Boosters

Our next group of stakeholders are those individuals who support the high school sport franchise. Go Team! This group is known as the "boosters." They enjoy the Friday night football game, the midweek basketball, baseball, and the track and field events. They support the strenuous and continual training of the high school athletes for these events and privileged status the players hold in the high school pecking order. The group is composed of parents, teachers, coaches, and administrators, and they have one goal in mind, which is to develop a winning team to give them bragging rights in their region.

An example of the "booster affect" recently occurred in the rich community of Allen, Texas, where a group of boosters were instrumental in passing a bond issue to spend $60 million on a new 18,000-seat high school stadium with NaturalGrass Matrix turf, a 75' x 45' HD video scoreboard, indoor golf, wrestling practice areas, customized weight room, press room, and private boxes for its boosters. Season tickets were immediately sold out. The new stadium replaced an older 14,000-seat stadium. At the same time, Texas funding for schools has dropped and the Allen High School is faced with reducing its teaching staff by 44 teachers, 40 support positions, and a budget deficit of $4.5 million. Supporters of the project have indicated that the stadium gives their students practical business experience, as students, for example, run the cash registers at the stadium beverage counter with its 45 wait lines.[4] Sounds like another upcoming minimum wage job after graduation to me.

With numerous web sites providing rankings of high school teams, sports may be the most important factor in a school's reputation. Yet, it might be important to know how our high school students are doing in their educational rankings, too. Beyond the federal assessment tests of No Child Left Behind, for which the students are prepared and the results are gamed, there are other tests of educational success. When the Organization for Economic Cooperation and Development (OECD) released the results from the International Student Assessment (PISA), a measure of how well students from more than 70 countries are educationally prepared, it showed that in the United States in 2009, 15-year-olds were 15th in reading literacy, 25th in math, and 17th in science. It's probably better to stick with local results—who cares what is happening in the rest of the world?

Really, How Important Is It to Be Able to Read?

"The hard truth," Secretary Duncan [Department of Education Secretary] said at Tuesday's PISA announcement, "is that other high-performing nations have passed us by during the last two decades. . . . In a highly competitive knowledge economy, maintaining the educational status quo means America's students are effectively losing ground."

Source: J. Johnson, "International Educational Rankings Suggest Reform Can Lift U.S.," *Homeroom* (official blog of the U.S. Department of Education), December 8, 2010.

Teachers, Sex, Unions, Drugs, and More Fraud

Enough said about the success of American students in throwing a
football. Our next group of stakeholders, who will be classified as a
single group, are the teachers and their unions. Teachers are different than administrators. They work on nine-month contracts, and
they get paid less than administrators. At one time, teachers had
the respect of the communities in which they worked, but not so
much anymore.

One of the first events I attended as a new high school teacher
was the quiet retirement party of a woman who had been teaching
business subjects for over 30 years. As part of her retirement "gifts"
she was given a framed copy of her very first teaching contract with
the school system. One clause in her original contract stated that
if she became pregnant, she would have to resign her position.
She explained that a pregnant teacher was not considered a good
influence on the young high school ladies. It is quaint to remember there was once a code of morals that extended to men and
women teachers. Such a past standard is hard to believe today as we
see more and more female teachers hopping in bed with their male
students to have their babies or just for sex.

Remember When All the Teacher Wanted Was an Apple?

In August, a jury convicted Colleps on 16 counts of having improper relationships with students. Though the students with whom she had sex—there
were five—were all older than the minimum age of consent in Texas, state
law prohibits any educator in a primary or secondary school from having sex
with any enrolled student, no matter their age.

Source: Jim Budreuil, "Teacher Who Had Group Sex with Students Says She's the
Victim," *ABC News*, September 28, 2012.

Amanda Sotelo, a married substitute teacher and mother of two has been
jailed pursuant to admitting that she had sexual relations with a 14-year-old
boy at the school where she from time to time substituted, which coinciden-
tally has led to her now expecting her third child.

Source: Scallywag, November 5, 2012.

(Continued)

(Continued)

A 24-year-old math teacher has been accused of having sex with at least four of her students. Ashley Nicole-Anderson is alleged to have confessed to a sexual affair with an 18-year-old student. She also performed oral sex on three other students, according to a criminal complaint. Anderson, a math teacher at Aplington-Parkersburg High School, in Iowa City, Iowa, also sent nude photographs of herself to students during an almost year-long series of illicit liaisons.

—————————

Source: Paul Thompson, "Math Teacher, 24, 'Had Sex with Four Students, Sent Them Naked Photos and Performed Oral Sex on Three Others,'" *Daily Mail Online*, October 21, 2012.

The moral code in teacher education is broken. If I were to guess the reason, I would trace it to the sexual practices these women (and men) followed as high school students and in their undergraduate college years. What is common sexual practice on the college campus has been transferred to the high school classroom. Regardless of the reasons, these acts are becoming more common, and it must be remembered that these are the cases that have been uncovered, not the ones that go unreported.

Discussing the teacher as a stakeholder cannot be completed without including the effect of unions. Teachers' unions try to keep change out of the school system. Their focus is on tenure, getting salary increases, protection against policy changes, reducing class sizes, and keeping jobs for incumbent teachers. The National Education Association (3.2 million members) and the American Federation of Teachers (about 900,000 members) are the two major teachers' unions representing elementary and high school teachers. As a former high school teacher and a member of the National Education Association (NEA), I appreciated their organizing efforts on my behalf. In my second year of high school teaching, the local NEA called a strike for higher pay. The strike was called after negotiations broke down and administrators insisted there was no money for teachers' raises. With one exception, everyone walked out of the high school. By the end of the first day of the strike, the school board found the money to give us 10 percent pay raises. We were back in the classroom after a one-day strike.

As a selfish person, I appreciated the stand the NEA took on my behalf against the school board. During those days, my only other experience with unionization was with a high school janitor. I had my students move chairs in an auditorium. Truly, this was a mistake. Our school janitor and union member, not the NEA, was irate. He explained to me that I was taking jobs from union members by having the students move the chairs instead of janitors. In other words, if the students did it, the janitors would not get paid for doing it. As the NEA matured and grew in membership from when I was a member, the attitudes among teachers changed and became closer to that janitor's perspective.

How can you nurture students when your concerns are related to analyzing your workload statistics or preventing your work activities from infringing on someone else's job activities? Don't move that book on the library shelf—that is the duty of the librarian. When did more effort start to be concentrated on building a wall around job functions and restricting those functions rather than concentrating on teaching students? Maybe this is why increasing expenditures do not correlate with increasing student performance.

The introduction of a union representative between the school administration and teachers may have the effect of demeaning the professional, as individual teachers have less responsibility to make independent decisions. When decisions about curriculum, workloads, and policies are taken out of the hands of the average teacher and passed to the union (or the federal government), the status of the teaching profession is diminished. When those choices are taken away from the classroom teacher, it also replaces the individual teachers' responsibility for the failure of the school system, and allows teachers to legitimately ask the public: "Why blame us?"

Why Blame Us for Failing Schools?

Indiana teachers frustrated by sweeping changes in the state's education system under schools chief Tony Bennett say they hope his successor will be able to slow the pace of change. . . . Teachers have been frustrated with the changes under Bennett, which include the nation's broadest use of school vouchers, the state's takeover of six schools, and changes that tie teacher pay to student performance. Many have said they feel that they are being blamed for failing schools.

Source: "Teachers Hope Ritz Will Help Slow School Changes," TimesUnion.com, November 17, 2012.

With all of this going on, it is always good to know that your school is in a protected "Drug Free Zone" except, of course, for all the legitimate drugs used by teachers to control students. Drug vendors provide all sorts of drugs for students that are doled out by school health nurses or school secretaries. Although this might seem to be a topic to be included under vendors, it is a teacher's recommendation that begins the process of identifying a student for drug treatment. For that reason, drug policy is covered here.

Ritalin is the number one drug pumped into today's K–12 students to control their behavior. It is a drug with the same chemical basis as the "bennies" widely used by long-haul truck drivers to stay awake on their drives. The side effects of Ritalin include addiction, heart palpitations, stomachache, decreased appetite, slowing of growth, blurred vision, and insomnia. But it calms the student in the classroom and makes the teacher's job easier.

Here's the warning label for Ritalin:

> RITALIN-SR IS A FEDERALLY CONTROLLED SUBSTANCE (CII) BECAUSE IT CAN BE ABUSED OR LEAD TO *DEPENDENCE*. KEEP RITALIN-SR IN A SAFE PLACE TO PREVENT MISUSE AND ABUSE. SELLING OR GIVING AWAY RITALIN-SR MAY HARM OTHERS, AND IS AGAINST THE LAW.
>
> TELL YOUR DOCTOR IF YOU OR YOUR CHILD HAVE (OR HAVE A FAMILY HISTORY OF) EVER ABUSED OR BEEN DEPENDENT ON ALCOHOL, PRESCRIPTION MEDICINES, OR STREET DRUGS.

Did you know there were shortages of Ritalin because the drug manufacturer could not produce enough pills fast enough for its increasing use in our K–12 students? Approximately *4 million* children are taking Ritalin, including preschoolers.[5] Finally, we have a way to have better children through chemistry.

My own children, a boy and a girl, were both placed on a Ritalin regime before they had entered middle school. My son's appetite dropped to the point where we were worried he would stop growing, and my daughter developed heart palpitations. We took them off Ritalin and eventually out of the school system. The elementary school they attended has two signs along the road in front of the school that said: "Drug Free Zone." It was quite amazing to me that all the parents endorsed this idea when more than 20 percent of the children in the school were taking the narcotic Ritalin. Once at lunchtime, I arrived in the school to pick up my son. As policy dictated, I went into the school office. To my amazement, I saw all these white paper pill containers on the large counter in the office. There must have been over a hundred paper containers on the counter filled with psychosomatic drugs for the kids. Well, that day I got my son out of the drug-free school before he got his bennies.

Still, teachers cannot be blamed for everything—truly. As international test scores of U.S. students in reading, math, and science continue to fall, it needs to be understood that teachers are not allowed to really teach in the classroom. There are restrictive curricula today that must require a great deal of time to be spent on social learning; teachers in many schools are not allowed to hold students back anymore; sports learning has replaced classroom learning; and it has been commonplace to assess incorrect work as acceptable because the student "did the work." After 12 years of schooling, these approaches develop an entitlement or "I don't care" view among those students in the upper grade levels and among graduating seniors.

Mommy, Mommy, Teacher Can't Read

When is it necessary to have receptionists teach Spanish . . . when this happens . . .

For 15 years, teachers in three southern states paid Clarence Mumford, Sr.—himself a longtime educator—to send someone else to take the [certification] tests in their place. . . . Each time, Mumford received a fee of between $1,500 and $3,000 to send one of his test ringers with fake identification to the Praxis exam [required as a qualification for entry into the teaching profession]. Authorities say the scheme affected hundreds—if not thousands—of public school students who ended up being taught by unqualified teachers.

Source: "Feds: Teachers Embroiled in Test-Taking Fraud," *New York Times*, November 25, 2012.

Parents

The next group of stakeholders has to be the K–12 parents. The first question of interest is: Where are the parents when all these negative effects are hitting their children? The answer is: Parents are busy. These parents can include the hardworking single mother who is trying to put food on the table and does not have time for anything else. Many of these parents don't know what is going on in their local school system until the "bad event" happens. Well, bad events have been brewing for a long time.

Parents are likely to leave their children's schooling up to the administrators and teachers without significant involvement in the process themselves. Absent and busy parents cannot provide needed support, especially in many dysfunctional school systems that cannot provide an adequate education for your child. My daughter was on the honor roll in the second grade, but we knew she could hardly spell her name. Of course, we had bragging rights that she was "on the honor roll." How long before parents recognize that their children are attending a school that is for show? Does student disillusionment and lack of concern follow? It is almost impossible for parents to truly influence change in any local school system. Only with a show of force similar to a union strike or by hiring an attorney will the school board and teachers react to the parents' concerns. Even then, the changes are minor, or they are only "show" changes. Although there is cooperation between parents and schools, especially in sports programs, there are innumerable "bad events" that eventually come to be recognized:

"**Parents Upset School Wants to Take Kids to see 'Charlie Brown Christmas' at Church**, November 20, 2012 (www.opposingviews.com/i/religion/christianity/parents-upset-school-wants-take-kids-see-charlie-brown-christmas-church).

"**Parents Press School Board on Elementary Standards,**" November 21, 2012 (http://capecharleswave.com/2012/11/parents-press-school-board-on-elementary-standards).

"**Utah Parent Sues School over Banned Book,**" November 15, 2012 (www.courthousenews.com/2012/11/15/52275.htm).

"**Riverview Parents Sue School District over Daughter's Death, November 1, 2012** (www.courthousenews.com/2012/11/15/52275.htm).

"Birmingham Parents Sue School District over Material Fees," November 12, 2012 (www.theoaklandpress.com/article/OP/20121112/NEWS/311129904).

"Brevard Parents Protest at Charter School's Groundbreaking," November 18, 2012 (www.cfnews13.com/content/news/cfnews13/news/article.html/content/news/articles/cfn/2012/11/17/brevard_parents_prot.html).

Most parents should be concerned about their children's education because it influences what happens to those children for the rest of their lives, both economically and socially. The common suggestions for parents to help their children is to read to your children; help with (but not do) homework exercises; take them to the library; discuss what is going on in school beyond what they are doing in the classroom; plan educational trips; and express positive attitudes toward learning. At the end of the day, these suggestions alone will not overcome a system that is incapable of preparing literate students as productive members of society. Many times, these suggestions are used to make the parents feel guilty and provide excuses for a failing school system.

Okay, are there any other stakeholders left?

Oh yeah . . . we can't forget the students.

Students

Now for the last and in many cases the least important of the stakeholders—the students. And they really are *stakeholers*, not stakeholders, because they leave the system as high school graduates in a hole. Although the local school system they attend is dysfunctional and dismal, the attitudes of most students do not help make the situation better. By the time many American students graduate, they have developed a hostile attitude toward their teachers and education. Most of them have an attitude of entitlement toward their schoolwork and a feeling of false achievement. For example, "If I do my homework, I should get the grade regardless of whether the answers are correct" (i.e., entitlement). After graduation, the logic follows: "If I come to work, I should get a raise" (i.e., entitlement). As a graduating senior, "I know I am good" (i.e., false achievement).

Forty-two percent of today's high school 15-year-olds with one college-educated parent are proficient in math compared with 75 percent and 50 percent same-aged students in Shanghai and Canada, respectively.[6] School systems may be able to show that they are doing better on the regional tests they administer, yet this may not be true on international tests. The results from the *2011 Trends in International Mathematics and Science Study* showed that U.S. fourth- and eighth-graders were 11th and 9th in math, respectively.[7] In science, the two grades scored 7th and 9th, respectively, on the international test.[8] If U.S. students could stop their education at the eighth grade, our students would be internationally competitive with students from other countries. Unfortunately, as U.S. students continue through high school and the math and science lessons become more complicated, their scores fall compared with the scores of students in other countries. On the 2009 international assessment exam *Programme for International Student Assessment* of 15-year-olds, U.S. students scored 14th in reading, tied with Iceland and Poland; 22nd in reading integration and interpretation; 31st in mathematics, tied with Portugal; and 23rd in science, tied with Hungary.[9]

Consequently, many graduates do not have the skills they need to enter the job market. On Day One, they find out they can't fill out their job application. With all the problems in our schools as teachers and administrators try to manipulate the state and federal government regulations to their advantage, it is small wonder that there is not enough time to spend with the students. Everyone seems busy.

Does it really matter? If everyone who graduates from high school is uneducated and illiterate, does it really matter? No one graduate will have an advantage over another student who graduates. For that reason, they are on equal footing when they compete for a job. Is that bad? It is bad because the competition will not come from your uneducated neighbor. The competition for a job will come from overseas, where the students are better educated and have the skills to perform well in high-tech jobs. Another reason to send jobs overseas is not just the lower wages but also to take advantage of the higher skill levels of overseas workers.

So What Are You and Yours Losing?

Families are losing their heritage. High school graduates are losing their future. These graduates do not have the skills to be part of the middle class. Financially, they will suffer for the rest of their lives. These graduates are unable to determine the total cost of the things they buy on credit because they cannot do the math needed to calculate the total interest cost of a loan. Consequently, they do not understand why they are living from paycheck to paycheck. Retailers understand their customers' lack of knowledge and disclose only monthly payment information in ads, not the total cost of a purchase.

Current students may be employed, but their earnings cannot match the purchasing power of earlier graduates who had a ready job, health insurance, and a pension waiting for them when they retired. Many of these graduates will never have the earning power needed to begin a family, buy a house, purchase health insurance, and be responsible citizens. They will create a permanent under-class in the United States that may one day object to how they have been manipulated.

Today, there is little demand for the young men who have only physical skills. No one needs the brawn and muscle in automated factories where machines do the work of 10 men. At one time, their strength to push inventory or carry bags of product were needed, but no more. These high school graduates are obsolete as soon as they receive their diploma. Without additional skills, they will continue earning slightly above the minimum wage.[10] The unemployment rate of young high school graduates not enrolled in college was 33 percent in 2010 and 31 percent through 2011.[11]

Many graduates who do not go to college do not realize what happened to them as they become disillusioned with their lives as divorced fathers or single mothers. Others who go to college and drop out because they don't have the patience to study their way through courses, or who don't have the reading, math, and writing abilities called for in their university studies begin to realize how little their high school contributed to their education. What happens is that they need to accept lower income for the rest of their lives and this reduces the opportunities available to their children and their children's children. The legacy is a lost heritage. Eventually, they are likely to develop a new way of life where they depend on government handouts or parental support to be able to continue with their diminished prospects.

Are There Choices?

Schools systems in the United States are preparing students to be second-class workers in a third-world economy. There are some choices. None of them are pleasant, and none of them are the simple silver bullet that everyone wants to find. Some of the choices mean that you have to give up your family's heritage of a middle-class life and accept your losses from a collapsing school system.

Here are seven choices:

1. *Hide your head in the sand.* Basically, this means that your family ignores the problem and resigns themselves to the belief that nothing can be done and really nothing is wrong. As the Pink Floyd song says, "We don't need no education." Here, the best approach is to enjoy the high school football games and let the students worry about the rest of it. The kids will take care of themselves. The financial losses using this approach to your children and their children will be substantial and uncorrectable. They will never be able to climb out the financial hole into which they have fallen.

2. *Get your children out of the public school system by sending them to a private school with an annual tuition of around $45,000 per child per year.* If you are rich enough, you have probably already taken this step. If you have the resources, get your kids out of the public school system and send them to a private school. Many private schools, and in some cases charter schools, are sprouting up to provide the K–12 education that is no longer provided in public schools. Yet, without your monitoring of the system, there still is no positive assurance that private schools can provide the type of education that is needed for your children, but the odds are better than keeping them in a collapsing public school system.

3. *Homeschool your children.* To start a home schooling program means a huge commitment by one parent, usually the mother. The commitment of time and concern is much larger than suing the school system or getting a hated teacher transferred out of a school, a step that many parents have taken and believe it shows they are taking an interest in their children's education. Although battles with the school system may be time consuming, they create only temporary changes. Further, these efforts are not anywhere near the huge time commitment it takes to homeschool children. Homeschooling means a total commitment to your child's educational development.

The homeschool curriculum can be set up by the parents, and although it may be overseen with periodic reports to the local school authorities, it can provide children with the skills that are no longer provided in public schools. Homeschooling does not mean studying in an isolated family group. Today, homeschooling can be combined with a homeschool group allowing for the social interaction of K–12 students without the bullying and the drugs found in public schools. Homeschooling in a homeschool group allows the parent to personally select the best curriculum for their children.[12]

4. *Try to change the school system.* A recently released Hollywood film titled *Won't Back Down* deals with this approach. In the film, two parents challenge a collapsing school system and try to make reforms. If you are ready to hire lawyers and start a battle that you have little chance of winning, this is the approach you should take. Even if you win and create reforms, the local school system will never fully implement these changes. The administrators running our public schools are experts at dealing with the ins and outs of regulation avoidance while seeming to meet the letter of any rule.

5. *Tell your kids they are as uneducated as everyone else and no one has a leg up on them.* The approach is a little different than choice 1. Here you recognize that the system is a mess and your children may be able to make up for it later as they go through life. The losses in your children's earnings will be life altering using this approach.

6. *If possible, after graduation, get them a job where an employer will teach them what the public school system never did—maybe the military.* For many high school graduates, there is only one choice for a job, and it is military service. The military will train them to the minimum level its needs for them to perform their jobs. Also, in the military, brawn and muscle are still the appreciated attributes in many jobs as they once were in manufacturing jobs. The problems develop after they leave the military and find they do not have the skills required in our service economy.

7. *If possible, after graduation, get them into a university or community college that has a high school remedial program that will teach them the math, writing, and science they should have learned in*

high school. If they have a high enough high school grade point average, they should be able to get into the remedial program at a community college. Remember a high school grade of "A" stands for adequate, and valedictorians graduate from our failing schools without being able to read. The remedial courses may not count toward their degree, but these courses are there to make up for the failure that occurred during their K–12 education.

Summary

I do not believe the collapsing school systems in the United States can be changed from internal or external pressures. Those pressures have not had an effect over the past 50 years, nor will they in the future. The way to improve K–12 education for your children is to step away from it. Step away and develop a private school or a homeschooling group that can teach the fundamentals and create graduates who have a better chance to compete with highly skilled international students. In either case, parents need to sacrifice income to ensure their sons and daughters have a place at the table of the new world economy. Without current monetary sacrifice, upward mobility in your family is forfeited as future generations fail to match the economic status achieved by past generations.

Thought I would close with the American Association of School Administrator's Statement of Ethics adopted in 1981 and my top 10 supplements to the Code.

The Code	The Forgotten Addition
1. Makes the well-being of students the fundamental value of all decision making and actions . . .	. . . when no one else is left.
2. Fulfills professional responsibilities with honesty and integrity . . .	. . . and sometimes with physical vigor.
3. Supports the principle of due process and protects the civil and human rights of all individuals . . .	. . . if they are watching us . . . closely.

4. Obeys local, state, and national laws and does not knowingly join or support organizations that advocate, directly or indirectly, the overthrow of the government . . .	. . . by lying.
5. Implements the governing board of education's policies and administrative rules and regulations . . .	. . . by gaming the system to our advantage
6. Pursues appropriate measures to correct those laws, policies, and regulations that are not consistent with sound educational goals . . .	. . . of course
7. Avoids using positions for personal gain through political, social, religious, economic or other influences . . .	. . . say what?
8. Accepts academic degrees or professional certification only from duly accredited institutions . . .	. . . even those fraudulently obtained
9. Maintains the standards and seeks to improve the effectiveness of the profession through research and continuing professional development.	I don't understand that?
10. Honors all contracts until fulfillment, release, or dissolution mutually agreed upon by all parties to [the] contract . . .	. . . you bet. See addition number 4 above.

Notes

1. http://www.goodreads.com/author/quotes/395622.Ron_Paul.
2. http://nces.ed.gov/surveys/ruraled/TablesHTML/5localedistricts.asp.
3. www2.ed.gov/about/offices/list/oig/invtreports/pa072012a.html. For a complete list of fraud cases prosecuted by the U.S. Department of Education, see http://www2.ed.gov/about/offices/list/oig/ireports.html.
4. See the *Huffington Post* at www.huffingtonpost.com/2012/08/08/dallas-suburb-unveils-new_n_1756434.html and Footballguys.com at http://forums.footballguys.com/forum/index.php?showtopic=649485.
5. www.salon.com/2000/03/31/ritalin_2/ or www.dadi.org/rtln_sax.htm.
6. Arthur Levine, "The Suburban Education Gap," *Wall Street Journal*, November 15, 2012, A19.
7. See http://nces.ed.gov/timss/results11_math11.asp.

8. http://nces.ed.gov/timss/results11_science11.asp.

9. www.oecd.org/pisa/ See www.oecd.org/pisa/46643496.pdf.

10. Cliff Zukin, Mark Sneltzer, and Charley Stone, "Work Trends," Rutgers University, June 2012, www.heldrich.rutgers.edu/sites/default/files/content/Left_Out_Forgotten_Work_Trends_June_2012.pdf.

11. U.S. Bureau of Labor Statistics. (2012). "College Enrollment and Work Activity of 2011 High School Graduates," Economic News Release, www.bls.gov/news.release/hsgec.nr0.htm.

12. Information about homeschool groups can be found at www.home-school.com/groups, for example. In addition, there are numerous homeschooling curricula available to help parents.

CHAPTER 9

Staying Poor in America

Poverty is the parent of revolution and crime.

—Aristotle

1960: It was a warm Saturday night in Kirkland, Texas. Saturday night in summer brought everyone into town. Farmers and their families came to town to shop in the local shops. U.S.-made products were displayed behind bright store windows. The downtown brick stores, built in the 1930s and 1940s, were busy, and shoppers were going from one store to another. The stores were family run, and their proprietors lived in Kirkland. On the sidewalk, some people stood in small groups laughing and talking with friends. Outside lights started to turn on as the evening sun sank down. High school students who owned cars "cruised the main" and showed off their cars. Occasionally, they drove into the local gas station on Highway 287. With a $2 fill-up, they got their oil checked and windshield cleaned. As night came, the streets cleared and the shoppers returned to their homes. It was another quiet but busy Saturday night in Kirkland.

2013: On any day, the main street in Kirkland is deserted. All the shoppers left long ago. Sidewalks are dusty, and weeds grow in the cracks. All the products have been taken out of the stores, and when a passer-by looks through the dirty store windows all he sees is emptiness. There are still a few stores and gas stations along Highway 287 that serve passing cars. But the downtown is silent and the stores look broken. There is no friendly laughter, and there are no people walking down the sidewalks. A community disappeared.

Did everyone move away and find a better life?

Today in the United States, slightly over 14 percent of the working population is unemployed. Note that this is not the percentage of unemployment, which is just north of 7 percent, but it is the total unemployed, which includes those who have stopped seeking work. The question that needs to be answered is: Even so, are we better off now than we were in previous generations? And if not, how can Americans afford to make stock or bond investments, or any investments, to increase their net worth and future wealth?

One way to begin to find an answer is to look at economic statistics about an earlier generation and compare it with today's generation. Although all sorts of distortions can arise when two time periods are compared, such as the effects of inflation, changes in standard of living, and a rise in the general level of "average" income or housing size, these comparisons still give us an indication of some of the generational changes that have occurred in our country and their implications for investment markets. If we are all poor, who has the money to make investments? And if not, do we have the inclination to invest for the future?

Rich or Poor?

U.S. poverty levels have essentially remained unchanged for the general population since the 1960s. In 2011, the general poverty rate was 15 percent. For those 18 to 64, the poverty rate was 13.8 percent in 2011, which is the highest since the early 1960s (in 1959 it was 17 percent).[1] For a family of four the poverty level threshold income was $23,021 in 2011. The poverty rate is determined by the federal government, and the basis for computing the "official" rate has changed over the years. "If the same basic methodology developed in the early 1960s were applied today, the poverty thresholds (income level) would be over three times higher than the current thresholds."[2] This statement means the poverty income level for a family of four would be $69,063 if changes in the measure had not been made by the government. For a complete analysis of the area, the federal government's adjustments to the poverty level must be reviewed in detail. The only major reduction in the poverty levels for any demographic group in the United States over this time period has been for those over the age of 65. In 1959, 35.2 percent of this group was classified as poor, whereas in 2011, it was 8.7 percent.[3] The change is due to the effect of Social Security, Medicare, and other pension payments that were not available or as generous in 1959.

According to the Tax Foundation,[4] the federal tax burden (as viewed through marginal tax rates) during the period from 1960 to 2012 has decreased for a family of four. In 1960, the marginal tax rate for a family of four earning between $31,026 and $62,952 was 22 percent, whereas in 2012 it was 15 percent.[5] During this period the consumer price index increased almost 10 times, from 29.6 to 229.6. While the marginal tax rates have decreased, the inflation "tax" created by the federal government has gone up close to 10-fold. It would be expected that inflation would increase over this period, but a $4 loaf of bread would have been unthinkable in 1960. The effects of less obvious inflationary increases are just as strong a driver of poverty rates as are increases in real taxes.

Beyond the federal government's income tax collections, there are other payroll taxes that Americans must pay. For example, Social Security (FICA) and Medicare taxes are deducted like income tax collections, and everyone must pay these at the same rate; that is, there is no marginal rate. In 1960, there were no deductions for Medicare because it was not enacted until 1965. In 1960, there was a deduction for social security taxes at the rate of 3 percent on first $4,800 of income.[6] In 2013, social security deductions are at their highest collection level ever at 6.2 percent of the first $113,700 of income, and in addition, all income earners have to pay 1.45 percent of their income (no upper limit) for Medicare. Now a question starts to form: Have taxes made me poorer?

Of course, the tax burden does not end with payments to the federal government. There are the states and the cities. Total taxes paid by residents as a percentage of their income to New York State is 12.8 percent.[7] In addition, certain cities require that a city income tax be paid if you work in their city. Don't forget property taxes paid on the more expensive McMansions that only the old wealth had in 1960. New Jersey residents pay 1.89 percent of their home value in property taxes.[8] An estimate is that most of us pay almost 10 percent our income in state and local taxes.[9] There are also taxes on cigarettes, gasoline, and liquor. New York State charges a cigarette tax of $4.35 per pack. But it doesn't end there because sales taxes need to be paid. Sales taxes are usually paid to the state but if you buy merchandise within a city, then the city can also charge a sales tax. The sales tax in Tennessee is 9.44 percent, but there are many states and cities where the sales tax is over 9 percent.[10] The county may also decide to impose a sales tax on purchases. Very few people pay attention to the amount of sales tax they are paying, and instead they are concerned with the retailer's selling price.

Are the levels of taxation and the increase in inflation (another form of government tax) helping to answer the question: Where did my money go and who took it? Well if you are paying a tax bill that amounts to 60 percent of your income, the answer should not be hard to find.

Further, are U.S. citizens better off today with all family members working than they were in the 1960s with one family member working?

Walmart customers and not Whole Food customers are representative of modern America. Remember the J.C. Penney stores in the 1960s and those women shoppers who still wore white gloves on their shopping trips. Don't look for them in Walmart. Today's Walmart woman is likely to wear pajama bottoms and flip-flops on her shopping trips. And today's Walmart man is likely to need a dentist. Sorry if that is a stereotype, but I am working with averages here.

Yes, the rich were present in the 1960s. But the view has changed, and our view today is more stark and typical of Latin American countries where enclaves of the super-rich—and, as we will see, pretend rich—are surrounded by the less affluent. These wealthy enclaves are not restricted to large cities such as New York, but they can also be found in rural areas with homes in gated communities that are patrolled by armed guards.

Many people and households find their financial situation under stress and cannot imagine saving for the future. In the 1960s, companies provided their employees with defined-benefit pensions. Defined-benefit plans provide the retiree with a fixed benefit for the rest of their life. Those plans are gone. Today's unfunded pension plans provide contribution plans where the employer and the employee make a contribution to the plan. The earnings, usually from the stock market, determine the final payments from the pension plan. Without supplemental retirement savings, these retirees will not be able to sustain themselves throughout their retirement years.

With high taxes, continual inflation, and sketchy employment patterns, how can anyone plan for the future and come up with a way to accumulate wealth if they are not already wealthy?

What Else? Business Models Have Changed Our Way of Earning a Living

Have you noticed that U.S. business models have changed? If you have gone through our dysfunctional secondary education system, the answer is probably not, and you are still looking for your father's job.

Business models have changed.

Fifty years ago, a third of U.S. employees worked in manufacturing.[11] Today, that number has decreased to one-tenth of the nation's workers.[12] New jobs are found in the service industry, not in manufacturing. These service jobs are in education, beauty shops, finance, photography, health care, check processing, and telephone service, for example. Many of these jobs pay less than factory jobs and do not provide the standard of living available to earlier workers. The job loss in manufacturing is continuing. Factory workers are losing their jobs by the millions. Their jobs are still being moved overseas or being replaced by robotic manufacturing operations. One community after another is scared that they will be the next Kirkland, Texas.

My high school graduating classmates in Michigan were faced with the choice of going to college or going to work in an auto plant and receiving a wage that provided them with the ability to have a family and buy a house and a boat. Many of them chose an immediate paycheck as college was too costly an alternative. Today's high school graduates and the skills they bring to the workplace can only result in unemployment or low-level service jobs as all the high-paying, entry-level union jobs have largely disappeared. In addition, many of today's high school graduates have gone through a dysfunctional education system that provides them with few marketable skills. Although the case may have been similar in the past, being unskilled was not such a disadvantage because low-level physical workers were needed, and they did not need to be literate.

An Old Problem That Just Stays and Stays

Since 1960, more than one-third of manufacturing jobs have disappeared from three states—Pennsylvania, New Jersey, and Delaware. In the last 15 years, job losses have accelerated, averaging more than 2 percent a year.

Source: Theodor M. Crone, "Where Have All the Factory Jobs Gone—Why?" Federal Reserve Bank, 1997, 1.

What has changed in America is that manufacturing does not need the large numbers of workers who were previously employed due to the increase in robotic manufacturing and transfer of jobs overseas. Today, the main jobs in manufacturing are for skilled professionals, not hourly workers. For example, there are 97,000 workers producing more products in the steel industry today than in 1980 when close to 400,000 workers toiled in this industry.[13] The old relatively unskilled and high-paying jobs for high school graduates will never return.

As intense physical-labor jobs have largely disappeared, service jobs have become more plentiful. Women are just as qualified as men to fill service jobs. Consequently, the percentage of women in the workforce has increased from about 44 percent in 1960 to around 76 percent in 2009; whereas men's participation rates during the same period decreased from around 97 percent to 90 percent.[14] These trends are reflective of the decrease in the number of entry-level manufacturing jobs held by men and possibly their lack of training for service functions. A consequence of all these changes is that there is a wider gap in the wealth than in the past, between the top 1 percent of households compared with the "median" household wealth.

These changes make it impossible for many Americans to increase their net worth—in other words, wealth—over their lifetimes. These Americans live from paycheck to paycheck. They cannot change their financial situation, nor do they have the financial skills to understand why. Consequently, they put their financial faith into the lottery, run by the government, continue to spend more money than they earn, and their financial future slips away.

As will be shown, there is a better choice, but it involves financial planning—and particularly more financial planning than walking into a convenience store and buying a lottery ticket.

Other Factors Making Americans Poor

The level of student debt has been explored in a recent study with some surprising results. In the 1960s, college student loans were relatively rare. Under California's 1960 Master Plan for Higher Education, student residents attending college did not have to pay tuition at the University of California and in the state college system.[15] For college students today, it is a different world—or at least a different university business model. In order for students to complete their educational programs, many must borrow money. Universities support easy loan initiation with their cadre of on-campus loan officers. Without such funding, universities would face greater enrollment and funding stress, as many students would not be able to attend college, and university enrollments would drop. Additionally, a shift in university funding has occurred as state governments privatize their university education systems, with historical and continuing cuts in appropriations. More public universities have to raise their tuition and fees to make up for these funding deficits.

The significance of indebted graduates is how such debt affects their ability to participate in the economy. Following homeowner mortgage debt, student loan debt is the highest debt load carried by U.S. households. At the end of 2012, it was $966 billion. In 2007–2008, around 67 percent of those receiving bachelor degrees borrowed from the government or private lenders. In 2012, 43 percent of Americans under 25 still carried student debt obligations, an increase from 2003 of 25 percent. Of course, these percentages are higher when all the borrowing from relatives and friends is taken into account. For 2011 borrowers, the average debt of students in college was $23,300, and 3 percent of these students owed more than $100,000.[16] Besides the fact that many borrowers are already defaulting on their loans and destroying their financial futures, the overall effect of such debt on their ability to increase their personal wealth needs to be taken into account.

When purchasing patterns of indebted college graduates are followed, it can be seen that these graduates are not buying homes as they have in the past. Although homeownership in the United States has fallen during the Great Recession, a noticeable change has occurred among those in the peak home-buying group of 30-year-olds. From 2003 to 2010, individuals with student debt had not been deterred from purchasing homes, and a higher percentage of them actually purchased homes than those without student debt. The trend changed in 2011 as those without student debt began to purchase more homes. It appears that at that time college debt levels began to decrease home purchasing patterns.[17] Many Americans' net worth is largely tied into the equity they have in their homes. If new graduates are unable to purchase a home because they are paying off their college loans, it means these individuals have lost a chance to create wealth for themselves.

Again it appears that another group of Americans, young graduates, are experiencing a financial situation that will turn into a permanent decrease in their net worth over their lifetimes. In this case, the detrimental effect comes from servicing their college borrowing costs and not having the financial resources to make other purchases, such as houses, or invest in stocks. Additionally, this college-educated group does not have the financial training to understand the long-term effect of these debt loads on their ability to achieve a better financial future.

Spend It if You Got It or Pretend to Be Rich Until You Are Poor

There is another issue at work today in the United States contributing to living poor in America. It is the fact that it has become patriotic to spend, spend, and spend. Consumer spending accounts for about 70 percent of the U.S. economy.[18] Our leaders tell us that we have a consumer economy and it is important for Americans to keep the economy going, so spend your money. Before the Great Recession, this was taken to the extreme as homeowners would take each small equity increase out of their homes as the financial bubble grew. The money was used to buy RVs, boats, ATVs, SUVs, second homes, electronics, jet skis, cruises, overseas vacations, home remodels, and other neighbor-impressing expenditures.

Translating a "Higher Standard of Living" into Real Wealth: Oh Sure!

In the twenty-first century, households throughout the country have purchased computers, televisions, iPods, DVD players, vacation homes, boats, planes, and recreational vehicles. They have sent their children to summer camps; contributed to retirement and pension funds; attended theatrical and musical performances and sporting events; joined health, country, and yacht clubs; and taken domestic and foreign vacation excursions. These items, which were unknown and undreamt of a century ago, are tangible proof that U.S. households today enjoy a higher standard of living.

Source: U.S. Department of Labor, U.S. Bureau of Labor Statistics, *100 Years of U.S. Consumer Spending Data for the Nation, New York City and Boston* (Report 991), May 2006, 70, www.bls.gov/opub/uscs/report991.pdf.

The quote from the U.S. Department of Labor reflects our nation's spending patterns. The government encourages spending patterns that contribute to the American economy and for you to *enjoy a higher standard of living* for a while. Although these purchases may raise a person's standard of living, they do not contribute to an individual's wealth. DVD players are replaced by new technology. Boats, expensive SUVs, and RVs depreciate; they don't grow in value. Numerous foreign vacations are fun, and so is an expensive latte, but they do not increase your net worth. Cell, Internet, and cable plans costing an arm and a leg don't help either; nor does eating out, which is recognized as the number one discretionary household expense.[19] Numerous advertisements bombard us to reinforce and justify our need to spend. Yet these expenditure patterns only help you remain poor in the long run. Are you willing to pay $20,000 over a lifetime for cell service? Without a doubt, no individual paid that much for a lifetime of phone service in 1960—even considering inflation.

Such spending is spending without growth. This is why seemingly "rich" Americans also live from paycheck to paycheck. These households carry the appearance of being rich while remaining basically poor in America. There is no valid argument in today's economic environment that can be made for saving any money in a bank. Today's bank interest rates are lower than inflation rates, and each dollar you save is worth less the day after you deposit it. So, please, don't save your money.

Do You Know if You Are Overspending?

About half of 3,000 Americans polled in a recent survey said that they're spending more than they earn at least a few months each year. However, just 10 percent said they were living beyond their means, according to the survey by Rasmussen Reports for Country Financial.

Source: B. Kavoussi, "Half of Americans Are Spending More Than They Earn, but Don't Realize It: Survey," _Huffington Post_, May 17, 2012.

A class of Americans has been created who live with a high standard of living as long as their paychecks keep coming, but the curtailment of even one paycheck can result in financial disaster. It is important for an individual to have the knowledge and ability to step away from such spending patterns. It is not necessary for households to follow a spending pattern set for them by others such as the government.

Governmental Solutions

As a naïve new university professor, I thought that if a student should unjustly accuse me of some act, I could rely on my university for legal representation. Another experienced professor laughed and told me that if that happened, the university attorney's only objective was to protect the university, not you. Eureka! I understood, and it helped me begin to understand government "solutions," too.

Although the government wants to help the poor and middle-income Americans, these policies for consumer spending are mainly solutions to stimulate the economy (and maybe help lobbying groups). Many Americans think the mortgage tax deduction is for them—it is not. The mortgage tax deduction is for banks. It encourages Americans to buy large homes and pay banks billions of dollars in interest. As realtor's say, "You can afford it; it's deductible."

It is estimated that 15 percent of all Baby Boomers will *not* get out of debt in their lifetimes, and that debt is largely mortgage debt.[20] Regardless of the deductibility of the mortgage interest, in the long-run the homeowner is paying a lot more for a home than its sticker price. If they bought a $250,000 house, its real cost to them could easily be $1 million. Many homeowners don't really have the financial literacy to understand the underlying nature of such purchases. Shame, isn't it?

Too poor to buy a house? Well, how about paying sales tax? As also noted by the National Center for Policy Analysis, the federal government allows for the deductibility of sales taxes in states where there is no state income tax. Unintended or not, this is another method that has the tendency to encourage consumer spending. "It's deductible!"

Government tax policies also discourage stock investments. In addition to the brokerage fees investors must pay to invest in the stock market, they also must pay a tax of possibly 15 to 20 percent on any dividends earned. A capital gain on stock appreciation is also a taxable event.

What else does the government discourage? How about just plain working. Americans are working longer as they try to provide for their underfunded retirements, but the government does not want you to work beyond the age of 70. If your nest egg allows you to retire at 30, 55, or 62, well great—this does not apply to you. For anyone working beyond 70, the maximum age for beginning Social Security payments, expect the government to continue to deduct FICA taxes (Social Security) out of your paycheck, but they will not be given back to you in the form of higher monthly Social Security payments. You are making those payments to someone else. Understanding of the law has caused older workers to move to Canada to work, but the Canadian government has a treaty agreement with the U.S. government. You cannot accrue any money in the Canadian retirement system if you are over 70 and currently receiving your U.S. Social Security payments. Gotcha!

Private Solutions

In the book *The Millionaire Next Door: The Surprising Secrets of America's Wealthy*, the authors interviewed individuals who had a net worth of $10 million or more to evaluate their lifestyle.[21]

The surprising secret of these millionaires was the frugal lifestyle they lived. They did not display the standard of living that would go along with their net worth because they concentrated on the accumulation of wealth, not spending it. A high-consumption lifestyle does not allow an individual to accumulate wealth. The authors call such a spending lifestyle an "earn and consume treadmill."[22] Those who support their high standard of living with only a high-paying job do not have the means to become wealthy. The continued purchase of the newest electronic devices, a new car every year, an annual $5,000 communication bill, and the Caribbean trips have the appearance of wealth, but eventually lead to a financial dead end. Those Americans without a high-paying job can still follow a similar spending pattern, albeit at Walmart. These less affluent spenders are headed to the same financial dead end. For both groups, there may be a way out.

Different Attitudes for Different Folk

After retiring at 30, my wife and I were subject to a barrage of skeptical questions from high-income peers who were still in debt years after we were free from work. Yet the reasons seemed so obvious: the bank-financed $30,000 cars and $2,500 road bikes, the 20-mile commutes, $50 haircuts, and the $100 happy hours every Friday.

"Little" things that are only a few hundred dollars a month add up to hundreds of thousands of dollars shockingly fast. But the lack of this understanding of the numbers is what keeps most middle-class people from getting ahead.

_____

Source: Kelly Johnson, "Meet Mr. Money Mustache, the Man Who Retired at 30, *Washington Post*, April 26, 2013, www.washingtonpost.com/business/meet-mr-money-mustache-the-man-who-retired-at-30/2013/04/26/71e3e6a8-acf3-11e2-a8b9-2a63d75b5459_story.html.

First, there must be an effort for those Americans who want to increase their wealth to become financially literate. There is more to this process than saving money. The more difficult part is determining how to invest accumulated cash to allow it to earn more money while you sleep. There are financial literacy programs conducted at local libraries through the American Library Association and the Financial Industry Regulatory Authority (FINRA) Foundation. These programs are usually free and are oriented toward helping the general public understand financial issues such as stock trading and mortgage financing. They are offered in the evenings and on weekends when working adults can attend. Some of these programs may even provide library story hour for children while parents attend financial literacy training. In the beginning, it is important to attend these seminars or free online webinars providing similar training, for example, *Money Smart* from the Federal Deposit Insurance Corporation (free registration at www.fdic.gov/consumers/consumer/moneysmart/mscbi/mscbi.html). An educated investor does not bet on the market or invest based on tips from their broker. For that reason, it is important to continue the education process with self-education from webinars and investment books. The objective is to have an understanding of the best way to make an investment, whether that is in stock, property, or bonds.

Second, there must be an effort by the wage earner to reduce their consumption spending to develop a surplus, no matter how small, after each payday. For many people, this requires a change in attitude from "if I got it, I'm going to spend it" to "the future counts." It is hard to understand *how* an individual, who is employed, is unable to have a small monthly monetary surplus. My Charles Schwab account holds eight cents (it's a long story). Can you save eight cents? If you can't, you can take eight cents out of the penny jar at the convenience store checkout counter where you buy your lottery tickets. It is easy to understand *why* they cannot stop spending: Our economy and our culture provide reasons to make you want to spend.

Third, it must be understood that investing small amounts in the stock market is going to be costly in percentage terms at the beginning. Broker fees will reduce the return and are a high percentage for these small investments, but as the amount invested grows, these fees will become a smaller percentage of the whole investment portfolio. The odds of growth in wealth through the purchasing of a diverse stock portfolio are likely to be higher than investing the same amount of money in lottery tickets. And if the purchase price of nonwinning lottery tickets is compared with brokerage fees, brokerage fees begin to look more reasonable. In order to keep those fees low, it is important to use an online discount broker such as E-Trade or Charles Schwab. Many online brokers require minimum deposits of between $500 and/or $1,000, but other online brokers have no minimum for a cash deposit account or retirement account to be opened (probably not 8 cents). ShareBuilder ($6.95 per trade), thinkorswim ($9.99 per trade) and MerrillEdge ($6.95 per trade) are examples of online brokers with no minimum requirement to open a cash brokerage account.[23] These brokers provide for investments in online banking, mutual funds, and dividend reinvestment plans, and will even add money to your new account balance to entice you to open an account. The exact nature of the investment into indexed funds, mutual funds, or exchange-traded funds are described in the book's other chapters and will not be repeated here.

Summary

It is possible to appear rich and not be wealthy as easily as it is to appear poor and be wealthy or appear poor and be poor. The accumulation of wealth allows one to be wealthy, not the spending every dollar in their paycheck. Many individuals are unable to make that choice and continue to live from paycheck to paycheck no matter how large the paycheck. Even Elton John had to go on a budget.

What comes from a consumption society is (1) a lot of people who have difficulty supporting themselves and their families; (2) seniors who eventually run out of money during their retired years and finally face a drastic reduction in their standard of living; (3) a large group of workers who have bought into the American dream that has been sold to us and the rest of the world about wealth in America; (4) the need for expensive transfer payments to support a consumption-oriented society during a financial crisis; (5) an extended recovery period from a recession due to lack of consumption from those not in the workforce.

Americans are aware of a growing divide between the really wealthy and paycheck-to-paycheck poor in the United States. The divide is greater than it was in 1960s, as the wealthy have multiplied the wealth difference between themselves and others. Many of the paycheck poor have attempted to mitigate those differences through high short-term consumption. These attempts cannot cover the gulf and eventually may lead to underlying resentment.

Such resentments have the potential to play out with attacks against the societal icons in our society.

Notes

1. Thomas Gabe, "Poverty in the United States: 2011," Washington, D.C.: Congressional Research Service, September 27, 2011, www.crs.gov.
2. Ibid., 3.
3. The calculation of poverty rates does not take into account improved standards of living over time periods.
4. http://taxfoundation.org/sites/taxfoundation.org/files/docs/fed_rates_history_real_1913_2013_0.pdf.
5. The marginal rate is the percentage of tax that must be paid on the next dollar earned within a specific tax bracket.
6. www.wsu.edu/payroll/taxes/hist-oasi.htm.
7. http://247wallst.com/2012/10/23/states-where-residents-pay-the-most-in-taxes/.
8. http://taxes.about.com/od/statetaxes/a/property-taxes-best-and-worst-states.htm.
9. These are state property and income taxes. http://money.msn.com/taxes/states-with-the-highest-and-lowest-taxes.
10. http://taxes.about.com/od/statetaxes/a/Sales-tax-rates-highest-and-lowest.htm
11. Productivity per worker has increased in the United States, but that is an outcome of the cut in factory jobs as well as new manufacturing methods, and expanding high-skilled tech jobs.
12. http://usatoday30.usatoday.com/money/economy/2002-12-12-manufacture_x.htm.
13. Editorial Board, "Manufacturing Jobs, Not Output, Have Left the U.S.," *Sun Journal*, April 12, 2013, www.sunjournal.com/news/our-view/2013/04/12/manufacturing-jobs-not-output-have-left-us/1346902.
14 L. Mishel, J. Bivens, E. Gould, and H. Shierholz, *The State of Working America* (12th ed.), Economic Policy Institute. (Ithaca, NY: Cornell University Press, 2012).
15. However, fees could be charged for housing, recreational, and health services, for example. See www.ucop.edu/acadinit/mastplan/MasterPlan1960.pdf.
16. A. Martin and A. Lehren, "A Generation Hobbled by the Soaring Cost of College," *New York Times*, May 12, 2012, http://www.nytimes.com.
17. "High Student Debt Is Dragging Down the U.S. Economy," *Washington Post*, www.washingtonpost.com/blogs; and M. Brown and S. Caldwell, "Young Student Borrowers Retreat from Housing and Auto Markets," 2012, http://libertystreeteconomics.newyorkfed.org/2013/04/young-student-loan-borrowers-retreat-from-housing-and-auto-markets.html.
18. www.investopedia.com/financial-edge/0512/the-spending-habits-of-americans.aspx.

19. http://247wallst.com/2011/02/24/ten-things-americans-waste-the-most-money-on/3/.

20. P. Villarreal, "How Baby Boomers Are Spending Their Money", National Center for Policy Analysis, September 2012, 7.

21. T. Stanley and W. Danko, *The Millionaire Next Door: The Surprising Secrets of America's Wealthy* (Boulder, CO: Taylor Trade Publishing; Reissue edition, November 16, 2010).

22. Ibid., 36.

23. The exact fee structure needs to be checked as these fees change frequently.

CHAPTER

The Federal Debt Bomb

HOLD YOUR BREATH (AT LEAST TRY)

Over the course of our deliberations, the urgency of our mission has become all the more apparent. The contagion of debt that began in Greece and continues to sweep through Europe shows us clearly that no economy will be immune. If the U.S. does not put its house in order, the reckoning will be sure and the devastation severe.
    —National Commission on Fiscal Responsibility and
    Reform, "The Moment of Truth," Debt Commission
    Report, The White House, December 2010

Blessed are the young for they shall inherit the national debt.
    —Herbert Hoover Address to the Nebraska
    Republican Conference, Lincoln, Nebraska,
    January 16, 1936

I once asked my economics professor if the United States could go bankrupt. He said, "No, because the government can tax you for everything you have." The answer has remained in my mind for 40 years. As I consider the question again, I know the government would create a political upheaval if they taxed away everyone's wealth to pay off the nation's debt. But maybe we can just take it

153

away from the rich, those that make over $400,000. One question: Who pays if the rich don't have enough wealth to pay off the debt?

Today, federal debt is out of control because of continual annual overspending by the federal government. Everyone knows it. The nation's enormous debt is the single most serious security threat to the United States, and consequently it is a financial threat to every U.S. citizen who holds anything of value that is denominated in U.S. dollars—savings, bonds, mutual funds, and many stocks. The threat is real, and it is only due to lucky financial developments elsewhere in world that the U.S. government's debts have not created a financial disaster. It is important to determine the financial losses a debt bomb can create for you. In this chapter, we will try to find ways to mitigate your financial losses as events unfold.

In a first step, the size of the federal debt needs to be put into perspective. Deficit spending contributes to the nation's debt burden. A deficit is created anytime more money is spent than is earned during a one year period, and excluding two past years, the federal government has been spending more than its income every year since 1960.[1] In order to fund the excess spending, the government must borrow money. Consequently, more and more debt is owed to those who buy government IOUs and fund governmental programs. The selling of U.S. bonds is the means the government uses borrow money. The U.S. Treasury prints those bonds and sells them to China, Japan, individuals, banks, and investment firms. In order to pay off maturing bonds, the government can sell more bonds to pay off its old bonds or it can just print money. Our governmental debt will continue into perpetuity as long as there is someone willing to buy bonds. The federal government has a lot of debt, and it is going up so fast any "current" debt estimate is quickly outdated. With that caveat, the federal debt as of December 21, 2012, was $16,336,217,360,826 or a bit over $16 trillion, and the interest rate on the debt averages around 2.8 percent, resulting in around $360 billion in annual interest payments.[2] The debt has continued to increase at close to $4 billion per day since 2007.[3] For the normal wage earner these amounts are unfathomable, but to put it in perspective, as of November 2012 to pay off the debt each person in the United States owes the government $53,378.[4] So get out your checkbook and pay off your share of the debt. It is our debt because it arises from government expenditures for innumerable social transfer payments, defense spending, payments to prop up foreign governments, special tax provisions for solar companies, subsidiaries to agriculture, tax loopholes for everyone, and interest payments for funding the debt. When we vote, we vote for these expenditures.

Is anyone in the United States willing to hand over $53,378 to the government? Even if the government were willing to increase everyone's tax to pay off the debt or if each American citizen felt a patriotic obligation to voluntary send in a check for that amount to the government, the results would be catastrophic to the economy. In an economy largely based on consumer spending, the withdrawal of this money from consumers would result in a business contraction that would rival the Great Depression of the 1930s. For individuals, the result would be substantially more losses than $53,378 per person and the recovery would take generations. Currently, the federal government is between the edges of two cliffs. At this point in the story federal officials have little wiggle room to get out of the situation that has been developing over the past 50 years.

Who Is Going to Take It Away?

Large debt will put America at risk by exposing it to foreign creditors. They currently own more than half our public debt, and the interest we pay them reduces our own standard of living. The single largest foreign holder of our debt is China, a nation that may not share our country's aspirations and strategic interests. In a worst-case scenario, investors could lose confidence that our nation is able or willing to repay its loans—possibly triggering a debt crisis that would force government to implement the most stringent of austerity measures.

_____

Source: National Commission on Fiscal Responsibility and Reform, "The Moment of Truth," Debt Commission Report, The White House, December 2010, 11.

Right now, the government has experienced a short-term reprieve from economic chaos due to interest rates being manipulated to historical lows by the Federal Reserve and the fact that the United States remains a safe haven for overseas investment. Currently, the interest rate on the federal debt is approximately 2.8 percent, which makes the interest paid on the debt only $360 billion annually. Should the interest rate on bonds increase, debt serving will become more difficult. If the interest rate should rise by threefold to 9 percent, then the annual interest payments will rise in parallel to an annual interest payment of over $1 trillion. These payments would largely be sent overseas. A 9 percent interest rate is not without precedent. In January 1980, the benchmark interest rate was 20 percent as the Federal Reserve attempted to reduce inflation.[5] With little complication, the federal government can find itself in a situation where the interest on U.S. debt is so high the ability of the U.S. Treasury to pay it may be questioned. Only so much money can be printed before investors devalue our dollars. These interest rates may begin to increase because foreign investors who buy our debt require a higher rate in order to continue to fund the U.S. government's operations or because the Federal Reserve has raised interest rates to fight runaway inflation.

Government Choices and Me

The choices to deal with an unmanageable debt are limited, and some choices are infeasible. The basic four choices are shown in Figure 10.1, which begins with the debt's ultimate effect on your net worth and financial prospects. Without careful planning, a loss of wealth is guaranteed no matter which road the government selects. Figure 10.1 shows that the results are the same; the only variation is how your wealth is going to be taken. The methods are different, as some are not a direct-in-your-face approach, such as

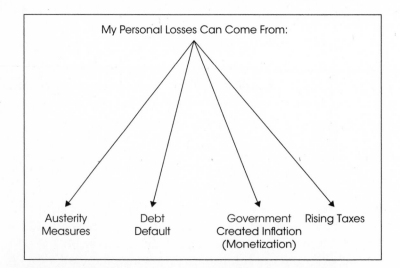

Figure 10.1   How Is the Government Going to Take Your Money?

personal tax increase or transfer payment reduction, but they are just as effective at appropriating your wealth.

Of course, these methods could be used in combination with one another. The nations in the European Union have raised taxes on their citizens while at the same time cutting government benefits from pensions to food support, laying off government workers, and cutting the salaries of government employees who remain. Right now, in Europe the conventional economic wisdom is to use tax increases along with austerity measures. In the United States, none of these measures have been agreed upon as a means to control the financial viability of the country.

Raising Taxes

Regardless of the outcome of the tax debates in Congress, tax increases cannot raise revenues enough to eliminate annual overspending and contribute to a pay-down of our debt. The new taxes that are needed to cover deficit spending cannot be instituted without creating political unrest in the United States. Additionally, when new taxes are instituted, they are already allocated for a specific purpose. For example, the new tax on investment income (above a specific criteria) is allocated to the Obama Health Care Law; federal fuel taxes are designated for road infrastructure; even general tax revenues are committed to other causes before they can be used to reduce the country's debt burden. The underlying purpose of many tax schemes is to redistribute the wealth from those who are better off to those who have less.

How *Not* to Work that Old Governmental Magic

Therefore, there must be two different ways of looking at the possibility of reducing inequality and abolishing poverty by deliberate redistribution. . . . At any given moment we could improve the position of the poorest by giving them what we took from the wealthy. But, while such an equalizing of the positions . . . would temporarily quicken the closing-up of the ranks, it would, before long, slow down the movement of the whole and in the long run hold back those in the rear.

Friedrich A. Hayek, *The Constitution of Liberty* (Chicago: University of Chicago Press, 1960), 48–49.

Social arguments for redistributing wealth by increasing taxes can take lawmakers to strange places. Is it financially fair for those who are well off to receive more Social Security payments than those who earned less during their working years? Does it also seem financially fair that those who followed a healthy lifestyle and may live longer may therefore collect more money from Social Security than those who followed a lifestyle predicated upon immediate satisfaction? All these differences could be considered reasons for changing the distribution of Social Security payments. Regardless of the side arguments about taxation, any choice is not going to stem the tide of annual deficit spending unless you first pay your share toward the reduction of the nation's debt now at $53,378.

Austerity Measures

Austerity measures are substantially different than tax increases, debt default, or inflation growth. The latter three methods target all Americans, causing equal suffering among everyone. With expenditure cutbacks (i.e., transfer payments), particular programs are targeted, and those specific programs and individuals receiving benefits endure the brunt of the cuts.

Today, so many people are dependent on one form or another of transfer payments, austerity or cutbacks in government spending is also an unlikely congressional choice. It is estimated that over 50 percent of U.S. households receive some form of benefit from the government.[6] Many U.S. citizens have been collecting money from the U.S. government for decades. These constituents and their government administrators have developed a symbiotic relationship. As more U.S. citizens receive transfer payments, the programs and those administering the programs become more important to our way of life. Can you imagine the result of these programs becoming successful and stopping their constituents' dependencies? One of the first steps would be a loss of jobs for the administrators of these programs. The governmental system encourages expansion, not corrections. Without the direst financial conditions, such as those currently experienced by Greece, austerity measures will not be instituted in the United States.

Welcome to the New America

... the plain fact is that the utilization of government entitlements benefits by American citizens registered what epidemiologists would call a "breakout" into the general population over the past two generations.

... the share of government transfer benefits in overall personal income for the nation as a whole rose from under 8 percent to almost 18 percent ... between 1969 and 2009.

—Nicholas Eberstadt, *A Nation of Takers: America's Entitlement Epidemic* (West Conshohocken, PA: Templeton Press, 2012), 47.

The government will not take your wealth and money through large increases in taxes, and they will not take away coveted transfer payments with austerity measures. The political costs for a democratically elected Congress are too great. Taking such actions results in senators and congressmen losing their seats in Congress. For the past 50 years, no Congress has voted to face that alternative, and it is unexpected that a new Congress would vote for such changes before a financial crisis hits the United States. At this point, minimum changes are not enough to make a difference in the debt story. The remaining two governmental choices, as shown in Figure 10.1, are debt default and inflation.

Debt Default

Debt default occurs when a government cannot pay the interest on its debt or its maturing debt, and consequently it requires a restructuring of its debt and its interest payments.[7] Debt repudiation, an unlikely event, takes place when a national government declares it will not pay its debt obligations. With a debt default, holders of the government debt can expect to only be repaid cents on each dollar owed them, as well as losing interest payments. A national government can always print more money, so default is likely to occur when no creditor will take the printed money because it is close to worthless. There have been 48 countries that have defaulted on their national debt over the 1971–1997 time period.[8]

The objective of a default is to eliminate debts the government finds so large that they will experience unacceptable austerity measures. In Europe, banks holding bond debt from national governments such as Greece and Italy have had to accept a reduction in the number of euros owed them. When this occurs, borrowed amounts are paid back at one tenth the original borrowing, for example, but the government does not repudiate its entire debt obligation. Thus, the government has only gone partially bankrupt. For the country, there are likely to be increases in all interest rates, devaluation of the countries' currency, inability to make international contracts, a contraction of the country's economy, and loss of purchasing power as all imported goods, from bananas to cars, become more costly.[9] If the United States were to take this approach, it would also mean that the dollar would no longer be considered the reserve currency of the world and further crash the value of the dollars as holders of U.S. dollars traded their holdings for other currencies. This approach will not be taken in the United States.

Argentina Is Not the United States and a Default Not Repudiation

. . . when creditors and their agents pushed crisis-stricken Argentina in 2001 to fully dollarize its economy in order to totally ensure it would pay it [debt] back, the result was the exact opposite: Buenos Aires first defaulted on its debt, and then devalued its currency.

. . . the Argentine government successfully forced its own renegotiation terms on foreign creditors and public-utility investors, making both take unprecedented cuts in the value of their holdings and incomes.

—Diana Tussie, "From Argentina to Greece: A Global Roller-Coaster," November 11, 2012, http://truth-out.org/news/item/12674-from-argentina-to-greece-a-global-roller-coaster.

Monetization

When government-caused inflation is instituted to order to use cheap dollars to pay off its debt, it is called monetization.[10] During the 2010–2012 period, the Federal Reserve instituted an interest rate policy to make people spend their money rather than save it.[11] During this period, interest rates were kept so low that those who saved money lost money. They lost their purchasing power because the rate of inflation, although low, was higher than the rate of interest savers received on their bank deposits. So each year that money was kept in an account, purchasing power was lost, and savers found themselves in worse financial shape. The Federal Reserve instituted this policy to force consumers, in a consumer economy, to spend their cash to help revive the stagnant economy. If the Federal Reserve has the ability to institute a policy to force Americans to spend money, the Fed can also institute a policy to create inflation in the economy. In fact, the current Federal Reserve policy is to focus on lowering unemployment levels and allow inflation to increase above previous rates as a way to stimulate the economy.

The basic purpose of allowing inflation to increase is to be able to pay off debt with cheaper dollars. Such a policy means dollars will buy fewer goods and debtors profit while creditors lose. For example, with a fixed-rate home mortgage of $200,000, you considered your ability to make monthly payments based on your current earnings at the time you made the purchase; that is Point 1. Assume hyperinflation rages for two years and your employer has matched inflation rates with raises in your salary. You are not receiving raises because you are promoted, due to seniority, or higher productivity. Now a $4 hamburger costs $12. At Point 2, you look at your mortgage and you see how you can pay it off with cheaper dollars. After two years, you now owe $198,000. Your balance and your interest rate have been unaffected by inflation. Your salary, however, has doubled or tripled and you are now making $198,000. You decide to pay off your home mortgage. Creditors, the bank or loan company, holding the mortgage get paid off in cheaper dollars, which are worth less than the dollars they loaned. The Federal Reserve can create this situation so the government does not have to default on its debt or cut its expenditures, but instead pays off debt with cheap dollars. This government policy is called the monetization of the debt. It is a more sneaky policy than visibly cutting program expenditures, raising taxes, or defaulting on the nation's debt, but it is still a conscious step toward debt repayment.

If the federal government decides to monetize its debt, it allows elected officials to say they did not raise taxes on the public or cut

Table 10.1 Policy Choices and Their Effect on Deficits and Debt

Effect on:	Tax Increase	Austerity Measures	Increase in Inflation	Debt Default
Government deficit	Possibly reduce the annual deficit	Possibly reduce the annual deficit	No effect	Direct reduction in interest payments and corresponding possible reduction in deficit
Government debt repayment	Possibly reduce the debt	Possibly reduce the annual deficit and future debt	No effect on balance but able to pay it off with "cheap" dollars	Cancels large portion of government debt in a restructuring

expenditures on the poor, but the overall effect will be the same. It allows politicians to say "we are on your side" as the deceptive effect of inflation creates a crisis for everyone on a fixed income or anyone owed money.

A debt default would have immediate international retaliatory effects, but increasing U.S. inflation does not create the outrage of a debt default. Yet defaults create similar losses among U.S. citizens as does inflation; except it gives the government an excuse to say "we are on your side." If expenditure cuts are made to government programs, it will create a huge outcry from the constituents of these programs and from members of Congress. Yet if inflation eats into the ability of these programs to provide services to their constituents, it is another matter. No programs were cut, but the same objective is achieved through rising inflation and it allows the government to say it is fighting inflation so that full services can be restored—that is, "we are on your side." Therefore, inflation is the only viable alternative for the federal government to alleviate its debt problem.

The specific effects of these policies are noted in Table 10.1. In Table 10.1, tax increases, austerity, increased inflation, and debt default are viewed from their immediate effects on the deficit and debt repayment. The direct consequences of these policies are shown in Table 10.2, but no changes in the economy are

Table 10.2   Policy Side Effects and Me

Effect on:	Tax Increase	Austerity Measures	Monetization	Debt Default
Your purchasing power	Tax increases do not affect the purchasing power of the dollar; there is just less money in the hands of the public.	Expenditure cuts will not affect purchasing power unless you are a constituent of the programs being cut.	All Americans experience a decrease in their purchasing power, especially with imported goods or services.	All Americans experience a decrease in their purchasing power, especially with any imported goods or services.
Worth of your "hard" assets (houses, land, cars), which is part of your net worth[13]	Does not affect the value of your hard assets.	Does not affect the value of your hard assets.	Inflation causes the value of your hard assets to increase in value but not in purchasing power.	Default is likely to cause hard asset to go up in value and any dollar-dominated asset, such as bonds, to fall in value.
Your overall wealth (net worth)	Every American experiences future wealth reductions due to tax increases.	Decreases affect specific groups and agencies where expenditures are cut.	Policy causes program dollars to be unable to cover program expenditures as prices increase resulting in a reduction of the numbers served (i.e., cutting program clients).	Immediate loss in value of any assets denominated in U.S. dollars.

that simple. For example, as has been indicated a debt default creates all sorts of currency, bond, and foreign exchange turmoil for a country. Several effects in Table 10.1 are qualified with the word "possible." The reason is because the immediate effect may be a reduction in the deficit, but it depends on whether governmental spending increases, for example.

What Am I Going to Lose in These Policy Choices?

Many of the effects of government policies to reduce the debt and deficit financial have been mentioned. Table 10.2 summarizes those effects on an individual's net worth, purchasing power, and value of their "hard" assets.[12] As has been stated, the most likely government plan to avert an immediate financial crisis is the monetization of its debt, so that is the policy scheme that needs to be investigated.

As monetization of the debt is the most likely policy scenario for the federal government to try to squeeze out of its financial situation, it is worthwhile to see how monetization affects different groups in the United States. The groups that will be considered here are the retired, salaried workers, bond and stock investors, the unemployed and disabled, and single small-business proprietors. These groups are not mutually exclusive from each other.

The Retired

After the Soviet Union collapsed in the 1990s, its workers' welfare system collapsed. Good comrades who had served communism and retired still received their pension payments, but the pensions did not buy much, and it was common to see news footage of these retired workers begging in the streets of Moscow. What happens to the retired if their pensions cannot increase to keep up with the rate of inflation?

No Need to Raise Taxes

With a $60,000 income at retirement and only a 3 percent inflation rate, you will need the following increases in income to support the same lifestyle you had at retirement:

$80,635 a year in 10 years
$120,000 a year in 20 years
$163,914 in 34 years (If you retire at 65 and live to 99, you have lived 34 years in retirement.)

Source: New Retirement, at www.newretirement.com/Planning101/Inflation.aspx.

All those living on fixed incomes or incomes that do not keep pace with the rate of inflation will suffer if monetization of debt becomes a government policy used to generate cheap dollars. If the retired own bonds, they will see the average interest rates on their bond portfolio rise, but their purchasing power from those payments cannot keep up with inflation. Consequently, they will lose their economic foothold just as they are losing it now with negative interest rates.[14]

My personal example of a loss of purchasing power relates to my mother and the amount she received when she retired. At the time she retired, her annual pension payments were just slightly lower than the salary I was earning. At the end of her life, her pension was so low she qualified for Medicaid. Quite a fate for someone who worked from the time she was 16, became an author, and retired as a university professor. At least she didn't have to use a tin cup on the sidewalk. God bless the U.S. government.

View from the Top

Lloyd Blankfein, CEO of Goldman Sachs, who made $16.1 million in a recent year, offers economic advice in an interview:

> You're going to have to undoubtedly do something to lower people's expectations—the entitlements and what people think that they're going to get, because it's not going to—they're not going to get it.

> You can look at the history of these things, and Social Security wasn't devised to be a system that supported you for a 30-year retirement after a 25-year career. . . . So there will be things that, you know, the retirement age has to be changed . . . maybe some of the inflation adjustments have to be revised . . . entitlements have to be slowed down and contained.

Source: "Goldman Sachs CEO: Entitlements Must Be Contained," *CBS Evening News with Scott Pelley*, November 19, 2012.

The government does not have to institute a tax increase to take your money to pay off its debt. Instead, the Federal Reserve can create inflation at a level that allows for all creditors to pay off their debts with dollars that are worth less.

Wage Earners

Okay, now suppose you are a working stiff. When inflation becomes rampant, what are you going to ask for in order to keep up with the level of inflation? Raises.

Will you get them? Probably, yes. Unfortunately, increased raises contribute to a never-ending increase in inflation through new price increases for products and services as employers raise their prices to cover their increases in cost, like your raise. Prices increase for everything, and they accelerate at a rate where wage increases cannot keep up with them. The inflationary spiral has started. Wage earners eventually find themselves in the same situation as retirees, except it will take them slightly longer to get there, but coming in second is not much fun either. If such a scenario occurs, it means the Federal Reserve has lost control of the economy. In our past financial history, this situation existed when Jimmy Carter was president and interest rates were raised to 20 percent to subdue inflation and regain control of the economy.

Under an inflationary environment, it makes less and less sense to save money as the dollars saved eventually will lose their purchasing power. In this environment, no one is saving and everyone is spending their earnings as fast as they can to buy goods before the prices go up again.

Investors

Investors are represented by three different groups. They are bond investors, stock investors, or a combination of these two groups. Here, we will consider the differential effects of inflation on bond investors and stock investors. As an investor in bonds that are not indexed to the rate of inflation (interest payments increase with inflation), you will suffer a loss in purchasing power as debtors pay you back with dollars that are not worth the dollars you loaned them in the first place. Although you may think it is possible to sell your bonds to someone else and not have to continue to receive interest payments that are worth less each day, it may be impossible to unload the bonds as no one else wants to buy them except at a steep discount. Investors in any sort of fixed-rate bond would experience significant losses in an inflationary climate.

Stock investors would fare better but would still lose purchasing power as the dividends they received would purchase less and less. The market price of a specific stock is likely to vary depending on the industry. Gold manufacturing companies are likely to see their stock price rise in the face of inflation. With other companies, the picture is more varied. Some companies are going to face constant cost increases as inflation continues to ravage their bottom lines. Those companies will see decreases in their share prices other things being equal. Other companies able to maintain profits in an inflationary economy or whose profits are denominated in currencies other than the U.S. dollar, such as oil companies, are going to see their stock price rise more than the rate of inflation.

During an inflationary economy, those companies with largely robotic operations and few manual workers will be better able to keep their costs down. The question about their operations that is important to answer is whether anyone will be interested in buying their products. For example, if you maintain a robotic manufacturing process to produce HD TVs that's good, but consumers do not need to buy your product during inflationary periods. However, with a robotic electric utility or a pharmaceutical manufacturer using robotic facilities, manufacturing cost increases are more limited and demand from consumers are not as likely to drop. Consumers need your product. High rates of inflation may lead to more speculation in stocks as it did during Germany's hyperinflation, but it depends on whether investors have any money remaining after paying an inflated price for necessitates.[15] Yet no one may benefit from the increase in the market price of stocks as investors hesitate to sell their shares due to the high taxes they would pay on inflated gains. Consequently, there is no easy answer as to the inflationary effects on stock investors as there is for bond investors.

Additionally, the inflationary effects on companies' financial statements that investors rely on to make stock investments will become distorted. The financial reports based on the assumption of a constant dollar will have to be adjusted in an arbitrary manner to take the effects of inflationary prices into account. In the past, this has been performed with price-adjusted financial reports.

In this scenario, it is assumed that the Federal Reserve is not taking any actions to decrease inflation by raising interest rates. It is assumed that the Federal Reserve is following a policy that allows rising inflation to purposefully allow the government to pay its debts with cheap money.

The Unemployed and Disabled

The unemployed will have difficulty paying for such basics as food and housing. Their transfer payments will buy less and less in an inflationary economy. The unemployed will face the same fate as the retired who are also essentially receiving transfer payments through their Social Security payments. The disabled will find no one willing to provide the services they need for the price they can pay. Or they will find that "free" charity services will handle fewer and fewer cases. The agencies providing services to the disabled will have to cut their roles in order to provide a minimum level of service to the remaining people enrolled in their programs. No politician can be accused of cutting services to the needy under these circumstances, but the result is the same as if program expenditures were cut. Who is to blame?

Small-Business Proprietors

Proprietors are those individuals or families who run a retail, manufacturing or service business. Proprietors do not include the large public companies such as General Motors or IBM. These are small companies, usually run by families, and they do not issue stock.

Inflationary effects on small business will vary, but general effects may result in speculation as managers concentrate less on their core business activities and try to secure inflationary gains. Thus, the efficiency of operations may begin to suffer as proprietors turn more to speculating on increasing prices of their production facilities. Or they may begin to make immediate purchase decisions they would otherwise delay. Purchases would be hedged in other currencies not affected by strong inflation. Hedging is done to guarantee the purchase price in constant dollars in an attempt to control price increases and anticipated future costs of operations. Profits on inventories would begin to become higher than profits on their core business operations.

The small businesses that will do best in this environment are the ones that provide essential services that must be purchased by consumers.

So How Do I Keep from Losing My Shirt—or at Least Survive an Inflationary Environment

Other issues aside, the inflation winners are those who owe money because they can pay off their debts with cheap dollars. The losers are those who have loaned money prior to the beginning of an inflationary period. So become a debtor before anticipated inflation is incorporated into a loan with higher interest rate.

Further, do not expect survival in an inflationary environment to come from wage increases. Survival cannot be dependent on the interest earned on bond investments. It has to depend on a product or services that can earn a profit when inflationary pressures are creating chaos in the economy. Although all "hard" assets owned by consumers such as houses, land, and cars will increase in value and give a false sense of wealth, the selling of these assets will not bring wealth, as the money received will not be enough to purchase a new asset. This is the "California effect," where Californians have held on to their houses for decades and have seen the price of their homes skyrocket in value, making them believe they are wealthy. When they sell their homes, they cannot repurchase another house in the same area and must move, usually out of state to a lower-priced area, in order to find a comparable home.

The characteristic of a truly profitable inflationary product or service is one that must be purchased by consumers, and can be provided without the continual business cost increases for raw materials, labor, or wholesale goods that drive up its own business costs. Such a product is one that is not subject to the full effect of inflationary pressures because those effects are delayed, or they do not seriously affect a product or service.

As an example, consider the services provided in a dental office with one dentist who owns his office (or has a mortgage), and therefore is not subject to inflationary rent increases. The number of patients coming in for a cleaning may drop as inflationary pressures cause consumers to spend on necessitates. Yet the fixing of a decayed or loose tooth is going to bring consumers into the dental office. The cost of materials used in tooth repair will rise along with other inflationary pressures, but it is a minor portion of the revenue earned by the dentist from repairing the tooth. The main cost component for the repair is the dentist's labor hours.

Thus, the added inflationary revenue for the repair is not for materials, and it goes into the dentist's pocket. The largest portion of increased charge to the patient is paid to the dentist, and the dentist does not have to pay it out to anyone else in cost increases. Compare this situation with a grocery store, which also represents a product, food, which must be purchased by consumers. For the grocery store owner, the largest cost component is the wholesale cost of goods, whereas labor represents a smaller portion of operational costs than with the dentist. For that reason, the grocer owner does not get to keep the increase in inflationary revenues, as they must be paid to vendors supplying the goods used to stock grocery store shelves. Essentially, the grocery store owner does not keep increased inflationary revenues but the dentist does as it is an inflationary charge for his labor services. Consequently, the dentist is advancing his financial position during an inflationary period, and the grocer is staying constant at best.

Consider the example of rentals or leasing as a business where inflationary pressures do not drive up the cost of doing business in direct proportion to inflation. Housing is a necessity just as are dental services. In the normal rental, the utilities are paid by the tenants. Therefore, the cost of running the rental is not affected by inflation and if the landlord has a mortgage, he can pay it off with cheap dollars as he raises the rents. The landlord can increase the rents in response to inflationary pressures without suffering an increase in operating costs that the grocery store owner faces. The landlord, like the dentist, is able to advance his financial position during an inflationary period.

The dentist and the landlord can independently raise their salaries or rents and keep the inflationary revenue increases for themselves. For that reason, their real return becomes proportionally larger than it was prior to the beginning of the inflation period. They do not have to match the inflationary cost increases dollar for dollar with their revenue increases. They are able to keep a larger portion of their revenues than before inflation occurred. The characteristic of an inflationary-protected organization is its ability to increase its revenues by raising its prices and not have these added revenues siphoned off by an equivalent inflationary increase in the cost of its operations.

Organizations providing professional services mitigate the effects of inflation. Rental and leasing operations, where purchase of new assets can be delayed, are examples of business operations that have the best opportunity of avoiding the damaging effects of inflationary cycles in the economy.

Summary

It is going to be difficult to improve one's finances during an inflationary period. Many of the strategies that are written about in the financial press are used to maintain a financial position but not improve it. Much of this advice deals with the purchase of hard assets such as gold or other precious commodities. These purchases will maintain your financial position in the economy when the value of the dollar is falling, but such techniques will not advance your financial position. In order to advance your position during an inflationary period, it is necessary to invest in a company or small business that does not face the full inflationary pressures on its cost structure. The objective is not just to maintain your finances but to improve them. One factor overlying all businesses is to focus on products or services that are a consumer necessity.

Individual survival tips:

1. Buy apartments, duplexes, or fourplexes now when the mortgage rates remain historically low and hang on to the properties as inflation begins to steep through the U.S. economy. Do not buy vacation condos or expensive rentals that renters can avoid renting during an economic emergency. Similarly, it is possible to invest in the stock of companies that lease facilities or equipment and that follow a cost structure similar to those in a landlord's business operations.
2. Work as an independent service professional where the major percentage of operating costs is related to your labor costs. Such a service allows you to independently raise your own salary to match or exceed inflationary increases.[16] An artist may be thought of as an example of such a profession, but the service must be one that consumers require, and that is not true for an artist.

Notes

1. See historical tables at www.whitehouse.gov/omb/budget/Historicals.
2. See TreasuryDirect at www.treasurydirect.gov/NP/BPDLogin?application=np.

3. See National Debt Clock at http://www.brillig.com/debt_clock/.
4. The *Weekly Standard* blog at www.weeklystandard.com/blogs/us-person-debt-now-35-percent-higher-greece_660409.html. It should be noted that in Greece the amount owed by each person is $39,384.
5. Trading economics: www.tradingeconomics.com/united-states/interest-rate.
6. Nicholas Eberstadt, *A Nation of Takers: America's Entitlement Epidemic* (West Conshohocken, PA: Templeton Press, 2012), 31.
7. For the United States, the debt limit has to be continually raised by Congress to keep the country borrowing more money so that it can pay its old debt off and keep spending.
8. Countries on this list include Chile, Czech Republic, India, Poland, and Turkey. Sebastian M. Saiegh, "Coalition Governments and Sovereign Debt Crises," January 2008, available at SSRN: http://ssrn.com/abstract=1017147 or http://dx.doi.org/10.2139/ssrn.1017147.
9. Purchasing power is the amount of goods that can be purchased with a U.S. dollar. If the value of the dollar goes down on international monetary exchanges, the amount that can be purchased is decreased and it is called a loss of purchasing power. Over the past 20 years, the purchasing power of one dollar has decreased. For example, a cup of coffee used to cost 25 cents, not $4.
10. "Debt monetization occurs when a government does not tax its citizens to repay the debt it incurs but instead prints money—or, in the modern equivalent, its central bank creates banking reserves by buying securities issued by its treasury department. The result is a larger amount of money chasing an unchanged amount of goods, which is a textbook explanation of inflation." Jerry H. Tempelman, "Will the Federal Reserve Monetize U.S. Government Debt?" *Financial Analysts Journal* (November/December 2009): 24. www.jerrytempelman.com/Jerry%27s%20website/Publications/01.%20Monetary%20Policy/01.%20Fed%20and%20Debt%20Monetization.pdf.
11. The Federal Reserve System is composed of 12 regional banks and a Board of Governors in Washington, D.C. The Federal Reserve sets monetary policy in the United States by changing interest rates and using other policies that affect monetary transactions.
12. Hard assets are sometimes called real assets. They are physical assets that have a value in and of themselves such as inventory and buildings. They do not have a value that is derived from the value of another valuation source such as most financial instruments.
13. Net worth is the difference between all your assets and all the money you owe.
14. Negative interest rates occur when interest on your investments is lower than the inflation rate.
15. Joe Weisenthal, "Here's What Happened to Stocks during the German Hyperinflation," http://articles.businessinsider.com/2011-11-26/markets/30443754_1_stock-market-speculative-mania-stock-exchange.
16. In a normal economy, prices cannot be raised above competitive marketplace prices, but in a highly inflationary economy accompanied by rapidly changing prices, a competitive marketplace price becomes harder to identify. Thus, the marketplace for professional services or rentals does not act as such a deterrent to price increases as it would in a stable economy.

11

Navigating the 2014 Recession

Arecession is coming. Are you prepared?

If you follow my newsletters, you'll know how I feel about the U.S. economy. We're in trouble. But let me review some of the highlights.

First, the economy is still recovering from the recession of 2008 and 2009, with unemployment still at an astounding 7.6 percent. Although that's down from its high of 10.0 percent in October of 2009, it's still unusual: Unemployment spent the years prior to the last recession ranging from roughly 4 percent to 6 percent. And the gradually improving numbers are, in my opinion, deceiving because each month a fraction of the unemployed become frustrated and stop searching for a job, which causes the unemployment rate to decrease.

Now, the payroll tax hikes that kicked in at the beginning of 2013—as well as federal spending cuts, additional tax hikes expected to follow the battle over the debt ceiling, and the added costs associated with health-care reforms—are weighing on employers and consumers as well. All told, they're enough to curtail incomes and that, it turn, will significantly dampen consumer spending.

But that's not the only problem we have. In an attempt to get the economy back on track, the U.S. Federal Reserve Board has significantly increased the U.S. money supply as part of its quantitative easing program, and an increased money supply decreases the value of each dollar out there. So not only will consumers see their incomes decrease; they'll be able to buy less with what money they do have. It's called inflation.

These factors—as well as others that are too complex to go into here—lead me to predict a recession starting in 2014. And my predictions are pretty good: I forecast the housing market correction of 2008 and 2009, the gold rally of 2008 and 2009, the recession of 2008 and 2009, skyrocketing unemployment in 2009, the flash crash in 2010, and the end of the bull market for bonds in 2012, as I detail later in this chapter.

Some of you may not be worried, thinking you're in the market for the longer term, and markets always recover. But I don't think you can afford to take the advice of John Bogle, the founder and retired CEO of the Vanguard Group, to ride it out. The S&P 500 Index returned an annualized 4.24 percent over the past 15 years ending June 30, 2013, and that included dividends. With inflation rising, 4.24 percent is barely a return at all. And, markets don't always come back. The Nasdaq Composite Index hit 5000 in 2000, and now, 13 years later, is only at 3500.

So, what should you do? I have some ideas. But before I go into more detail about the 2014 recession and how to survive it, let me tell you more about my background. After all, there are a lot of economists and investment professionals who feel differently than I do. Why should you take my word for it? What experience do I have?

Beginnings

In the summer of 1984, when I was in college studying economics, I got a job as a stockbroker's assistant, thinking it would teach me about the investing business—but I learned everything I needed to learn about being a stockbroker my first day on the job.

The market opened at 9:30 A.M., and at 9:31 A.M., the stockbroker for whom I was working got his first call from a client. The client wanted to know about the stock that I'll just call Company ABC. The stockbroker didn't offer an opinion about the stock until after the client indicated that he wanted to buy it. Then the stockbroker had a whole list of reasons why the client's feelings about the stock were correct. Within a minute or so, my stockbroker had placed the order and garnered hundreds of dollars in commissions.

At first, I thought perhaps I was making assumptions, but then the stockbroker hung up the phone, turned to me, and said, "My job is to figure out which way clients are leaning and give them all the reasons in the world to execute the trade, even if I make them up on the spot. It's all about the trade."

Before I could digest what had happened, the stockbroker was on his next call, and his next, and his next—and I saw him do the same thing, time and time again. After a few weeks of observing this behavior, I realized being a stockbroker was more about making transactions and less about understanding economics. I soon after moved on to my next summer job.

Although I was never paid a penny by this weasel, the lesson I learned was priceless. That summer, I lost the desire to push stocks onto naive investors. However, I didn't lose my love for economics. I still wanted to find a way to combine economics and investing, and I hoped to find a way to document my macroeconomic forecasts, and apply those forecasts to investment models.

Luck struck 20 years later, in 2004, when I was doing some due diligence on an investment firm whose stock I was looking to acquire. The owner of the company I was researching told me he'd just sold another one of his businesses—a fairly new and small investment newsletter—and the new owner had bitten off more than he could chew and he might be interested in a new partner.

It was the opportunity I had been waiting for. There were three separate newsletters—*The Fidelity Navigator*, *The No-Load Navigator*, and *The Sector Navigator*—with thousands of loyal readers. I reached out to the owner, and within a few weeks, a deal was cut, with my purchasing a 50 percent stake in the investment newsletter business. I took over management of the models on July 1, 2004.

It turned out that I didn't buy the investment company I was researching, but my hard work turned into an incredible opportunity because in the middle of 2005, I purchased the remaining 50 percent of the investment newsletter business and assumed the role of publisher, meaning I wrote the articles as well. It was a perfect fit given my interest in economics and investing.

Today, I still operate these newsletters. *The Fidelity Navigator* and *The No-Load Navigator* are identical in style and content, but *The Fidelity Navigator* focuses on Fidelity mutual funds and models, and *The No-Load Navigator* focuses on Vanguard mutual funds and models. *The Sector Navigator* is geared toward investment professionals, focusing on the investment philosophy that the so-called buy-and-hold strategy is antiquated and that the next generation of investing involves a sector-rotation strategy. You can get a free subscription to this newsletter using the code provided in Chapter 7.

"Mark Grimaldi is a genius."

—Suze Orman

When I began publishing investment newsletters in 2004, as I noted, I was doing exactly what I wanted to do—but I still saw room for growth. So in early 2011, I partnered with Suze Orman to create a brand new newsletter.

Suze, if you haven't heard of her (but I'm guessing you have), is a financial adviser turned author and television show host. Suze began her financial career as a financial adviser at Merrill Lynch, and in 1983 became the vice president of investments at Prudential Bache Securities. In 1987, she founded her own business, the Suze Orman Financial Group. By 2002, she'd taken her wisdom public with the launch of *The Suze Orman Show;* and she later wrote a number of bestselling investment books.

The mission of our monthly newsletter is to provide a real-time guide to investing—geared toward the public, not the investment community—for each stage of an investor's life. To do that, we decided to use the advice in Suze's upcoming book, *The Money Class: How to Stand in Your Truth and Create the Future You Deserve,* so the newsletter was an extension of the book. In addition to the monthly newsletter, we also planned quarterly conference calls and real-time alerts.

The book and newsletter hit the market in March 2011, and both were a hit. *The Money Class* went on to reach the top of the *New York Times* bestseller list, and here's what Suze had so say about me in it (on page 156, if you want to check):

> Mark Grimaldi is the chief economist and portfolio manager of the highly respected *Navigator* newsletters, monthly newsletters that offer information on the economy and investment advice for no-load mutual funds, ETFs, and 401 (k)s. Mark has an uncanny record: He accurately forecast the bursting of the housing bubble, the economic recession, the great gold rush, and other market milestones. I am an admirer of Mark's work, so I was thrilled by the idea that together we could offer

something special for readers of *The Money Class* who are interested in learning more about ways to invest.

I received many accolades for the newsletter, from Suze herself, who tweeted again and again about my calls. On August 11, 2011, for example, she wrote, "Well congratulations Mark Grimaldi the chief economist for my money navigator newsletter. You called it 100% correct in our May newsletter." Even Oprah Winfrey's OWN network featured *The Money Navigator,* tweeting on January 31, 2012, "Did you watch last night's #MoneyClass with @SuzeOrmanShow? Click to get her FREE Money Navigator Newsletter http://ow.ly/8N2HN."

Behind the Accolades—Accurate Forecasting

So what led to this level of success? To start, I believe it was the accuracy of my historical forecasts, particularly leading up to the financial crisis. Here's just a sample.

The Housing Market Correction

I forecast the housing depression of 2007, writing in the March 2006 *Navigator* newsletters, "In the next five years, house values are going to return to their 1997 levels plus inflation." In the second quarter of 2006, the S&P/Case-Shiller Home Price Index reached an all-time high of 188.93, and as I had forecast, in the second quarter of 2009, it hit a low of 111.11.

The Gold Rally

I forecast the gold rally, writing in the January 2007 *Navigator* newsletters, "My long-shot prediction of the year is gold (the single worst asset class over the last 10 years) will rally." In the January 2008 *Navigator* newsletters, I continued this thought, writing that gold would reach $1,000 per ounce, and in the January 2009 *Navigator* newsletters that gold would reach $1,100 per ounce." At the time of my initial forecast, gold was selling at $625 per ounce. In May 2008, it reached $1,000 per ounce, and on November 6, 2009, it reached $1,100 per ounce.

The Recession of 2008 and 2009

I forecast the recession months before anyone knew it had started, writing in the December 2007 *Navigator* newsletters that the "recession risk increased from 60 percent to 70 percent in 2008, and in the January 2008 *Navigator* newsletters that "a recession begins in the middle of the year." In December 2007, growth of gross domestic product (GDP) was 2.1 percent. From July 2008 through June 2009, GDP growth was negative for four consecutive quarters. Looking back, we now know that the recession formally began in December of 2007, and lasted 18 months, until June of 2009.

Skyrocketing Unemployment

I forecast skyrocketing unemployment, writing in the January 2009 *Navigator* newsletters that unemployment would reach 10 percent nationally. The national unemployment rate began 2009 under 7 percent, and on November 6, 2009, in line with my forecast, unemployment broke 10 percent nationally.

The Flash Crash

I forecast the quick drop in stock prices that occurred on May 6, 2010. In the January 2010 *Navigator* newsletters, I called for "the first 1,000-point down day in the history of the Dow Jones Industrial Average in 2010." In the flash crash, the Dow plunged approximately 1,000 points (around 9 percent) in one day! It was the biggest one-day point decline on an intraday basis in Dow's history. I refer to this forecast as a "Jackpot."

The End of the Bull Market for Bonds

I forecast the end of the great 29-year bond market rally, writing in the January 2012 *Navigator* newsletters, "It's as simple as this: When you have interest rates this low, eventually inflation starts to come back. And the way you tame inflation is by increasing interest rates. And when interest rates go up, bonds prices go down." By 2013, it had happened: Bond yields entered the year near all-time lows. "Ouch," said a June 15, 2013, *Barron's* article entitled "What Goes Up Must Come Down." "Bond investors knew they could be in for pain this year, but maybe not the body blows that have battered them from all directions over the past six weeks."

This is just a sampling of my forecasts, but I think it's important to provide more. After all, I'm an economist, and it's my job to make accurate forecasts. Reviewing my past predictions is the only way to check up on how well I'm doing my job. Too many talking heads on financial news channels are masters of predicting what just happened.

To build credibility regarding my forecast of a 2014 recession, in the appendix, I provide excerpts from a number of articles I wrote before and after the Great Recession. As you'll see, if you take the time to read them, I had begun to see the cracks developing in the U.S. economy as early as January 2008. I felt strongly that these cracks would widen as the year progressed, leading up to a recession starting in the middle of 2008. I conclude the appendix with my all-time favorite article, "This is Not Your 2006 Economy," which I wrote in May 2009, around the same time the $863 billion economic stimulus package was passed. In it, I used my love of classic muscle cars to illustrate where I thought the economy was heading—and, unfortunately for most Americans, I was correct.

I hope you'll read these articles because they were written in real-time, without the benefit of hindsight. They'll show you that my forecasts about what the so-called Great Recession would look like were pretty accurate. Seeing that, I believe you'll listen more carefully to my advice on how to best navigate the 2014 recession.

Our National Ranking

In October 2013, *Hulbert Financial Digest*, which ranks investment newsletters, had some good news for the *Navigator* newsletters: *The Sector Navigator*, *The Fidelity Navigator*, and *The No-Load Navigator* ranked number 2, 4, and 5, respectively, among 41 newsletters on a risk-adjusted basis for the last 10 years. *The Sector Navigator* ranked number 4 among all newsletters ranked on a total return basis over the last 10 years.

Rankings are based on risk-adjusted return, which is represented by Sharpe ratio. Sharpe ratio measures an investment's performance per unit

(Continued)

(Continued)

of risk over a given period. The higher the Sharpe ratio, the better the risk-adjusted return.

To understand why, consider two hypothetical investments with similar returns. Investment A gained an average of 12 percent a year over the past three years, but had a risk (represented by standard deviation) of 30 percent, giving it a Sharpe ratio of 0.4. Investment B gained an average of 10 percent a year over the past three years, but had a standard deviation of 20 percent, giving it a Sharpe ratio of 0.5. (The higher the standard deviation, the greater the risk.) So, while Investment A had a better return, Investment B delivered more return for the amount of risk it took on.

Hulbert Financial Digest 10-Year Mutual Fund Newsletter Risk-Adjusted Rankings (out of 51 newsletters): Year-to-Date as of October 2013

Rank	Newsletter	Annualized Return	Risk	Risk-Adjusted Return
1	*No-Load Mutual Fund Selections & Timing*	6.1%	35.3%	0.25
2	**The Sector Navigator**	**9.3%**	**68.5%**	**0.22**
3	*InvesTech Research Portfolio Strategy*	10.4%	78.5%	0.22
4	**The Fidelity Navigator**	**7.6%**	**60.1%**	**0.19**
5	**The No-Load Navigator**	**7.0%**	**61.2%**	**0.18**

The 2014 Recession

"The poor visit money, the middle class rent it, but the rich own it."
—*Mark A. Grimaldi*

My next prediction, as I've written, is a recession starting in 2014. The 2014 recession may not be as deep as the last one, but it will most likely be longer, because the Fed is running out of options. Think about it. What can the policymakers do to fix the problem this time? Can they quadruple the debt—again? Can they print even more money than they have already printed? It didn't work the first time; why would it work now?

It won't, and the markets will be hit hard when the economy tanks, so we're entering a new world of investing for each age group.

Those who are aged 20 to 40 will see that real estate prices can go down even further, and real estate is extremely illiquid—not a good mix. But they'll have nowhere to turn, with assets in their 401 (k) plans obliterated. This will make them much more cautious, and they'll be reluctant to invest at all—but not investing in an inflationary environment isn't a good option.

Those who are aged 40 to 60 already suffered a recession, during which they saw their net worth cut in half in just 12 to 18 months. They've most likely pushed out their retirement dates as a result, and they're investing more cautiously because they're experienced enough to know that anything that happened before can happen again. But, they need the 20- to 40-year old investors to inject new money in the markets to support their distributions—and that generation is just too cautious to do that.

Those who are aged 60 and older were affected the most by the last recession. Most didn't factor a stock market collapse and a 1.5 percent yield on U.S. Treasuries into their retirement plans. Some managed to enter retirement debt free and make the spending adjustments to make ends meet, but they may see their assets obliterated again. Those with debt, who could not retire, are in even worse shape.

Recession Rules to Live By

Your only choice is to navigate the recession, but that's easier said than done. It will take some hard work as well as some sacrifice. Here are my suggestions.

Live below your means. In times of peace, it's important to prepare for war, so start a war chest today. Avoid accruing debt by never using credit to take a vacation, go out to dinner, or finance a car for more than four years. Save a little each month—even if it's just the change in your pocket.

Don't try to ride it out. As I've noted, the S&P 500 Index returned an annualized 4.24 percent over the past 15 years ending June 30, 2013, and that included dividends. With inflation rising, 4.24 percent is barely a return at all. And, you could actually lose money because markets don't always come back. The Nasdaq Composite Index hit 5000 in 2000, and now, 13 years later, is only at 3500. The list of stocks that hit an all-time high then never reached that price again is almost endless. Remember Apple at $700 per share.

Learn to say NO to your kids. I have three children (two adult) of my own, so I can speak as a parent. Never tap your retirement account for your children's needs, other than medical, of course. You need to retire more than they need a new phone, a vacation, a car, new sneakers, and so on. Yes, this includes education. I know this is a hard one, but *never* touch your retirement, even to educate your kids. I am not saying that you shouldn't help to pay for education. But if you need to withdraw money from your retirement plan, pension and/or 401 (k) to do it, you can't afford it.

Save after-tax money outside of your retirement accounts. During the recession, you'll need money you can access without penalties.

Keep some money in cash. Even with today's very low interest rates, cash must be a part of everyone's portfolio.

Invest the rest in a no-load mutual fund. Many have monthly minimum investments as low as $100, so open an account today and set up an automatic monthly investment account (as long as it's not a target-date fund, as I explained in Chapter 5). Good, all-weather, no-load mutual funds with very low monthly minimums include Oakmark Equity Income Fund (OAKBX), PIMCO Total Return Fund (PTTDX), American Century Equity Income Fund (TWEIX), Vanguard Wellington Fund (VWELX), and Schwab 1000 Index Fund (SNXFX).

If you're already retired, protect yourself even more. Move two to three years of distributions to a high-yielding money market fund to ensure you have enough cash to cover expenses in the event of a market downturn.

Do not retire until your debt is. Retiring with debt is like filling a swimming pool that has a leak in it. You don't really know how much water you are going to need. I find I am doing more and more retirement plans for individuals and couples who plan on carrying debt into retirement. When someone asks me "when can I retire?" I always say the soonest is the day after you are debt free.

Ensure that you keep your portfolio risk low. As I've shown you, two similar investments with different levels of risk can produce dramatically different returns. If you don't know your portfolio risk, you have the wrong financial advisor. And don't assume you can set it and leave it; do regular portfolio checkups to ensure you're portfolio risk remains low.

Don't be afraid to take profits. Remember, an investment's gain isn't yours until you sell the investment. Taking a profit is the only way to make money in the stock market. Trim the winners that are the most risky.

Get a financial adviser. I know brokers and financial advisers are ranked only barely above politicians when it comes to public trust, but you can't let that stop you from getting help when it comes to investing. You simply can't go up against the professional Wall Street sharks on your own. My advice is to ask a trusted friend or colleague who they use (but under no circumstances should you hire a friend; money does strange things to people and even stranger things to friendships). When you have some candidates, consult any one of many good web sites that list the questions you should ask an adviser.

Special Investor Alert

There is one investment that outperformed the S&P 500 Index from September 30, 2007, to December 31, 2012, without having a single down day. In other words, it didn't lose money during the so-called Great Recession—not a penny. It didn't lose money during the Great Depression, either. If we're heading into another recession, as I believe we are, doesn't it make sense to invest in something that didn't lose any money during these difficult times? Especially when macroeconomic conditions have never been better for this investment than they are today? To learn what this investment is, please go to www.grimaldieconomics.com, click on the tab marked "Jackpot," and enter the code "Grimaldi."

Navigate Carefully

There you have it. I've showed you that I saw the Great Recession coming, and I gave you a road map for surviving and possibly even thriving during the next one—and it all comes down to economics.

I know, the eight steps I provided don't seem economic in nature. But every major decision you've ever made involves economics. Whether you realize it or not, we're all a tiny part economists. The economist in you subconsciously helped you select the college you attended or didn't attend, the last car you bought, the last vacation you took, even your life partner.

That economist helped you by telling you how to evaluate what you were getting and what you were giving up with each choice. So if you remember one thing from this book, it's this: Take that tiny part of you that's an economist and apply it to your investments. Ask yourself, before you choose an investment, "What am I getting and what am I giving up to get it?"

For example, if you're thinking about investing in a government bond, what you're getting is a fixed interest rate and a promise to pay back your principal, and what you're giving up is an opportunity to grow your investment at a much higher rate. Or if you're thinking about investing in an aggressive-growth mutual fund, what you're getting is access to a part of the market that will appreciate the most in up markets, and what you're giving up is not putting your principal at substantial risk.

So I challenge you to put the economist in you to work, because I believe most of us have the ability to see what we're getting and what we're giving up on a daily basis, even when it comes to investing. Practice it a few times, and it will be old hat in no time. If you can answer the question and are comfortable with your answer, then I think you've made a good investment choice. But if you (or your financial adviser) can't answer what you're getting and what you're giving up to get it, just say no.

My Fiscal Solution

A fiscal mess, in part, is leading us to the 2014 recession, but I have a way out of it. Politicians may not listen, but you will, and remember, you vote in elections.

1. Cut corporate income taxes to 25 percent. It will unlock the billions of dollars sitting in foreign banks and encourage more businesses to invest their capital.

2. Cut capital gains taxes to 10 percent. We *must* encourage all of us to grow our capital. Remember, when capital is created, so are new taxes and jobs.

3. Move toward a cashless society, thereby eliminating the tens of billions of dollars of business transacted each month that goes untaxed.

4. Create a progressive national sales tax that will tax the wealthy more than the middle class, and will capture off-the-books earnings when money is spent. (Basic necessities such as food and clothing should be exempt.)

5. Ratchet up Federal Insurance Contributions Act (FICA) tax contributions to the poverty level (because no one should pay a penny in payroll taxes until they reach that level), and raise the corresponding amount above the cap to make up the difference.

6. Provide Social Security benefits only to those who need them, because Warren Buffett, Derek Jeter, Brad Pitt, Sofia Vergara, Matt Lauer, and Oprah Winfrey don't really need a benefit that was designed to keep retirees out of poverty.

7. Install a millionaire tax on all income above $1 million.

8. Create a national lottery with proceeds that go directly to pay our ever-growing national debt.

Appendix: The Grimaldi Forecasts

To build credibility regarding my forecast of a 2014 recession, I provide excerpts from a number of articles I wrote before and after the Great Recession.* Articles have been edited for editorial style to ensure consistency, but the content has not changed. As you'll see, I had begun to see the cracks developing in the U.S. economy as early as January 2008. I hope you'll read these excerpts because they were written in real time, without the benefit of hindsight. My commentary below each excerpt will show you that my forecasts about what the so-called Great Recession would look like were pretty accurate. Seeing that, I believe you'll listen more carefully to my advice on how to best navigate the 2014 recession.

January 2008 *Navigator* Newsletters

From the Crow's Nest: "Looking Over the Bow"

"What's in store for 2008?" I wrote in this newsletter article. "The first half of 2008 will be a continuation of the conditions that dominated the second half of 2007: housing woes, credit crunch, lower interest rates, inflation concerns, and market volatility."

Navigator outlook #1: Home prices continue to drop. The government bailout plan backfires.

I wrote, "Credit is going to be hard to get, and this will decrease the number of eligible homebuyers that are in the market. Fewer buyers will mean less demand, which, in turn, will equate to lower purchase offers."

---

*Articles have been edited for editorial style to ensure consistency, but the content has not changed.

Looking back, here's why I was right: Later that year, in a December 1, 2008, press release, Freddie Mac announced, "Conventional Mortgage Home Price Index Purchase-Only Series registered a 7.3 percent annualized decline in U.S. house prices during the third quarter of 2008." This followed a downward revised 0.9 percent annualized drop in the second quarter. And, the median U.S. home value dropped from $232,400 to $208,600 between January 2008 and January 2009."

Navigator outlook #2: The Federal Open Market Committee (FOMC) reduces interest rates in the face of growing inflation.

Looking back, the FOMC dropped the discount interest rate a total of 4.0 percent in 2008. A Federal Reserve press release on December 16, 2008, stated, "Since the committee's last meeting, labor market conditions have deteriorated, and the available data indicated that consumer spending, business investment, and industrial production have declined. Financial markets remain quite strained and credit conditions tight. Overall, the outlook for economic activity has weakened further."

Navigator outlook #3: A recession begins in the middle of the year.

I wrote, "If the Fed cuts too much and too soon, it could stimulate an already bubbling inflation pot. This would almost ensure a recession."

Looking back, a December 23, 2008, press release from the Bureau of Economic Analysis, which stated that real GDP "decreased at an annual rate of −0.5 percent in the third quarter of 2008." We now know a recession started in December of 2007.

Navigator outlook #4: 401 (k) contributions will drop.

I wrote, "Even in the wake of the new law requiring all employees of companies with ERISA regulated 401 (k) plans to be automatically enrolled into the plan, I foresee cuts in retirement plan contributions. . . . The "Smiths" are going to find their budgets even tighter in 2008. Water always finds its own level, and the reservoir will be dangerously low; people will look for ways to cut expenses. 401 (k) contributions will be viewed as "overhead," and the "Smiths" will view 401 (k) contributions as nonessential."

Looking back, this prediction had clearly come true by June 18, 2008, when Christine Dugas wrote in an article in *USA Today* that Americans who are struggling to stave off eviction or foreclosure were raiding their 401 (k) retirement accounts to pay their bills. An estimated 3.1 percent of participants stopped contributing to their employer's plan in 2008 below the prerecession level in 2006, when 2.5 percent of participants stopped contributing to their employer's plan.

Navigator **outlook #5: At least one major financial company files for bankruptcy protection, and the CEO is unfairly held responsible**.

Looking back, my outlook was proven true when Lehman Brothers—the primary dealer in the U.S. Treasury securities market—filed for bankruptcy protection on September 15, 2008. The filing of Lehman Brothers—which had regional headquarters in London and Tokyo, as well as offices located throughout the world—was the largest bankruptcy in U.S. history.

Navigator **outlook #6: Gold continues to soar**.

I wrote, "You could see $1,000 per ounce by midyear."

Looking back, at the end of 2007 gold closed at $833.75 per ounce. The precious metal reached $1,000 per ounce on May 14, 2008. That is an increase of 19.94 percent in less than five months.

Other predictions I made in this newsletter article are as follows:

"Expect several very good buying days (a drop of 2% or more) during the first quarter of 2008." There were nine of these days in January.

"Famously, the Fed sat on its hands heading into the 1992 and 2000 elections . . . which means the Fed needs to act early and often at the beginning of the year." The Fed's emergency cut of 75 basis points on January 22, 2008, lowered the federal funds rate to 3.5

percent. Another 50-basis-point cut to 3.0 percent followed on January 30, 2008.

"If we find ourselves in an economy where inflation is over 3.5 percent and the federal funds rate is under 3.5 percent, a recession is almost inevitable." At the time, annualized core inflation was 4.08 percent, and subsequent data would show we were already in the Great Recession.

February 2008 *Navigator* Newsletters

From the Crow's Nest: "Warning Shots"

In this article, I wrote that "I believe the worst is yet to come," and explained that it is "because unlike many other corrections (1987, 1997, 1998, 2001, and 2002), this time all American homeowners have their biggest assets on the table, their houses."

"Many Americans," I wrote, "are still suffering from 'not here-itis.' I talk to subscribers all over the country, and almost every one says the same thing when it comes to real estate: 'The market is bad, but not here.'"

"Let me tell you something: Other than some remote areas of the country, everyone has been hit hard. If you have not been hit, then you probably did not participate in the boom in the first place. Over the last 10 years, billions of dollars of home equity loans were taken on houses. Every time you pull money out of your house, you just repurchased it for a higher price. Now, the prices are dropping and teaser rates are resettling. To editorialize, the government plan is a drop in the bucket to fix the problem because it will help some people keep their homes, but it will not create new buyers."

Today, more than five years later, the housing market has still not recovered.

March 2008 *Navigator* Newsletters

From the Crow's Nest: "No H.E.L.P. on the Horizon"

"I think a topic yet to see the media spotlight is Home Equity Loan Period (HELP)," I wrote in this article. "This is a stipulation in most of the $9.7 trillion worth of home-equity loans that were outstanding in this country at the end of 2006."

"What is a 'loan period'? As stated by the U.S. Federal Reserve Board (Fed), many home-equity plans set a fixed period during which you can borrow/draw money, such as 10 years. At the end of this draw period, you may be allowed to renew the credit line. If your plan does not allow renewals, you will not be able to borrow additional money once the period has ended. Some plans may call for payment in full of any outstanding balance at the end of the period. Others may allow repayment over a fixed period (the repayment period)—for example, 10 years."

"Let's dissect this. HELP is the length of time that a home-equity loan or line of credit will allow withdrawals. After the draw period is over, the line of credit is withdrawn. The Fed is correct in stating that a new line of credit can be established. However, remember that in order to do that, there must be at least 20 percent equity in your home (equity being the difference between the current value of your home and the current debt you owe on it). If an individual wants to re-establish a line of credit, there is a high likelihood that the equity was maxed out on the prior line of credit. My guess is there will not be enough equity in the home to qualify for another line of credit. In other words, no HELP is on the way. Equity is created in two ways: either by reducing the principal debt of the property or by the property increasing in value. Conversely, equity can be reduced in two ways: either by increasing the amount of debt on the property (tapping into the line of credit) or by the value of the home decreasing. Nationally, home prices are suffering the biggest decline on record."

"When the end of the draw period is reached, one of two things will happen. Either a one-time balloon payment will be required or the bank will amortize the loan for a period of 10 to15 years. Either way, the house ATM is closed and now it is time to repay all that equity and interest. Some people will be able to make the payments, some will not. Some will lose their homes, some will not. Some will try to refinance again, some will apply for a reverse mortgage. Many will stay afloat, some will not. For most of the United States, HELP is not on the way."

Looking back, we all know what happened. Low interest rates—designed to spur economists and market growth after the dot-com bust—sent Americans on a shopping spree. Everyone was a real estate investor, and everyone could afford it, thanks to the new mortgage products offered by banks who were willing to overlook the ordinary due diligence measures. But it was unsustainable. National home sales and prices both fell dramatically in March of 2007. Home sales were down 13 percent to 482,000 from the peak of 554,000 in March 2006. The national median home price was down nearly 6 percent to $217,000 from the peak of $230,200 in July 2006. The plunge was the steepest since 1989. Economist Nouriel Roubini warned that the housing sector was in "free fall" and would derail the rest of the economy, causing a recession in 2007. He was a couple of years too early, but he was right.

June 2008 *Navigator* Newsletters

From the Crow's Nest: "Navigating without a Compass"

In this article, I offered "a couple of thoughts about the 'recession' we may be in or are about to enter."

"I called for a 70 percent chance of a recession to start in the middle of 2008. I have not changed my forecast. In fact, using 'government math,' we are already in a recession," I wrote.

I expanded as follows: "On May 15, 2008, the government reported that the Consumer Price Index (CPI) increase was only 0.2 percent in April and a moderate 3.9 percent for the year. Core CPI (which excludes food and energy) rose only 2.3 percent. As part of the reading, the government reported that gasoline prices dropped by 2.0 percent in April 2008. Yes, dropped by 2.0 percent!"

"Here's government math in action. The average U.S. price for a gallon of regular gasoline was $3.28 on March 31, 2008. The same gallon would cost you $3.60 on April 30. That's an increase of 9.75 percent. However, the government forecast was for gasoline to increase by more than that so according to the government, gasoline prices actually declined. You cannot make this stuff up."

"So, using government math, we are already in a recession. Why? Gross domestic product (GDP) grew by 4.0 percent in the third quarter of 2007, then it dropped to a growth rate of only 0.6 percent in both the fourth quarter of 2007 and the first quarter of 2008. If the government were consistent with its math, we would be in a recession already."

"Why does the government want to keep CPI numbers in line? More than one third of the federal government's budget consists of entitlements, the costs of which are adjusted based on a change in the CPI. Many readers will know these as Cost of Living Adjustments (COLA)."

In this article, I also explained what I called "government math in the private sector," writing, "If, at this year's holiday party, I announce that everybody is getting a 10 percent raise in 2014, that would make the *Navigator* team very happy. However, when they get their first checks in 2014, they see a raise of only 2.0 percent. On the pay stub is a disclaimer that says the 10 percent raise is on any day worked except Tuesday, Wednesday, Thursday, and Friday. So the 10 percent raise is in reality only 2.0 percent."

Looking back, we were already in a recession. And, there was no COLA on Social Security benefits in 2010 and 2011—interesting.

November 2008 *Navigator* Newsletters

From the Crow's Nest: "A Recession Starts Mid Year: The Credit Markets Could Freeze Up"

At this point, many Americans—though perhaps not all—knew we were in a financial crisis. Bear Stearns and Lehman Brothers had folded, and the credit crunch had begun. So I speculated how we got there, noting that "there are five parties that caused this financial crisis."

"Alan Greenspan," I wrote, noting that "in an October 3, 2007, episode of *60 Minutes* interview about the housing crisis, Leslie Stahl asked, 'If you knew these practices were going on, or even maybe just suspected something illegal or shady, why didn't you speak out? I mean you had a huge megaphone, people really listened to Alan Greenspan.' Greenspan responded, 'I was aware a lot of these practices were going on, but I had no notion of how significant they had become until very late. I didn't really get it until very late in 2005 or 2006."

"The Republicans," I wrote, noting that "the Republican controlled federal-government-spent money like they were printing it themselves, which they were. They mishandled the war in Iraq, making a two-year conflict last six-plus years. At the height of our economic expansion in 2006, they did nothing in preparation for the impending slowdown. They pushed as many people as possible into houses that they could not afford."

"The Democrats," I wrote, noting that "since taking control of Congress in January 2007, the Democrats could not detect a "category-five" financial crisis. This past July, Representative Barney Frank said that Fannie Mae and Freddie Mac "looked very good going forward." Less than 75 days later, they collapsed. Senator Chris Dodd got a sweetheart mortgage from Countrywide. It was the Clinton administration that pressed Fannie Mae and Freddie Mac to ease underwriting requirements in the first place."

"Wall Street," I wrote, noting that Lehman Brothers was massively overleveraged (30 to 1), and the same is true of Bear Sterns. Their CEOs were either incompetent or neglectful, and either is bad—not to mention the problems at Merrill Lynch, Washington Mutual, Wachovia, and AIG.

"The public," I wrote, noting that we got drunk on home-equity loans. We got greedy and lazy, and abandoned all of our financial common sense. We lived in a dream world of credit, and now the alarm clock has rung."

As it turned out, we were all to blame. Conservatives tend to blame Greenspan for keeping interest rates too low as the real estate bubble inflated, spurring a frenzy of irresponsible borrowing. Liberals are more likely to focus on Greenspan's aversion to regulation, which led to the emergence of an unsupervised market for exotic derivatives such as credit default swaps and collateralized debt obligations. In an earlier chapter, I talked about the role the election played in Greenspan's choices. But Wall Street and the public have also been widely held responsible for the Great Recession as well.

I also wrote that "2009 will be an unprecedented year. More banks will fail in 2009 than in 2008." As it turns out, 140 banks fell in 2009 versus 30 in 2008.

I added that "home prices will continue to decline." On December 30, 2008, the S&P/Case-Shiller U.S. Home Price Index recorded its largest year-over-year drop. Since that point, the housing market has not fully recovered.

"Will the recession end or extend into a depression?" I asked in 2008. "Right now, I feel all signs point to lower equity markets, lower commodity prices, and lower interest rates. Consumer activity makes up two-thirds of the economy, and the consumer will continue to struggle. Unemployment will reach 10 percent, and household income will decline. In 2002 (the year after our last recession), the S&P 500 Index lost 22 percent."

The S&P 500 Index lost 26 percent of its value in 2009, and commodities showed similar losses. The federal funds rate—which couldn't go any lower—remained steady. Unemployment was 9.3 percent. So I was pretty close.

May 2009 *Navigator* Newsletters

From the Crow's Nest: "This Is Not Your 2006 Economy"

In my all-time favorite article in the *Navigator* newsletters, I explained why the interest-rate cuts leading up to the Great Recession were like adding high-performance equipment to the engine of your sports-utility vehicle (SUV).

"Look at it like this. In 2000, our economy was humming along, then the technology bubble burst and trillions of dollars of capital evaporated, sending the economy into the recession of 2001. Then U.S. Federal Reserve Board (Fed) Chairman Allan Greenspan cut the federal funds rates from January 2, 2001, through June 25, 2003, to only 1 percent."

"The Greenspan rate cuts were like adding high-performance equipment to the engine of your sports-utility vehicle (SUV). The first series of rate cuts in early 2001 were the equivalent of adding fuel injection, which increased the horsepower from 200 to 325. Additional rate cuts increased the airflow by adding a high volume exhaust system and filters, increasing the horsepower to 400. By 2002 the engine was humming along like a 465 horsepower Z/28 Camaro with a four-speed manual transmission. The final rate cut in 2003 pushed the engine to over 600 horsepower! Government deregulation of Fannie Mae and Freddie Mac was the high-octane jet fuel and nitrous oxide that rocketed the engine to over 800 horsepower! Now you have a racecar that could give NASCAR's superstar Jimmy Johnson a run for his money, and the economy/markets soared. The Dow Jones hit 14,000 and GDP mushroomed to $14.2 trillion annually. But as we now know, the economy could not sustain that performance for very long. With all that stress and all those moving parts causing heat and friction, something had to give. Some parts had to start to wear out, and that is exactly what happened."

"The first sign of trouble was on August 17, 2007; the engine sprang an oil leak, causing a slight loss in horsepower. The Fed (pit crew) fixed it by dropping the discount rate half a percentage point. Jimmy Johnson (consumers) felt the problem was fixed, but the pit crew knew the fix was only temporary and hoped the car would reach the finish line (the presidential election)."

"The next problem was a loss of compression in cylinder one. This was caused by the Bear Stearns collapse in March 2008. Before the pit crew could fix the problem, cylinder two gave out when Bank of America saved Merrill Lynch from bankruptcy. Citigroup and AIG seized up, and Washington Mutual was gone. By then, pit crew chief Henry Paulson knew he had real trouble on his hands. The engine was losing oil and started to overheat. He called for an emergency pit stop (September 2008) and said the engine would seize up immediately without a $700 billion rebuild to protect the damaged cylinders. The driver was not convinced the car would finish the race, so he persuaded the car owner (taxpayers) to rebuild the troubled cylinders. Only a few laps after the rebuild, four cylinders were blown and the car lost the third and fourth gears (October 2008)."

"The car was able to finish the race, but crossed the finish line (the inauguration of President Barak Obama) with massive engine damage and only first and second gears."

"After the race season ended, the team owner voted in a new pit crew and crew chief. The new team started with the same eight-cylinder 200 horsepower engine. But instead of adding performance enhancers, the government is installing performance governors, or restrictors, in the name of taxes, social programs, and national debt. President Obama signaled this during his April 16, 2009, appearance at Georgetown University where he said, 'Even as we clean up balance sheets and get credit flowing again, even as people start spending and businesses start hiring—all that's going to happen—we have to realize that we cannot go back to the bubble-and-bust economy that led us to this point.'"

"I am not passing judgment on the president's policies; I am just reporting as an economist what I believe will be the macroeconomic effects of said policies. I am forecasting that the rebuilt engine of the future will be a clean burning, low compression, aggressively filtered, gas sipping, electronic hybrid PCV (politically correct vehicle) with only 125 horsepower. I envision a cross between a Toyota Prius and a Moped. I am okay with all of this. But this PCV will not have the power of a NASCAR or even a Honda Accord; so do not expect the economic pull of one."

Looking back, I couldn't have been more correct. Since I wrote this column, the economy has plodded along, but hasn't completly recovered from the Great Recession. Sure, the markets are back, for the most part, but look at the economy. Unemployment is still at an astounding 7.6 percent, and the situation is getting worse, because the payroll tax hikes that kicked in at the beginning of 2013 and Obamacare are weighing on employers and consumers alike. And, the Fed has created a new problem when, in an attempt to get the economy back on track, it has significantly increased the U.S. money supply. Sound familiar? Boom, bust, boom, bust. Unfortunately, I think we're in for another bust.

CHAPTER

Changing Job Patterns and You

People at Bear Stearns get tens of millions for doing a terrible job at manipulating financial markets. And people get minimum wage for taking care of our grandparents.
        —Professor Barry Bluestone, Director of the Dukakis
                Center for Urban and Regional Policy at
                        Northeastern University

It's a recession when your neighbor loses his job; it's a depression when you lose yours.
                        —Harry Truman (1958)

In Chapter 10, "Staying Poor in America," a brief review of the changing manufacturing jobs in the United States was made. In this chapter, more detailed information will be provided as to exactly how manufacturing has changed in the United States, the reasons for those changes, and if there is any way for those who relied on those jobs to once again feel they have a way of getting back into the mainstream of the job market.

The Old Jobs Are Not Coming Back

Although manufacturing has long been shrinking as a proportion of America's expanding workforce, the number of industrial jobs stayed more or less the same between 1970 and the late 1990s. Since then, however,

(Continued)

(Continued)

manufacturing employment has fallen in every year . . . since 1996 the number of manufacturing jobs has shrunk by close to one-fifth in America,

―――――――――

Source: "Britain and Japan: Industrial Metamorphosis," *The Economist,* September 29, 2005, www.economist.com/node/4462685

The chart in Figure 12.1 from the Bureau of Labor Statistics illustrates *Employment, Hours, and Earnings from the Current Employment Statistics* (National) in U.S. manufacturing jobs from 1970 to 2013.[1] The change in jobs (in the millions) dropped from 18,500 to 11,800. Six million, seven hundred thousand jobs disappeared when the labor force was increasing in size making the need for more jobs critical. Many economists tout the fact that manufacturing jobs have been eliminated as excellent progress because productivity has increased. But, that is not the point. The point is that the U.S. manufacturing has deindustrialized itself to the level where a consumer-based economy does not have economic strength to rapidly pull the country out of a recession. Consumers do not have the money to buy products if they do not have good paying jobs. Yes, some consumers have weathered the Great Recession, but the millions of others who used to have good paying jobs are now scraping by, and this is contributing to the lack of

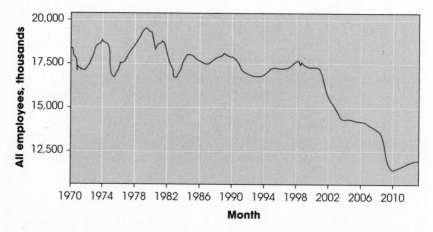

Figure 12.1   Change in Number of U.S. Manufacturing Jobs from 1970 to 2013

a real recovery even when the Federal Reserve has taken unprecedented steps to boost the economy.

Additionally, as the United States has limited its manufacturing capacity, the country must import manufactured products such as electronics, washers, and almost everything else. We learned in school that this was the economic policy followed by England when the United States was a colony. At that time, the United States would export low-value products such as wood to England. English craftsmen would convert the wood into high-end furniture and sell it back to the colonies. The increased value of converting a raw material such as lumber into furniture meant there was a constant higher outflow of money from the colonies to England as real value was added in England. England's colonial policy made many businessmen in England very rich. Not since the United States was a colony has this pattern been used to bleed resources from U.S. consumers. Today, those resources are flowing to China where high-end products are manufactured and many businessmen in China are now very rich, too.

Harvard economists with their Harvard educations tell us that this loss of jobs is good because now Americans are more productive. Not all Americans feel that way. Attending dysfunctional school systems where learning is a far off myth, with little or no job training outside of high school, with no jobs like their father's, these Americans want to know what are they going to do? In the next breath, many politicians, businessman, and intellectuals lament the increasing level of Americans receiving transfer payments from food stamps, disabilities, unemployment, and other state and federal programs.

Productivity Is Up, but. . .

Since 2001, the country has lost 42,400 factories, including 36 percent of factories that employ more than 1,000 workers (which declined from 1,479 to 947), and 38 percent of factories that employ between 500 and 999 employees (from 3,198 to 1,972). An additional 90,000 manufacturing companies are now at risk of going out of business.

Source: Richard McCormack, "The Plight of American Manufacturing," *The American Prospect,* December 21, 2009, http://prospect.org/article/plight-american-manufacturing

How Could This Happen?

We remain one of the best countries in which to live despite the lines of hungry Americans looking for handouts from the government. The question that needs to be asked is: How did we get into this mess?

It goes back a lot further than the 1960s or 1970s.

It all began in England around the turn of the century. At that time, manufacturing production was handled in a much different fashion. The manufacturing plant in England was called the "works." The works was constructed by rich Englishmen, such as a lord, wanting to make more money. The lord provided the land, building, and the equipment from his own resources, and he or others employed by him brought in the manufacturing jobs for the works. The works itself was run by a skilled foreman who assigned jobs to skilled craftsmen within the facility to complete orders. The job order would be received and then the foreman would arrange for the craftsmen working under him to schedule and produce the product. The lord would pay the foreman a prearranged and agreed-upon price and the completed product would be sold to the customer. Thus, the internal production was handled by the foreman and he was handsomely paid by the lord to deliver the product. The portion of the profit from the product's sale was basically split between the foreman and the lord and then distributed to the men in the works who had constructed the product. Soon, it became clear to the owners of the works that a large share of the profits was going to the foreman and the men in the plant— a larger share than was being received by the owner who had put up all the money for constructing the facility.

The owners wanted to change this situation. Eventually, the way it was changed was to standardize the jobs so that a high-paid craftsman was not needed to produce the product. If the different processes of production could be standardized into distinct units of work, then a craftsman was not needed, and the pay for unskilled workers would drop labor costs. Thus, allowing more of the profits from the sales to be paid to the owners of the plant, and this is what actually occurred. The skill level for a worker was reduced to what any unskilled worker could perform.

In the United States, the change in jobs from craftsman to laborer began with the heralded assembly line instituted in the Ford Motor Company by Henry Ford. The purpose was to reduce the cost of making a vehicle, but at the same time, it reduced the skills need by workers who only performed one job and did not need the skills to work on the entire car. For example, it was not necessary to be a craftsman if your job was to put a wheel on a car all day long.

These changes turned craftsmen into laborers who were interchangeable and consequently did not have to be paid as highly as a craftsman.

The next important change responsible for the drop of manufacturing in the United States was unionization of the labor movement beginning in the 1930s. The labor movement had a great growth period from the 1930s to the late 1950s as they increased their membership across the United States. The objectives of the unions were to ensure that their members would not lose their jobs, and to increase wages and benefits for their members. The salary for union workers in the auto industry in 2007 was around $28 per hour, and with benefits it was much higher. By 2015, GM's total cost for wages and benefits will be about $59 an hour, which is lower than in the past (estimated to be $70 per hour).

Unions had driven up the wages and benefits for a group of relatively unskilled factory workers in American factories. Factory jobs such as putting covers on seat belts or placing passenger seats in a vehicle on the assembly line are not craft jobs. Soon, managers realized that American unskilled workers could be replaced with overseas workers and the pay scale would not include benefits or a high unionized hourly rate. Consequently, the exodus of manufacturing jobs to overseas locations began.

Another job killer was the North American Free Trade Agreement (NAFTA) enacted in 1994 during Bill Clinton's presidency. The 2,000-page agreement opened free trade between the United States, Mexico, and Canada. It is estimated that since the agreement has been in effect 682,900 jobs have been lost, largely manufacturing jobs, in the United States as our trade surplus with Mexico has changed into a trade deficit.[2] The economic consequence is that domestically produced goods and jobs in the United States have been replaced by jobs in Mexico as imports from Mexico increased and replaced domestically produced goods in the United States.

The overall result of these changes has been that American manufacturers have left the United States in order to reduce their labor costs, and the jobs that had once been available to Americans are gone forever.

Did You Leave the Middle Class on Purpose?

In order to stay in America's middle class, it is necessary to have enough money to be more than self-sustaining. The poverty income for a family of four in the United States was $23,681 in 2012.[3] Today's minimum wage is $7.25. Many workers must work less than 30 hours per week; otherwise, the employer has to provide their employees with health insurance under Obama Care. Assuming a worker earns $7.25 per hour and works 28 hours per week. They will bring home a weekly pay of $203, monthly of $812, and yearly $9,744 before taxes. Assuming they pay a minimum state and federal income tax of $1,000 as well as sales tax of 5 percent on their retail purchases ($8,744 × .05) $438, it leaves one worker with a net income of $8,306. Even if both husband and wife are both working at minimum wage jobs, their net together is below the poverty level for a family of four, $23,226. At this point, no one in their family has health coverage. Once Obama Care kicks in they will be required to purchase health insurance or have to pay a fine, reducing their net pay even more. A company pension plan . . . well, that is just a distant dream. If the minimum wage is raised, it will only cause employers to try to cut their workforce to save money.

Welcome to the new middle class . . . the barely self-sustaining.

One More Time: The Jobs Are Gone

The industrial worker core had been declining for some time, a result of both new technology and offshoring, and now its decline became precipitous. The statistics tell the story. In 1960 out of a total nonfarm workforce of 54,274,000, there were 15,687,000 manufacturing workers representing 29 percent of the total. By 2009 out of a total of 134,333,000 nonfarm workers, there were only 12,640,000 manufacturing, representing just 9 percent of the total. That is, manufacturing workers fell in the last 50 years from almost one-third of all workers to less than 10 percent.

Source: Dan LaBotz, "What Happened to the American Working Class," *New Politics* XII-4 (Winter 2010), http://newpol.org/content/what-happened-american-working-class

The barely sustaining are people who may work two jobs, they have little stake in the country, and they don't care about the Founding Fathers, if they even know what that means. They are exhausted and they live paycheck to paycheck. They did not leave the middle class on purpose because they never got that far up the economic ladder in the first place. They grew up with parents who lived from paycheck to paycheck, and this seems normal for them.

Then there are those who were part of the middle class while they were growing up but left it once they left home as adults. These individuals grew up in a middle-class environment and did not suffer from being deprived in any way. Although these individuals had parents who earned enough to be part of the middle class, these individuals are no longer part of that group. They have made choices that will keep them out of the middle-class lifestyle for the rest of their lives. For example, they made a choice not to go to college even though they had the ability and grades to attend college. Not going to college is acceptable if those who forgo college have a high-value trade skill, such as machinist, allowing them to earn a middle-class income. Without that alternative, the lack of a college degree will reduce their standard of living and allow them only to earn poverty-level wages. There are others who decided to go to college and borrow their way through school while earning a degree in a major that makes them completely unemployable (regardless of what their college professors told them). These people will find they are having difficulty repaying their college loans while working at jobs that do not require a college degree and pay little.

There are still young adults who have not gotten the word that grandpa's factory job no longer exists. They believe that all they need to do is drop out of school and sign up for that lucrative, high hourly factory job that grandpa had—it's just waiting for them. Unfortunately, it's not true.

The Job Recovery from the Great Recession

The loss of jobs during the Great Recession, which they tell us is over, was horrendous. Now the number of jobs being generated by the economy is bringing hope to the Federal Reserve and policy-makers. It is important to take a look at the type of jobs that are being generated to "bring the economy back on track."

Part-time and melt-away jobs are the rage in hiring new employees during this part of the recovery cycle. These jobs allow employees to scrape by with limited discretionary money. The June 2013 employment report showed that the biggest gain in part-time jobs was in restaurants and bars with an increase in employment of 51,700.[4] These jobs account for 9 percent of all private-sector nonfarm payrolls. The average weekly earnings are around $351, which is reflective of low-shift hours as employers try to keep their workers below 30 hours per week to avoid paying for health insurance under Obama Care.

Melt-away jobs are part-time jobs for temporary workers. Once the job is complete, the worker disappears or melts away. These contract employees or freelancers are the new trend in hiring since the recession ended. It is easy for employers to hire temporary workers, even those who normally would have to be hired as a full-time employee, such as lawyers, substitute teachers, nurses, doctors, and accountants. The employer has no commitment to these workers other than making sure they do a good job or submit a quality work product. Today, these workers represent about 12 percent of everyone with a job.[5] These jobs provide generally low pay and no benefits. Employers are able to eliminate approximately 20 percent in costs that they would have to pay full-time employees.

Yes, employees are being hired, but they are not being hired for the jobs that existed before the Great Recession because up to this point those jobs are gone, too.

Societal and Economic Effects

There have been structural changes in the job patterns in the United States as employers are able to lower their labor force costs.

- The traditional middle-class jobs that were available to employ people with low-level skills and still provide them with a middle-class life are gone forever.
- The new work environment is one where workers become gypsy workers as they go from one contract job to the other.
- Most new jobs provide part-time work along with wages that do not allow workers to fully participate in the economy.
- The working poor rely on government handouts to close the gaps in their ability to live.

A new subclass of people is being created in the country. For them, the United States of America will be the greatest nation on earth in which to stand in a bread line. There has always been a subclass, but it should not be growing and, specifically, it should not be growing because families are being bumped out of America's middle class. The jobs that put people into poverty include babysitters, dental assistants, hospitality workers, certain hospital staff, waitressing, clerks, bartenders, cashiers, domestic help, and child and senior caregivers. As a consequence of the weakened power of labor, more profits from large corporations are being passed on to equity owners and executive managers.

Return to Capital versus Return to Labor

In terms of functional income distribution, which concerns how national income has been distributed between labour and capital, there is a long run trend towards a falling share of wages and a rising share of profits in many countries. The personal distribution of wages has also become more unequal, with a growing gap between the top 10 percent and the bottom 10 percent of wage earners. These internal "imbalances" have tended to create or exacerbate external imbalances, even before the Great Recession, with countries trying to compensate the adverse effects of lower wage shares on consumption demands through easy credit or export surpluses.

Source: "Executive Summary," Global Wage Report 2012/2013, International Labour Organization, International Labour Office, p. VII, www.ilo.org/wcmsp5/groups/public/—dgreports/—dcomm/documents/publication/wcms_194844.pdf

One of the societal changes that is notable is the division of American society into two distinct classes. As has been shown here, many Americans are living from paycheck to paycheck, but the upper income groups, the upper two of income earners, are having no problems. In fact, it has been reported their income is growing while the majority of Americans find their income stagnating. The well-off are strengthening their economic positions with well-diversified portfolios that range from stocks to investment funds, bonds, and property investments, whereas Americans in lower-income groups find their main asset, their home, has lost value. The effect is that America is being divided by income into two separate groups: those with the money and those without. It is necessary for those without much discretionary money to find some way to increase their net worth.

The restructuring of the corporation into a money-generating, highly efficient organization has resulted in an increase in dividends and profits for investors. At the same time, this restructuring has resulted in many jobs disappearing and the workers who performed those jobs becoming obsolete. The efficient corporation is producing more widgets than can be purchased by consumers who do not have discretionary purchasing power to buy these products. When I was a freshman in college in 1960, they told us the United States was a self-sustaining economy. In our economics textbook, the U.S. economy was illustrated with a big circle showing that we produced all the raw materials, goods, and services we needed without the necessity of any of these resources coming from outside our country. We may not have been efficient, but at least everyone was employed.

Today, no one would expect to work for any company for 30 years and retire with a gold watch anymore. Tenure at a company is limited, and moving to another company does not mean an increase in pay. Most of today's "permanent" jobs are temporary compared with those of the past, making it hard for employees to vest into any company pension plan; thus, they must rely almost entirely on Social Security for their retirement. Another societal change in the new work environment has been the increase in single mothers running a household.[6] This is typical of what has occurred in the workforce as male employment has dropped as a percentage of the total workforce. What is the use of having an unemployed husband who is not working and having to support him as well as the children in the family? The result is an increase in single-mother families, with many of those families living in poverty. The work environment, not entirely by itself, has changed the family unit.

The new work patterns have changed who is employed and who is not; it has changed the family structure; and it has changed the way Americans look at their future prospects. Today, it cannot be expected that an increase in the wealth of the rich few will "trickle down" to the many and allow them to live a life without financial stress. The income trickle down that existed since the end of WWII is not coming back. As these divisions become clearer, the result is likely to be the development of political unrest in the United States as more groups organize to control political power. Regardless of people's view of the Tea Party or Take Over Wall Street Movement, these groups should be recognized as the first political groups to start this process. We have been a very politically stable country, but it was because everyone had a stake in the country through home ownership, a decent paying job, and a stable family. Take those cornerstones away and the result has to be more instability and discord among competing groups.

A Possible Solution?

Poverty advocates say the solution is to raise the minimum wage. It won't work. The Democrats say raise taxes on the rich and spread the wealth. It won't work. Today's free market will not work either by allowing income distribution patterns to change back to the 1960s and 1970s. It won't work with today's multinational and totally flexible corporations that owe nothing to any nation as they search for the lowest wage rates anywhere in the world. The solution starts with the individual.

The first step is to determine your level of illiteracy. It does not matter whether you graduated or did not graduate from high school or even college. What matters is your level of literacy or illiteracy.

If you see this number, $112,000, and you say "one, one, two, zero, zero, zero" instead of "one hundred twelve thousand dollars," you have a literacy problem. If you don't know that each new sentence starts with a capital letter and that most paragraphs have more than one sentence, you have a literacy problem. If you see the following subtraction as a trick question: "Subtract $3.75 from $4," and you think it is a trick question because there is nothing above the .75 when you write the numbers on a piece of paper, you have a problem with literacy. If your instructor tells you to turn to a page number in a text, and you don't know where to find the page numbers, someone has shortchanged you. If you can't find the city where you live on a map, then again you have a literacy problem. If you can't fill out a job application correctly, then you need help.

Step 1: Academic Skills. Individuals need to improve their reading and writing skills so they can get a higher-paying job that allows them to have more financial choices. It is a small step-by-step process. If you have not finished high school, some of these problems may be alleviated if you get a general equivalency degree (GED), which will cost around $325. Many community colleges provide a GED program as well as additional skill development in math and basic academic skills.[7] If you are a high school or college graduate, you may still need to go through one of these programs in order to be able to deal with today's high-tech world. No one expects the graduates of our educational system to be illiterate, yet they are illiterate. Graduates with these levels of illiteracy are unemployable except for menial low-paying physical work, and without an improvement in their skills, they will essentially remain in these jobs. The solution to leaving this cycle of poverty rests with the individual who is willing to increase their academic skill level. It is not dependent on government handouts. Yet if an individual is not going to make the effort, my recommendation is to read the chapter on gratuity government and apply for as many transfer payments as possible.

Although the GED program usually requires a payment for tuition and books, there are numerous free ways to upgrade an individual's writing and math skills within an organized program. For example, Coursera is an online education company that provides hundreds of free online education courses (www.coursera.org). The courses range from songwriting to mathematical methods for quantitative finance. One of these courses can enroll hundreds of thousands of students from around the world. Nationally known professors from the University of Michigan, Princeton, Vanderbilt, and Harvard teach these courses. Most of these programs provide certificates of completion but they do not provide university credit at this point. Khan Academy (www.khanacademy.org) provides free learning materials for K–12 students as well as for other levels of learning. Open Culture (www.openculture.com/freeonlinecourses) provides many free educational materials including audio books and online courses. For a list of free courses from MOOCs see: *MOOCs: Top 10 Sites for Free Education with Elite Universities.*[8]

Academic Earth (academicearth.org/online-college-courses) also provides free courses from Practical Math to Introduction to Financial and Managerial Accounting. Although the Open University in the United Kingdom has been providing free courses for 65 years (www.open.ac.uk/about/main/the-ou-explained/the-ous-mission), many of these online educational providers are in their infancy.

Step 2: Building Net Worth. As has been noted in this chapter, the profits from corporations has long ago tilted toward large returns to investors. With that understanding, there should be no argument as to why it is important to become an investor. For most of us, with little money, there is only one way to try get out of a low paying job life style or off welfare and it isn't easy. It means working at a low-paying job and making extreme efforts to save small amounts of money that we can invest to build net worth while we try to increase our academic skills as a means of entry into a better paying job. If paychecks are completely spent without holding something back, it will be impossible to earn more money in the future or raise your standard of living. If that discretionary money is spent on a leisure fishing boat, it is not going to help increase your future wealth. Small stock investments provide the easiest way to become an investor. With stock investments there is the risk of loss, but in a diversified fund that risk can be reduced as been explained in other chapters. If more money becomes available, other types of investments, such as real estate, can be used to provide a safer return to the investor.

Learning new skills and increasing your intellectual investment means taking advantage of every free training offer provided by your employer. It means using the Internet to find webinars on specific topics related to our jobs that allow us to improve our literacy level so that we can qualify for a better job. Many Americans have the will to take these steps. There are those who will work at fast food outlets or large box stores until they become managers. But it takes more than promotions; it takes the ability to set aside monies for investments and employment skill upgrades. Education and training are also investments into intellectual capital as an individual grows their skill set.

What is the solution? It comes from the individual who is willing to sacrifice to increase his or her education. It comes from the individual who is willing to set aside moneys for investments in capital markets or in intellectual capital. The good-paying jobs in the economy are not growing as they have in past recoveries; therefore, there is more competition for the available jobs. Success in finding a good-paying job is directly related to an employee's skill level.

Summary

Letters to the newspaper editor will continue to decry the fact that we need to buy American products (i.e., American steel). Such letters to the editor are surely to be repeated and sent to editors as long as there are editorial pages. Yet it will not make businesses or the individuals purchase more expensive American products over the less expensive overseas products. Urgings to "Buy American" are not going to change the situation. What is needed is new training, apprenticeship programs, effective school systems, workers with skills that cannot be matched by workers in overseas countries, and a work force with a strong work ethic. What is not needed are more psychology majors, political science, finance majors, and more people receiving transfer payments from the government. A tall order; yes, but one that may still be able to be accomplished. How much longer will it be possible to make these changes? I think we will find out as most of the country sits around waiting and arguing for governmental solutions and watch the government become unable to pay its bills.

Notes

1. http://data.bls.gov/timeseries/CES3000000001?data_tool=XGtable.
2. Robert E. Scott, "Heading South U.S.-Mexico Trade and Job Displacement after NAFTA," *Economic Policy Institute,* May 2011, http://epi.3cdn.net/fdade52b876e04793b_7fm6ivz2y.pdf.
3. www.census.gov/hhes/www/poverty/data/threshld/index.html.
4. Jeffrey Sparshott, Eateries, Bars Show Big Appetite for Hiring," *Wall Street Journal,* July 6–7, 2013, A2.
5. Christoper Rugaber, "Temporary Jobs Becoming a Permanent Fixture," *USA Today,* July 7, 2013, www.usatoday.com/story/money/business/2013/07/07/temporary-jobs-becoming-permanent-fixture/2496585.
6. Single-mother families are defined as families headed by a female with no spouse present—living with one or more of their own, never-married

children under age 18. In 2009, there were about 18.1 million children in the United States living in single-mother families. www.prb.org/Publications/PolicyBriefs/singlemotherfamilies.aspx.

7. For example, see Bergen Community College in New Jersey: www.bergen.edu/pages1/pages/611.aspx.

8. www.bdpa-detroit.org/portal/index.php?option=com_content&view=article&id=57:moocs-top-10-sites-for-free-education-with-elite-universities&catid=29:education&Itemid=20.

Gratuity Government

SHOULD I TAKE THE FREE BUTTER?[1]

The art of government consists of taking as much money as possible from one party of citizens to give to the other.

—Voltaire, 1764

A democracy cannot exist as a permanent form of government. It can only exist until the voters discover that they can vote themselves largesse from the public treasury. From that moment on, the majority always votes for the candidates promising the most benefits from the public treasury . . .

—possibly Alexander Fraser Tytler

As you read the book's chapters, you may decide that the U.S. education system is not helping your children achieve their full potential, you may decide that credit card companies have replaced old, loan shark gangsters except the gangster charged less interest, and you may also notice the numbers bookie has been largely put out of work by state lottery systems that make it legitimate and easy to gamble. Of course, the government can come to your rescue if you have the right group of lobbyist on K Street. Whether an individual realizes it or not their potential has been taken from them. Is there any way for me to become a *taker* who can take something back from the government?

This chapter is written for the single individual who is asking that question. The chapter describes several government handout programs that a single individual should be able to apply for and receive government transfer payments. It is assumed our hypothetical single individual has graduated, or not, from a dysfunctional secondary education system and has few job prospects other than earning an unlivable minimum wage. These are the individuals who used to find work in the automobile factories and steel mills and earned a wage that would allow them to start families. The chapter is not written for the family of four who are only barely surviving through the receipt of transfer payments. The difference between these two examples is that the single individual may be able to set aside moneys from their transfer payments to begin building a small group of investments, whereas the transfer payments for a family of four do not allow for any residual monies at the end of the month.

The underlying question for people is: should I take the free butter? My answer is: Take it before it is all gone.

My neighbor, who we will call Ted, has been taking payments as a disabled firefighter for at least 30 years. He has a great disability package because every time a new firefighter is hired at a higher pay rate, my neighbor's disability payments increase. The payments are not based on cost of living but rather the salary of the most recent hire at his old fire station. Ted has a boat for lake cruising, a tractor for moving dirt around his property, and he has built and sold at least three houses since becoming disabled. He decided long ago to take the free butter.

The government provides programs for its citizens to take money back from the federal government and to do it legally. This chapter is not a moral lecture that says no one should take free butter. Rather, it is an argument for stating that if you are going to take the transfer payments from the government, then make sure to spend it in the best way to create an increase in your net worth. It may be the payments that you receive are just enough that allow you to get food on the table. But that is not true for everyone receiving transfer payments through state and federal programs.

Therefore, the argument here is that if you take it, and you have an ending balance, no matter how small, invest it, and don't just spend it on toys. Without a deliberate and thoughtful investment plan, no matter how small the investment, it is impossible to get out of a long-term financial decline that many people in the United States are facing and seem unable to ever leave.

Once I was sitting at a table in an unemployment office with others who were trying to get unemployment benefits. The guy next to me pointed to a notebook on the table, pointed to the title on the notebook, and asked me what it said. It said *Job Listings*. If your secondary education has been so poor that you cannot fill out applications, these government programs are not going to work for you. The forms that you will have to fill out are going to be like tax forms.

Let's take a look at successful taker trends in the United States.

Taker Trends: Get Wise and Do Less for Yourself

Takers get their money through transfer payments. Transfer payments are those payments made to individuals who do not have to give up any resource in return for the payment. Transfer payments are made to corporations and other organizations in the form of subsidies, but the focus here is on payments to individuals. Social Security, unemployment compensation, and welfare payments account for the bulk of transfer payments made by the U.S. government, but within those three areas there are multiples and multiples of smaller programs. Examples of such transfer payments are disability payments, unemployment compensation, temporary assistance for needy families, veterans' programs, state and local payments for health care, housing assistance, energy assistance, school lunches and breakfasts, payments for supplemental nutrition assistance programs (in the old days called food stamps), Medicare, Medicaid, supplemental Social Security, and Social Security payments. Social Security recipients worked to get those payments, and unemployment is paid only to those who lost a job. Yet, none of these recipients are asked to do anything for the payments they are currently receiving. For that reason, the payments are called transfers.

In the United States, from 1990 to 2009, transfer payments increased from $566.1 billion to $2,076.1 trillion.[2] In plain terms, this means that transfer payments from the government are more than the total taxes paid by 60 percent of U.S. households in 2009.[3] In 1960, government transfers represented 6 percent of all personal income in the United States, whereas today it is 18 percent, and over 12 million working-age Americans received disability payments in 2011 or 1 in every 18 adults in the 18-to-64 age group.[4]

Nicholas Eberstadt, a well-known demographer and social scientist who holds the Henry Wendt Chair in Political Economy at the American Enterprise Institute, states that transfer programs have widely expanded their coverage. For example, Aid for Families with Dependent Children originally established for orphans, has expanded to provide support for the children of unwed mothers. He further states that over 50 percent of American voters are obtaining one or more benefits from the government.[5]

Most writers bemoan these statistics as a sign that America has fallen apart and lost its edge.

My view to government largesse is: Get it while you can. Should you take the free butter? Yes, you better take the free butter before there is none. The long-term debt burden created by these programs and the continual increase in their annual expenditures makes the financial sustainability of the federal government questionable, as has been explained in previous chapters. The financial situation created by the federal government will eventually create a financial meltdown. But use as much of the government's largesse as you can now to make yourself an investor. With the small balance available at the end of a month for a single individual receiving transfer payments, there are not many choices to becoming an investor. The easiest method to invest these balances is by making small investments in the stock market with the hope of increasing stock values. Few other choices are available for making small investments. For that reason, many people see their only chance for financial security is to buy lottery tickets. Consequently, they are using any remaining moneys to gamble. If you want to gamble, the odds are better in the stock market.

Entrance to the Land of the Takers

There are many doors that open to the land of the transfer payment takers. We will explore several of them here and their characteristics. The programs described here do not have limitations based on an individual's net worth. If you have a high net worth, you may still qualify for the program. In other words, you can be a millionaire and still get unemployment, for example.

Disabilities[6]

There are three programs that can provide for disability payments from the federal government. There is disability under Social

Security, disability under Supplemental Social Security, and disability under benefits for children with disabilities. Each program has different rules and slightly different criteria for qualifying for disability payments. The focus here will be on receiving disability under the Social Security program criteria. Before getting started, it needs to be understood that there are millions of people who are truly disabled and need these payments.

It's a Fact

The Social Security Administration approved 76,983 disability applications nationwide in April 2013, bringing the total disabled receiving federal aid to an all-time high of 12 million people. More than 80 percent of them, or 8.8 million people, are disabled workers. About 18 percent, or 1.9 million, are children. And fewer than 2 percent, or 160,000, are spouses of disabled workers. Compare that with 1990, when there were barely more than 3 million recipients of federal disability benefits. Alabama, Mississippi, and West Virginia each have more than 10 percent of their adult workforce on disability.

Source: Michael Miller, "Ranks of Those Receiving Federal Disability Benefits Swell Amid Struggling Economy, *Press of Atlantic City,* June 9, 2013, www.pressofatlanticcity .com.

The basic criterion to qualify for Social Security disability payments is having "a medical condition that is expected to last at least one year or result in death," and, in addition, the disability prevents an individual from working.[7] The point to concentrate on in that sentence is "a medical condition." There are a whole host of medical conditions that prevent someone from working, and they do not all lead to death. If you have a minimum work history under Social Security, you are likely to qualify for disability payments. Disability payments are one of the few personal income growth areas in our country.

> In 1960 an average of 455,000 erstwhile workers were receiving monthly federal payments for disability. By 2010 that total had skyrocketed to 8.2 million (and by 2011 had risen still further, to almost 8.6 million).
>
> —N. Eberstadt, *A Nation of Takers,* 2012, p. 52.

The chances of obtaining disability payments depend on several factors. For instance, if your claim is heard by an administrative law judge (ALJ), your chances are better for obtaining disability payments. Over half the claimants who appeal lower-level administrative decisions to an ALJ received disability payments more than half the time, whereas only 35 percent of claimants initially receive them at the administrative level. Those claimants who have the patience to go through the system are more likely to obtain disability payments. After the ALJ, appeals can be made to an Appeals Council and finally in a U.S. federal district court. At each level, more cases are favorably settled for the claimant.

Additionally, the state jurisdiction where the claim is filed affects the outcome of a disability claim. In New York, initial filings granted disability payments to 66.8 percent of claimants in 2011. In Oklahoma, the rate of approval at this level is only 28.6 percent. Claimants who are represented by an attorney tend to have more success in obtaining payments. Those claimants with less education and who are older are more likely to receive disability payments because your ability to do hard work is limited as well as your ability to do office work if you are illiterate. Thus, those with less skills and little future potential are the ones most likely to receive disability benefits.

One of the most important aspects of qualifying for disability is to find a supportive physician. Two disabilities that are hard to verify are mental disorders or back pain that cause the claimant to be unable to work. For back pain, there needs to be a specific diagnosis for its cause as identified with X-rays or MRIs. A diagnosis of a mental disorder rests more on the opinion of a psychiatrist. Mental disorders include obsessive-compulsive behavior, posttraumatic stress, social phobias, agoraphobia, attention deficit–hyperactivity, autism, severe antisocial behavior, schizophrenia, bipolar behavior, and mood disorders such as depression. These conditions must be recognized by a doctor and be serious enough to prevent the claimant from working. Today, it is easier to be diagnosed with a mental disorder. The American Psychiatric Association has recently released broadened definitions of mental illness in the fifth edition of the *Diagnostic and Statistical Manual of Mental Disorders*.[8] For example, in the past it was necessary to have specific delusion or hallucinations to be classified as a schizophrenic, but no more; now to qualify for unspecified schizophrenia, it is not necessary to have delusions, only distress from unspecified symptoms. This is also true for unspecified ADHD—unspecified symptoms. The fuzziness of these diagnostics also includes *unspecified mental disorder*, which is classified as not meeting any other disorder. Consequently, the revisions make it a lot easier for claimants to be identified as having a mental disorder and qualify for disability payments.

Claiming these conditions is no guarantee that a claimant will receive payments. The conditions need to show specifically how they limit the claimant's ability to work.

Even with all these steps to apply and receive disability payments, the ranks of those receiving those benefits are growing exponentially. It must also be remembered that disability payments do not only come from federal disability payments through Social Security. Beyond Social Security, disability payments are available for firemen, railroad workers, veterans with disabilities, federal workers, some state and local government workers (not under Section 218 agreements), and other organizations that do not pay into the Social Security program.

To determine the amount of your Social Security disability payments, see the online calculator at http://www.ssa.gov/retire2/AnypiaApplet.html. The amount is dependent on your work history, disability level, and age. Most amounts range from $300 to $2,200 per month.

"There Ain't No Fraud in This System!"

SAN DIEGO (CNS)—Roberto J. Velasquez, a clinical psychologist from National City, California, was sentenced Wednesday to nearly 21 months in federal prison for fraudulently winning government disability benefits for claimants via a scheme in which the Social Security Administration was swindled out of at least $1.5 million in disability payments over a six-year period. For a fee of $200, Velasquez fabricated patient histories, test results, symptoms, and complaints that did not exist. He admitted to falsely certifying that dozens of patients were disabled and therefore eligible for disability benefits.

Source: www.10news.com/news/psychologist-accused-of-selling-medical-forms.

Housing Assistance

Housing assistance is paid for monthly rent, and this assistance comes in all forms and amounts, mainly through various state or local programs. The transfer payments are made to low-income individuals or single mothers, for example. The government organizations providing these payments vary all over the map from city government to state government, depending on the situation. Housing assistance includes living in public housing but that is not discussed here.

Section 8 or Housing Choice Voucher Program from the U.S. Department of Housing and Urban Development provides rental assistance payments, which are paid directly to private landlords. This program offers eligible participants the ability to rent housing and pay no more than 40 percent of their income for rent. The subsidies are for one-, two-, three-, and four-bedroom homes, including apartments, mobile homes, duplexes, or any kind of dwelling that meets the standards set by the program. To qualify for assistance, families must generally earn an income 50 percent or below the area's median income. If the individual owns income-generating assets, that income must be counted in making a determination for housing assistance.

In some programs, rent is only 30 percent of a family's monthly adjusted income. Rent includes the monthly cost of shelter plus water, sewer, trash pickup, and allowances for electricity and gas. The rent you actually pay is based on 30 percent of your adjusted gross monthly income. Consequently, if a program participant is receiving disability payments of $1,500 a month and 30 percent qualified under housing assistance, their housing support would be for any rental payments above $450. Rent payments above $450 would be provided under a housing assistance program and paid directly to the landlord. The net amount from their disability payment would be reduced to ($1,500 − $450) $1,050.

Who Would Steal Housing Assistance Funds? Really!

STATEN ISLAND, N.Y.—An Elm Park man is accused of collecting more than $11,000 in federal housing assistance, even though he and another member of his household took in a combined $82,000 a year. Okema reported that he had only taken in $9,360 in annual household income that

(Continued)

(Continued)

year, but an investigation proved otherwise, according to court papers. He had been employed by both Coca-Cola Enterprises and Domino's Pizza, and another household member, Amenan Kouame, was working for the Carmel Richmond Healthcare and Rehabilitation Center in Dongan Hills, court papers allege.

Source: John M. Annese, "Staten Island Man Accused of Housing-Assistance Fraud," April 10, 2013, www.silive.com/news/index.ssf/2013/04/staten_island_man_accused_of_i_1.html.

Food Stamps

Food stamps are another transfer payment program from the government. It is now called the Supplemental Nutrition Assistance Program (SNAP), and monthly benefits payments are recorded on the back of a plastic card. This is a federal program administrated through the Department of Agriculture since 1975 and run by the states. In 2012, $74.6 billion in food stamp assistance was distributed to program participants. The average benefit per individual in 2013 was $133.44 per month for 47.68 million individuals.[9]

Low-income single individuals can use an online calculator to determine the amount of benefits for which they might be eligible.[10] Assuming a single individual with no assets who grosses $1,000 per month in other transfer payments and pays rent of $675, the calculator shows they will receive monthly food benefits of $109 per month. If the individual has assets such as a bank account, the amount receivable will be reduced. If you own a home and property, it will not count toward the reduction of benefits. The final allocation of benefits is based on the results of an interview with agency administrators and the paperwork needed at the interview.[11]

Unemployment Insurance

Currently, there are around 11 million unemployed Americans. There are even more Americans who have given up looking for work or who have had their unemployment benefits run out and are therefore not counted as part of the 11 million. The minimum and maximum amount of unemployment is usually between \$143 and \$604 per week, respectively; or \$572 to \$2,416 per month.[12] In order to qualify for unemployment, an employee must have worked 680 hours during the past year and lost their job through no fault of their own (i.e., was not fired due to misconduct).

The total weeks of unemployment receivable vary with the state. For example, in New Jersey, it is possible to collect 73 weeks of unemployment, whereas in Wyoming it is 40 weeks. Unemployment payments are based on both state and federal programs. Most state benefits are for 26 weeks, with the additional weeks coming from federal government in the emergency unemployment programs and funding.

Getting unemployment requires a certain level of previous earned wages. With some exceptions, job loss can be based on firings due to a lack of an "employment fit," but not misconduct such as theft. General company layoffs would qualify an individual to receive unemployment. If you quit because of family or health concerns or a hostile work environment, you may qualify. The rules for qualification depend on the state employee at the unemployment office asking you for information and interpreting your responses. Further, the criteria to receive unemployment may be eased as the overall economic situation worsens. Here are some suggestions as ways to get fired for poor performance and still collect unemployment[13]:

- Pretend that you don't know how to do something. This works especially well if you are asked to do something new.
- Do just enough to scrape by. If anyone is going to be laid off, it is you.
- Work very, very slowly.
- Spend time forwarding "funny" e-mails. Become a workplace disrupter.
- Treat work as your personal social club. Go around and sit in other people's work area and gossip.
- Be constantly upset, angry, or depressed—anything but happy.
- Have a lot of ongoing personal problems.
- In inconsecutive sequences, miss work; these are unavoidable events for flat tires, sickness, missing dog, and so on.

What you are creating is the work image of a slacker, and if anyone has to be laid off, it should be you.

Am I Disqualified Because I Am Rich?

In 2009, 2,362 millionaires received unemployment benefits, down from 2,840 the year prior, according to a study from the Congressional Research Service, a nonpartisan arm of U.S. Congress that provides policy and legal analysis. Of the 2,362, more than 1,000 receiving unemployment benefits had a household adjusted gross income of $1.5 million in 2009.

Source: Lyneka Little, "Thousands of Millionaires Collect Unemployment," *ABC News,* Consumer Report, October 2, 2012.

Transfer Payments and a Hypothetical Monthly Budget

If you are a recipient of transfer payments, it may be possible to save a small amount from your payments at the end of each month for making investments. Of course, as these investments grow in value, the amount of your transfer payments may be reduced. One way to determine how much of your transfer payments are available for investment is to set up a monthly budget. Two simple budgets are set up in Tables 13.1 and 13.2 for a single individual who is receiving transfer payments. These budgets are hypothetical, as

Table 13.1   Hypothetical Monthly Budget with Disability

Source of Monthly Funding Estimated*	Amount Received
Disability	$1,250
Food stamps	$110
Other sources	$50
Total monthly income	$1,410
Rent of $625 after housing assistance (.30 of disability)	$375
Food after using food pantry ($6 per day)	$180
Miscellaneous expense	$200
Total monthly expenses	($755)
Net remaining at end of month	**$655**

*Does not take into account any health costs, which should largely be paid by the government.

Table 13.2 Hypothetical Monthly Budget with Unemployment

Source of Monthly Funding Estimated*	Amount Received
Unemployment	$2,000
Food stamps	$110
Other sources	$50
Total monthly income	$2,160
Rent of $625 after housing assistance (.30 of unemployment)	$600
Food after using food pantry ($6 per day)	$180
Miscellaneous expense	$200
Total monthly expenses	($980)
Net remaining at end of month	**$1,180**

it is very difficult to accurately determine the amount of transfer payments received by an individual. It must be remembered that the only method to get out of a situation where transfer payments are your only means of living is to make small investments that increase your net worth. The only type of investment that can be easily made in small increments is a stock investment.

The following two budgets are for one individual. In case one, they are receiving disability and in case two they are receiving unemployment compensation.

Table 13.1 shows that even on disability, there should be monies remaining at the end of the month from these transfer payments. In our example, the recipient has an ending monthly balance of $655. If our hypothetical individual is receiving unemployment compensation, the amount remaining at the end of the month would be expected to be even more, as shown in Table 13.2.

With unemployment, the net remaining at the end of the month is $1,180. Although these are estimated amounts, the budget shows that for a single individual receiving disability or unemployment along with housing assistance and food stamps, a balance is likely to remain in their pocket at the end of each month.

This budget does not take into account payments for cigarettes, alcohol, expensive cell phone plans, car payments, cable, or satellite bills. Nor does the budget take into account other entertainment expenditures such as lottery purchases or casino gambling.

These balances can serve as a basic source of investment for these individuals. The investment objectives for someone with a disability, which is a lifelong payment, are expected to be different from those individuals receiving unemployment. Unemployment benefits have a finite end to them. Therefore, investment objectives should be to develop supplemental income. For example, such a portfolio more likely would include stocks that provide a rate of dividend return (possibly 3 percent) to the investor, thus supplementing their sources of income when unemployment payments stop. However, those with a disability may be more interested in long-term appreciation in the value of any stock purchased as they look for market gains in the value of the stock.

Summary

The government's role at one time was limited to protecting property rights, establishing transparent markets rules, providing capital infrastructure for trade, and defending the nation. Today, the government has bought its way into the social fabric of the nation influencing marriage rights, the unborn, health services, and a host of other personal activities.

Today's government provides more and more supportive services for the citizens of the United States. As the government faces financial constraints, the quality of such services is reduced or rationed, causing those dependent on such services to remain in limbo. Dependency on these services can result in abject poverty for program participants without any way to get out of a web of failed government programs. Many of the people in these programs do not have the literacy or other skills to move from welfare to self-sufficiency. They have gone through dysfunctional school systems that have contributed to their illiteracy. They are faced with the choice of taking welfare and finding ways to increase their welfare payments or take jobs that pay them less than they receive under welfare. Their future potential has been stolen.

Our "greatest generation" came out of World War II and the Depression. Many of these people had a code that would not allow them take any sort of government handout. Today, with all respect to those people, I say take what the government will give you and try to use it to get out of poverty. Take what the government will give you before the government's continuing deficits and misspending cause a financial meltdown.

Notes

1. No suggestions are being made in the chapter that readers should attempt to fraudulently receive transfer payments.
2. U.S. Census Bureau, *Statistical Abstract of the United States: 2012*, Table 539, "Government Transfer Payments to Individuals—Summary: 1990 to 2009," 351.
3. Scott Hodge, "60 Percent of Households Now Receive More in Transfer Income than They Pay in Taxes," The Tax Foundation, October 4, 2012; www.taxfoundation.org.
4. Nicholas Eberstadt, "Yes, Mr. President, We Are a Nation of Takers," *Wall Street Journal*, January 25, 2013, A13; and Nicholas Eberstadt, *A Nation of Takers* (West Conshohocken, PA: Templeton Press, 2012).
5. Ibid., 33.
6. For a full examination of disability payments, see D. Morton, *Nolo's Guide to Social Security Disability* (Berkeley, CA: Nolo, 2012).
7. Social Security Disability at www.socialsecurity.gov.
8. Leonard Sax, "Unspecified Mental Disorder? That's Crazy," *Wall Street Journal*, June 27, 2013, A21.
9. www.fns.usda.gov/pd/34snapmonthly.htm.
10. www.ndhealth.gov/dhs/foodstampcalculator.asp.
11. To find out how many people in your zip code receive food stamps, go to www.slate.com/articles/news_and_politics/map_of_the_week/2013/04/food_stamp_recipients_by_county_an_interactive_tool_showing_local_snap_data.html.
12. www.esd.wa.gov/newsandinformation/faq/unemployment-insurance-benefits.php.
13. http://finance.youngmoney.com/careers/get-fired-and-still-qualify-for-unemployment.

About the Authors

Mark A. Grimaldi

Mr. Grimaldi received a BA degree in economics from Albany State University in 1985. His career in money management began in 1986 as an investment coordinator at Meyer Handleman Company in New York. After two years, he joined Prime Financial Services as Director of Operations. In 1992, Mr. Grimaldi accepted a position as manager, Securities Operations, at Marshall & Sterling Consultants in Poughkeepsie, New York. In 1996, he cofounded Navigator Money Management, Inc. and The Prestige Organization, Inc. In 1997, he earned the Certified Fund Specialist (CFS) designation. From 1989 through 2005, Mr. Grimaldi coordinated and taught securities training classes at Dutchess Community College, Poughkeepsie, New York. In 2004, Mr. Grimaldi became chief portfolio manager of the *Navigator* newsletters. Mr. Grimaldi is the portfolio manager of The Sector Rotation Fund (NAVFX), a pure no-load mutual fund. In January 2011, Mr. Grimaldi formed a strategic partnership with one of America's most trusted financial experts of CNBC TV. They created a new and exciting newsletter called *The Money Navigator*. Mr. Grimaldi acts as chief portfolio manager and economist on this joint venture.

G. Stevenson Smith

G. Stevenson Smith is the John Massey Endowed Professor of Accounting and chair of the Department of Accounting and Finance in the John Massey School of Business at Southeastern Oklahoma State University. He is a CMA and a CPA. Professor Smith received his PhD from the University of Arkansas and his

MBA from Michigan State University. Dr. Smith has authored three books dealing with nonprofit financial management for the American Library Association. His most recent title is *Cost Control for Nonprofits in Crisis* (ALA, 2011). He has authored numerous articles on forensic accounting that have been published in *Journal of Forensic Accounting, Journal of Financial Fraud, Fraud Magazine, Digital Investigation,* and the *Journal of Digital Forensics, Security and Law.* His HTCIA White Paper on RFID hacking received the Best Paper Award at the HTCIA's International Conference in 2007. He is the coauthor of *Forensic and Investigative Accounting* (CCH, 2013). His professional experience includes working for the Securities and Exchange Commission in Washington, D.C., as a financial analyst. He has been a visiting professor at the University of Victoria in Wellington, New Zealand, and a visiting fellow at the University of New England in Armdale, Australia. In 2011, he was a Fulbright Scholar at the University of Pula in Croatia, where he lectured and developed research on forensic issues in eastern Europe.

Index